A Passionate Life

Other books by Helen Caldicott:
If You Love This Planet
Nuclear Madness: What You Can Do
Missile Envy

DR HELEN CALDICOTT

A Passionate Life

RANDOM HOUSE
AUSTRALIA

Random House Australia Pty Ltd
20 Alfred Street, Milsons Point, NSW 2061

Sydney New York Toronto
London Auckland Johannesburg
and agencies throughout the world

First published in 1996

National Library of Australia
Cataloguing-in-Publication Data

Caldicott Helen.
A passionate life.

Includes index.
ISBN 0 09 183106 7.

1. Caldicott, Helen. 2. Pacifists - Australia - Biography.
3. Nuclear disarmament. 4. Physicians - Australia - Biography. I. Title.

327.174092

Design by Philip Campbell Design
Cover photograph Peter Solness/Fairfax
Photo Library
Typeset by Midland Typesetters, Maryborough
Printed by Griffin Paperbacks, Adelaide
Extract from *On The Beach*
by Nevil Shute (William Heinemann)
reprinted by permission of Reed Books

To cynomys with love

Special thanks to Jacqui Kent

C O N T E N T S

Part 1
Early Days

CHAPTER 1

When I was nineteen, I read a book that changed my life.

It was a novel, barely read these days, called *On the Beach*, by Nevil Shute (later made into a popular film). It tells the story of the final months in the lives of five people living in a world doomed to be destroyed by radiation after a nuclear war that had begun by accident in the northern hemisphere.

'Couldn't anyone have stopped it?'

'I don't know . . . Some kinds of silliness you just can't stop,' he said. 'I mean, if a couple of hundred million people all decided that their national honour requires them to drop cobalt bombs upon their neighbour, well, there's not much that you or I can do about it. The only possible hope would have been to educate them out of their silliness.'

'But how could you have done that, Peter? I mean, they'd all left school.'

> 'Newspapers,' he said. 'You could have done something with newspapers. We didn't do it, no nation did because we were all too silly. We liked our newspapers with pictures of beach girls and headlines of indecent assault, and no Government was wise enough to stop us having them that way. But something might have been done with newspapers, if we'd been wise enough.'

Something might have been done with newspapers, if we'd been wise enough . . .

Shute's story haunted me. Millions of words have since been written about nuclear war and its consequences, and much of the literature is more horrific and emotive than anything Nevil Shute wrote or perhaps even imagined. But his novel was set in Melbourne, the city where I had grown up. It described places I knew, devastated by nuclear catastrophe. Nowhere was safe. I felt so alone, so unprotected by the adults, who seemed to be unaware of the dangers.

> She passed the grammar school away on the left and came to shabby, industrial Corio, and so to Geelong, dominated by its cathedral. In the great tower the bells were ringing for some service. She slowed a little to pass through the city, but there was nothing on the road except deserted cars at the roadside. She saw only three people, all of them men . . . At the end she turned left away from the golf links and the little house where so many happy hours of childhood had been spent, knowing now she would never see it again.

I had already decided to be a doctor, and I came from a family who encouraged me to believe that if I worked hard, I could do anything. But after reading *On the Beach*, I knew I wouldn't just go through medical school and settle into a nice, cosy, well-paid niche somewhere, as doctors in Australia were apt to do. I wanted a husband and a family, certainly, but somewhere in me was a conviction that I had other work to do as well.

When I read *On the Beach*, I started to realise what that work might be.

Nobody with Polish and Irish ancestry—as I have—has any right to expect a quiet, easy life. If I hadn't found that out for myself, I could have learned it by considering the lives of my forebears.

Gracius Jacob Broinowski, my great-grandfather on my father's side, was a Polish baron, born in 1837, who began his career by avoiding conscription in the Russian army. After escaping from his upstairs bedroom window in the Polish town of Weilun by the time-honoured method of tying sheets together to make a rope, he travelled to Germany and then to England. In about 1857 he came to Australia, where he eked out a living by painting landscapes and scenes of various towns as he travelled around the eastern side of the continent. He married a pretty girl named Jane Smith who smiled at him from her Melbourne window, and after some years they settled in Sydney with their six sons and daughter. Gracius taught painting to private pupils and at colleges, lectured on art and exhibited at the Royal Art Society.

His greatest claim to fame, however, was as an artist of Australian native fauna. In the 1880s he supplied the school classrooms of New South Wales with pictures of Australian birds and mammals, and between 1887 and 1891 prepared a series of six volumes called *The Birds of Australia*, which have since become collectors' items. His bird prints hang on the walls of my house to this day.

One of my great-grandmothers on my father's side, Mary Sanger Creed, was a forthright woman and an early feminist. The first woman to matriculate in Australia, she applied to enter medical school in Melbourne. In the 1870s the idea of a woman wanting to be a doctor was considered ridiculous enough to be featured on the front cover of the English satirical magazine *Punch*; the drawing shows the chancellor of the University of Melbourne holding up a grave, dismissive hand as my great-grandmother attempts to enter the sacred portals. (The first Australian woman to train in medicine didn't receive her degree until 1893, and even then it was from Edinburgh University.)

Mary married a progressive Anglican minister, the Reverend Jonathan Evans, and had four children. She hated being a minister's wife and living in the small Tasmanian town of Deloraine, and she turned to writing. Soon she became known as an excellent journalist, whose articles on a variety of topics appeared in local and national newspapers. When her children were still young, she and Jonathan Evans agreed to part, and he moved to the Riverina district of south-western New South Wales. Obviously harbouring his own ambitions, he left Australia for England, where he became an actor, while the four children remained with their mother.

In the 1890s the irrepressible Mary and her children moved to a seventy-acre (30 hectare) property near Wyong, north of Sydney, where she started a cooperative silk farm for other single women and their dependent children. All the families worked together, growing mulberry trees to feed the silkworms, spinning the silk and selling it. The silk farm was successful for a number of years.

My grandmother, Grace Creed Evans (whom for some reason we called Dais, short for Daisy), was the oldest of Mary's four children. A talented musician who played the violin and piano, she helped support the family by performing music on the ships that plied the cities on the eastern seaboard of Australia. Later she became a music teacher. Her youngest sister, Win, was an early Montessori governess who taught the children of Ethel Turner, author of *Seven Little Australians* and one of Australia's most famous early writers.

Grace married Gracius's son, Robert Broinowski, in Melbourne in 1905, where Robert was Usher of the Black Rod in Federal Parliament for some years. It was not a happy marriage, as Bob was known to go on bushwalks with various women. He was a prickly, talented man, an amateur poet. Many of his own verses reflect his dalliances and affairs. Others, such as this one, highly descriptive of the Australian bush and its ubiquitous flies, show his irreverent sense of humour.

The road comes winding down the range
Each moment bringing to my eyes
Some point of beauty new and strange—
Oh damn the flies . . .

Ten thousand furies blight the stinking swine
Bright parrots flash with eerie cries;
The lyrebird sings his chorus divine—
Oh, flaming bastards . . . the flies.

Dais and Bob had two sons, my uncle Bob and my father, Theo Philip, who was born in 1910 and was called Philip. In 1927 Parliament moved from Melbourne to its permanent home in Canberra, Australia's brand new federal capital and the site of a former sheep station about 300 kilometres south-west of Sydney. The move gave Bob the excuse he needed to leave Dais and the boys in Melbourne; he eventually married another piano teacher and they had a daughter, Ruth. My grandfather became clerk of the Senate in Canberra and the designer of the Senate rose garden. His portrait hangs in Parliament House.

My father was about eleven when his parents separated, and he told me that every night he used to pray that they would be reconciled. The divorce was finalised when he was fourteen, leaving Dad bitter and disillusioned, never to believe in God again. When I was a child, Grandfather Broinowski hosted and presented a radio program called *The Poet's Tongue* on Australia's national network every Sunday evening, and Dad always turned the program off because he could not bear to hear his father's voice. Not until Grandfather was an old man were he and Dad reconciled at my mother's instigation. They were similar in many important ways: both had red hair, the long Broinowski nose, an irreverent sense of humour and a bad temper.

Mum's side of the family were just as tumultuous. One of her great-grandfathers was a vitriolic Scot named William Kerr, who immigrated to Australia in 1832 and fourteen years later founded the Melbourne *Argus*. This twice-weekly broadsheet that mirrored Kerr's own independent views—for instance, he was a great opponent of convicts entering Melbourne from the state of Tasmania, where they were sent by the British penal system—became one of Melbourne's two morning daily newspapers (the other being the *Age*), and continued to be published until 1957. William Kerr was also Melbourne's second town clerk. My mother had a high regard for him.

As I write about this man, I realise that I am very like him in many ways. I have taken on the establishment in society, I tend to have independent views which are often not popular initially, and I am impelled to speak the truth with little regard for the prevailing norms of society. And I am known to be irascible from time to time.

Another great-grandfather was Henry Coffey, an Irish sea captain who arrived in Australia in the 1860s, met and married William's daughter Helen, and took her back to England. Henry was a passionate Anglophile, who unwisely persisted in wearing an orange buttonhole during St Patrick's Day marches in Ireland. Their first child was born in London, and they then returned to Melbourne, where Helen gave birth to three more children, including my grandfather James, the second son.

Soon after their fourth and last child, Wilhelmina, was born, Henry, who had invested a great deal of money in a shipbuilding firm in Williamstown, the old part of Melbourne, lost it after going guarantor for a builder whose business failed. This disaster was compounded when Henry and

Helen, who shared a taste for Irish whiskey, were both carried off by it when their eldest child was only fourteen.

Despite his difficult childhood, James grew up to become a personable young man, well dressed and a member of the Walking Club of Melbourne, a society whose members were Melbourne's genteel—or would-be genteel—citizens. Social position being important to him, he became engaged to Ethyl Clarke, from a wealthy, established Melbourne family. Unfortunately, Ethyl's father wasn't any better with money than James's father had been. Charles Ernest Clarke started off as a wealthy sharebroker, and Ethyl was raised in the lap of luxury, but her father borrowed far beyond his means during the land boom of the 1890s; he was ruined and was jailed for almost five years. The scandal remained the skeleton in the family closet. Mum told me about it only once, in hushed tones.

Ethyl had few skills that would enable her to support herself. She played the piano beautifully, as befitted a young lady of her social position, and even after her family fell on bad times, she continued to uphold certain standards of behaviour. She had a mop of beautiful auburn hair, about which she was very vain. Mum told me that Ethyl used to position herself under the light as she played the piano so that her hair shone golden red and everybody could admire it.

But Ethyl's standards became increasingly difficult to maintain. Her mother died when she was only eighteen, leaving a family of five, including a baby boy. Ethyl stepped into her mother's warm shoes and raised this family single-handed. The youngest brother, of whom Ethyl was very fond, was later killed during the First World War.

Shortly after, Ethyl married James Coffey. He went to war as well in 1914, returned without money or a trade. Like many other veterans, he thought he would become a farmer, and was allotted a soldier's settlement block in the scrub of north-east Victoria. Again like so many other returned soldiers, he failed as a farmer, forfeiting his farm at the end of the 1920s, and went back to Melbourne. He bought a house in the eastern suburbs with money borrowed from Ethyl's family. It was here that Ethyl bore and brought up six more children, the eldest of whom died of meningitis when he was only a year old.

James never succeeded in accruing money of his own, and in desperation he joined the Melbourne Tramways Department as a clerk. Poor old Pop, as we called him, was somewhat inadequate. He was considered by his wife to be a failure, he never helped Ethyl (whom we called Nanny) with the large family, and he suffered from asthma. When I was little, he spent hours in his room, inhaling strange-smelling medications. But he wasn't beaten; I remember his sparkling Irish eyes and wicked sense of humour.

Nanny, also, could be very funny, even though she was so often exhausted. Her boys—Owen, Earle, Terence and Selwyn—all slept at the back of the house in an outside screened porch. Every year on the first of April Nanny woke them at dawn, saying, with great excitement: 'There's a ship on fire in the bay!' She persuaded them to scale the tallest tree in their pyjamas, just to look, and only when they reached the top did she announce: 'April fools!' They never seemed to learn.

Mum, born Mary Mona Enyd Coffey in 1911, was the second youngest child in the family and the only girl. She was a pretty little thing, with Irish colouring, delicate features and bright blue eyes, dark hair and a fair, soft skin that you could hardly feel when you kissed her cheek, even as an adult. Like most parents of the time, her mother and father believed that a woman's place was in the home, and Mum often told me how resentful she used to feel, ironing her brothers' shirts while they went out on the town. Being Cinderella rarely turns women into saints, despite the fairy tales, and her frustration might have triggered the dark side of Mum's personality. She had a violent temper, and when we were kids, she was racked by inexplicable bouts of uncontrollable rage. I was the main target of these attacks, and I never knew when they would strike.

After Mum died in 1969, I asked her brothers whether they had been psychologically or physically abused as children; my medical training had taught me that the kind of fury Mum demonstrated can stem from child abuse. They adamantly denied any such thing. But a question mark remains at the back of my mind and I've discussed Mum with my sister Susan, who is a psychologist. We'll never know the truth now, of course, but I suspect that Mum was abused in some fashion when she was a little girl.

Mum was one of the most intelligent women I ever knew. Her birthright was her enquiring mind and her hunger for information and knowledge. She was a brilliant student at University High School, Melbourne, and qualified for university entrance, an impressive achievement for an Australian woman in the 1920s. However, she did only one year at university without completing her degree—I never knew why. She had been promised a job as a journalist on the *Argus* (which, of course, had been founded by her great-grandfather). However, when she applied, she was informed that she would have to start at the bottom as a typist, which outraged her so much that she left in high dudgeon and got a job in a bank.

Even though her own career ambitions had received such a setback, she firmly believed that women could do whatever they set their minds to. She was, in fact, an early feminist before the word was coined. I grew up with these admonitions as an article of faith, and she frequently talked about women she admired. When I was a child, I heard a great deal about her friend and my godmother, Mary Holdsworth, who went to law school late in life and topped her year. Mary was one of Mum's role models, and mine, too; others were the intrepid, strong Australian women who stepped into their men's shoes during the Second World War and did dangerous jobs such as driving buses around perilous country roads.

Mum read voraciously. She was fascinated by politics and history, and kept abreast with everything. My first memory of her finely tuned political instincts goes back to when I was four and was standing in the kitchen when she suddenly announced: 'Hitler has turned on Russia—thank God, we're saved.' She was right. Hitler couldn't win the war by fighting on two fronts simultaneously; but he could have beaten Britain if he'd not been tempted to attack Russia. Her political intuition was unerring; her analyses of events were rarely those in the newspapers or on radio, but in the long run, she was almost always right. She had nightmares about Hitler killing the Jews in 1940, long before the world officially recognised the dreadful truth. Forty years ago she worried about the consequences of world overpopulation, and as early as 1960 she could see that computers would eventually put people out of work. Her perceptions were always sure, and from her I think I inherited my political intuition.

But she wasn't just interested in things intellectual. When I was very young, she retaught herself to play the piano—she had learned as a child—and I remember lying underneath the piano by the pedals on sunny mornings as she played Schumann's *Scenes from Childhood.* This music still evokes my own scenes from childhood. Because we were quite poor, she supplemented Dad's income by sewing. She smocked peasant blouses, which were popular in those days, and made the most delicate nightgowns and blouses from silk chiffon and inserts of the finest lace. Then she had another interest, which I imbibed at the time but didn't exhibit until later. I grew up with an intimate knowledge of plants and their botanical names. One of my passions as an adult is gardening and another is music. She also taught me to sew, and at the tender age of ten I cut out my first dress on the back lawn.

And she was always reading. When we were kids, she took us shopping in central Melbourne every Friday, returning with a huge pile of books. During the week, she would tie a scarf around the bobby pins in her hair, vacuum the carpet or do whatever household tasks had to be done, then sit down for a cup of coffee with a cigarette and a book. I can still see her reading in the wooden chair that Dad made with maroon cushions that she made, the opalescent blue smoke swirling above her head, while we children played outside.

Mum met Dad in the mid-1930s because he played tennis with her brother Terence. Philip was tall, six foot two (188 centimetres), with freckles and curly red hair, and in the time-honoured Australian tradition, he was known as Blue (the same sardonic sense of humour that leads to men with black hair being called Snow). The family story is that he was standing in the Coffeys' living room when Mum, five foot two (157 centimetres) and looking very pretty, wandered in cradling a cat in her arms, and Dad fell in love with her immediately. He later took her to the theatre, and when he held her small hand in his big one, she immediately felt safe and knew that they would eventually be married.

Dad's life had not been easy either. He had to leave the public boys school Scotch College at fourteen when his parents divorced, because his father had ceased to pay the bills, and he took whatever jobs he could get, including selling advertising for the *Argus*. This was a precious source of income during the depression. One particularly traumatic day the manager lined up all the salesmen and pointed at those who were about to be dismissed. Dad was one of a few lucky ones: he stayed.

When he eventually left the *Argus*, he was offered a job with Mum's brothers, who ran a large lighting company called Kempthorne, named after one of their illustrious ancestors, Sir John Kempthorne, a vice admiral in the British navy. During the depression the boys, desperate to find work, started making outdoor lights out of kerosene cans in the back garage, and it grew into a thriving company. During the Second World War they won a contract with the Royal

Australian Navy to make emergency lighting systems for warships, and they never looked back.

Dad had the bad temper typical of redheads (my hair has a tinge of red in it, too). An excellent tennis player—he had been coached by Harry Hopman and was considered at one point to be potential Davis Cup material—he was known to become so furious during a game that he would smash tennis balls miles out of court. On one famous occasion he hit a ball right over the golden statue of the Virgin on top of the Camberwell Catholic Church. But despite his temper, he was always reliable, sweetly understanding, irreverently funny and unassumingly shy. Like Mum, he was passionate about many things, read a great deal and could be very persuasive. Well known writer Frank Hardy acknowledged that during the 1930s Dad converted him from Catholicism to socialism during arguments they had over lunch in Melbourne.

Mum and Dad had a great deal in common. Both considered ideas, books and music to be extremely important; both came from families who, though relatively poor, had had money and influence at one time. Like many Australians of their generation, my parents took their cues of 'correct' behaviour from England, particularly the manners of the so-called upper classes. They both 'spoke well' and were pretty savage if, for example, we children said '*Ee*-vonne' instead of 'Y-*vonne*' or 'washerlady' instead of 'washerwoman', or if we failed to hold our cutlery correctly, with our elbows in. Today they might be considered snobs, but they felt, I am sure, that they were simply teaching us how to behave in society.

Australia in those days was an interesting social study. The depression had a profound effect upon many Australians, who became insecure and never forgot it. The bulk of society in the 1930s was working class; people lived in suburbia on their quarter-acre blocks, the men cut the lawns and cleaned the car on the weekend and the women were classic housewives. Liberation was never thought of then.

Mum and Dad, both agnostics, had a strong sense of social

justice. They were, in a way, more progressive in their thinking at that time than most Australians. As I've said, they read widely, and they especially liked the work of progressive social writers like George Bernard Shaw (I still have mother's copy of *What Every Woman Knows*, inscribed by Dad). In their courting days they loved the theatre, and they also went to the opera, including Melbourne's rare productions of Wagner. When they married and had children, all this stopped: bringing up a family left little money or time for such luxuries, and making ends meet was not easy; the carpet in our house became so threadbare that my brother Richard would pull threads off the bare spots and use them for kite strings. We were given basic uninteresting, boring English-type food (mutton and boiled cabbage, and bread and butter pudding); I never saw a navel orange until I was a teenager.

Interestingly, despite my parents' lack of religious persuasion, from a very early age I dressed myself in my best clothes on Sundays and took myself off to church in the morning, Sunday school in the afternoon and church at night. Intuitively I knew there was some higher power or a God, but although I tried every neighbourhood denomination, I never found any evidence, so I gave up the search as a bad job at the age of seven.

My parents were also progressive in other ways. They told us at an early age about how babies were made, a thing never discussed in this still quite Victorian society, and I was not very popular when I saw it as my duty to educate the neighbourhood kids about the fundamentals of life. I had no idea that this was unacceptable behaviour until I told Judith Wiggerham and soon after her mother became quite cold and forbade her to play with me again. What had I done? This was one of the first of what were to be the many times in my life when I realised that I had said or done the wrong thing without knowing why—a very lonely feeling that occurs to this day.

I was a much wanted and waited for baby. My parents had experienced difficulty conceiving and were thrilled when I appeared on the scene. As he drove his labouring wife to hospital on 7 August 1938 though, poor Dad ran out of petrol, and he felt forever guilty.

My first eighteen months were blissfully happy as far as I can remember, despite the fact that Mum did not mother intuitively and fed me on the hour every four hours whether I needed it or not. She had attended a Truby King child care course to learn how to mother, which is surprising as she came from such a large family herself. One very hot summer afternoon old Mrs Miller across the road heard me screaming at the top of my lungs. She knocked on the door and tentatively suggested to Mum that, schedule notwithstanding, I might be thirsty. Apparently I was; I gulped down a whole bottle of boiled water, much to Mum's astonishment.

A very significant event occurred when I was eighteen months old. Mum was six months pregnant again with Richard and because she was very tired Dad decided to take her away for a holiday, so they placed me in an institutional home that cared for babies. I vaguely remember that this place was very cold, the nurses wore stiff white starched uniforms and high white hats, and my metal cot was pale green. I remained here for a fortnight—two weeks that were to have a profound effect on my life.

It has been very difficult to reconstruct that time because memories are dim, but during meditation, I recalled being placed upon a cold metal table and forcefully held down by a pair of huge hands covered in black hair as I struggled and screamed blue murder while they placed a cloth over my face and a ghastly smell filled my nose and lungs—chloroform. Years later when I became a paediatrician, I discovered that when a baby is suddenly abandoned by its parents, it screams for about two days to no avail and then gives up and sits in the corner of its cot, uncommunicative and severely depressed. It often takes months for the baby to forgive its parents, and it may never completely return to normality and a state of trust. This is my story. At the end of two weeks when Mum and Dad came to collect me, I had developed severe otis media (middle ear infection). These were pre-penicillin days; I had a raging fever and could have died—indeed I believed I was about to die when I was on the operating table.

These events changed my life. From being a trusting, happy child, I put a wall around myself and never really trusted anybody again, and to this day I let very few past this barrier. I feel that I am basically alone in life and that I must handle everything myself, and when I do decide to develop an intimate relationship, I have a great and recurring fear of abandonment. I also developed an intense and unreasonable fear of death, which has plagued me all my life. Clearly this is one of the reasons I decided to study medicine.

Of course, Mum and Dad had no idea what they had done to their daughter, except that when they returned to find me so desperately ill, Mum was inconsolable. To comfort her during my operation, Dad took her to the theatre, where they saw a film about a dying child being flown to hospital, and she wept throughout. Life is so unpredictable; a seemingly small event in the life of a child can have enormous consequences.

My brother Richard was born when I was twenty one months old. During Mum's confinement I stayed, happily, with Dais in her flat. Dais adored me because I was her first granddaughter. She let me wear her satin shoes with pointy toes and pencil-thin heels, and I staggered around pretending to be a grown-up. She had a wardrobe full of beautiful chiffon tunics glistening with bugle beads in the dressing room where I slept. She always left a perfect yellow banana, which I can still smell today, beside my pillow so I would wake up and eat it without disturbing her too early.

Dais had silver hair done in a bun at the nape of her neck and twinkly, quite wicked brown eyes. I lay in bed with her in the mornings, snuggling into her large soft, cushiony body.

She was about the only person with whom I felt relatively safe during my childhood. She gave me porridge for breakfast with cream from the top of the milk bottle, that somehow magically looked pink to me, and I was fascinated by the way she held a loaf of bread under her arm, buttered the end, then sawed the slice off with a breadknife.

Sometimes she played the violin for me. Her style was passionate, the violin resonating with vibrato as she swayed to the strains of *Air for the G String* by Bach. She once played in a concert before Dame Nellie Melba, who told her that she performed beautifully. She lived on that memory until she died. My love of classical music surely came from Dais.

She also had an interest in the occult. She took part in seances, where people joined hands around a table in a darkened room. Sometimes the table elevated and spirits appeared and spoke to people present. When I was little, she read my tea leaves and my palm, and told me I would have a long, turbulent life that would be interrupted by a serious illness (the last part has certainly turned out to be accurate). Dais gave me a tin tea set, and I spent countless summer hours under the trees at the back of her flat, making mud pies and feeling very grown up.

Her flat, in a large elegant building with red tiles and a terracotta dragon surmounting the roof, was in Kooyongkoot Road, Hawthorn. It was fronted by a bouncy buffalo grass lawn and a sweeping curved drive with an old cabbage tree palm smack in the centre of the lawn. She played bridge and when she proudly took me to visit friends for cards and afternoon tea, she wore a pink silk dress and a large hat covered with pink cabbage roses.

Judging by family photographs, Richard began life as a chubby baby, but when he was fifteen months old and we went on holiday to Phillip Island in Bass Strait, the home of those beautiful fairy penguins that have always been a great tourist attraction in Victoria, he became very ill with diarrhoea. During this illness he became extremely thin, and he's been skinny ever since. I had little time for him as an infant because it was clear that although Mum was kind of liberated, she was thrilled that she had given birth to a boy, and my time in the sun was eclipsed. However, we became quite good mates in childhood; we fought a lot, but we also played together for hours. As he grew older, he developed a love for aeroplanes that has persisted. He would walk very slowly around the house for hours, holding a toy model aeroplane, imitating the sound of its engine in his very deep voice. Even though he is now a diplomat, his childhood passion persists and planes are still one of his great loves.

Susan arrived twenty months after Richard, and Mum's life became, as she often told us, a round of household drudgery caring for three young children. Years later she told Susan that she had been a 'populate or perish' baby, quoting a popular slogan in Australia during the late 1930s and early 1940s. In those days Australia had a very small population (less than ten million), and we felt vulnerable living adjacent to the 'teeming millions' of Asia. Women were advised to increase the population as this would help to ensure our survival. To this day the government awards a sum of money, called 'child endownment' until recently, to each mother for every baby that she delivers.

This did not make Susan feel any better. She knew that Mum had her more out of duty than desire. Susan was a good baby; she rarely cried, and I was very fond of her. She was shy during childhood, never asserting herself, instead remaining in the background. She didn't have the forceful personality that I must have displayed; Richard and I dominated the scene. She had light blonde hair which she wore in a fringe and I remember thinking how pretty she looked when she wore a red tartan skirt and red jumper.

Fear of the 'yellow peril' or 'yellow hordes'—the racist tag given to Asians—not an admirable trait, has persisted in the Australian consciousness, but at one time in our history it certainly seemed vindicated. The Japanese bombed Hawaii's

Pearl Harbor on 7 December 1941, when I was three, and immediately moved south-west, closer and closer to Australia. This signalled a dreadfully anxious time; we had heard tales of Japanese cruelty in Burma and China. What if they invaded us? And how could we prevent their gaining access to our vast natural resources, our mineral wealth?

Panic really set in when Singapore fell in February 1942; nothing, Australians felt, could stop the Japanese from coming here. And in retrospect it seems there was every cause for fear. The Japanese repeatedly bombed Darwin, and only three months after the fall of Singapore, on 31 May, their midget submarines actually entered Sydney Harbour.

Even though this attack failed, threat of the Japanese invaders continued to permeate our daily lives. Like all houses, ours had blackout blinds on the windows at night, so if enemy planes flew overhead, they would be unable to see the lights of Melbourne. Scary air raid sirens frequently sounded, and searchlights filled the sky. Dad dug an air raid shelter in the backyard, basically a big yellow clay pit that filled with water every time it rained, because they couldn't afford a better one. If the Japs, as we called them, had flown over, we would probably have drowned before they could shoot us, whereas the Millers, a childless and relatively wealthy couple across the road, had a beautifully constructed dry shelter. This infuriated my parents, who somewhat injustly felt that because they had young children, they had a greater right to it.

Sometime during the war Dad was called up to serve in the army but because he had lousy eyesight he could not go overseas, so he worked in an ammunition depot at Keilor, north-west of Melbourne. One afternoon he came home, having received a commission. His digger's hat had been replaced by a flat officer's hat. Mum met him at the front door with a look of enormous pride; she fell into his arms and they had a long passionate kiss. I must have been four years old as I watched, and decided that that was what I was going to have when I grew up.

Petrol was in short supply for civilian use during the war and the fuel was charcoal-burning gas producers, cumbersome tanks that people attached to the backs of their cars. They caused the engine to backfire, and on the evenings when Mum and Dad had parties, I hid under my blankets, afraid of the combination of loud, laughing voices that seemed out of control and the terrifying explosions of the gas producers.

Many Australian families were so worried about the impending Japanese invasion that they fled the coastal cities and headed inland. Several times towards the end of the war Mum took us to Horsham, some 300 kilometres from Melbourne, to stay with her mother's sister Auntie Selma and her lawyer husband Uncle Reg for weeks at a time. I never understood how the location of Horsham would help us escape the Japanese. The back fence of their house abutted the main railway line to Melbourne and every day trains laden with tanks and other military equipment thundered up and down, pulled by enormous puffing steam engines. Clearly this transport route would have been a primary target. Several times as we climbed the fence to watch the steam engine, the train driver blew his terrifyingly loud whistle to surprise us, and Richard got such a shock he would hide under the bed for hours.

Rationing was a way of life during the war. We all had ration books and never saw butter, chocolates or other luxuries. But then, after the Battle of the Coral Sea in May 1942 and the victory of the US marines on Guadalcanal, greater numbers of Americans came to be stationed in Australia, training for the offensive in General Douglas MacArthur's 'island-hopping' strategy against the Japanese.

Occasionally Dad took us for a drive to Port Melbourne, where we would board a gleaming grey US warship. The sailors wore beautiful white uniforms—so different from the rather sloppy and sometimes ill-fitting clothes of their Australian counterparts—and the officers took us to their cabins.

They were lonely for their families, so they showered us with treats: chocolate bars and chewing gum in long grey strips. We thought this was wonderful, and admired the Yanks greatly. Mum also benefited from their generosity; they gave her silk stockings. These were impossible to buy in wartime and, like Australian women everywhere, Mum used to cover her legs with brown pigment or liquid makeup to get a similar 'look'. All this convinced us that the United States was an exotic land of plenty, inhabited by warm, kindly people.

I was four when I went to kindergarten at Strathcona private school. On hot days we sat under a weeping peppercorn tree, smelling its sweet herbal scent as we ate our lunches out of brown paper bags. The ground was dry and dusty, drilled full of cicada holes. We used to fill our lunch bags with water and pour it into these holes, and when the beautiful insects emerged shaking their lacy fairy wings, we carefully put them into matchboxes with air holes punched in the lid. One day some of us got into terrible trouble in class when the cicadas started their deafening *scree scree*. Now, whenever I hear cicadas, whose song has been described as 'the sound of heat made audible', I remember kindergarten and the smell of the peppercorn tree.

I was sitting in the classroom at my primary school in August 1945, just after my seventh birthday, when suddenly we heard the long wail of fire sirens.

'What does that noise mean?' asked our teacher, a pleased smile on her face.

I shot up my hand and said: 'The war's over.' And it was. How did I know? I suppose Mum had been talking about the war's end at home.

To celebrate, we were let out of school at lunchtime. I walked home through the sunny warmth of the early afternoon smelling all the flowers that hung over people's front fences and feeling very happy. Little did I know that the price of peace had been the explosion of two atomic bombs over Japan and the incineration of 350 000 people.

CHAPTER 2

When I was five, I went to Surrey Hills State School, a typical suburban government school. They initially put me in the first grade, but one of the teachers became concerned that I knew too much for that class, so I was promptly transferred to the second grade, where Mrs Hobsen, a rotund woman who sat at her desk on an elevated platform, taught us how to write cursive on our slates with pieces of chalk; we also learned the multiplication tables by rote, which we droned in a sing-song voice day after day.

The school was a two storey pile built of dark red brick, a labyrinth of classrooms that accommodated about three hundred children. The bare wood floors were noisy, the banister beside the stairs had protruding nobs every few feet to prevent the fun of sliding down on our bottoms. I visited the school recently for old times' sake and nothing has changed after fifty years. It even smells the same—a combination of lead pencils, new exercise books and faint, lingering smells of sandwiches and stale orange peel. I really didn't like school very much; it felt like a boring prison from which I would never escape.

I had various forgettable teachers until I reached the sixth grade with Mr Reynolds, a veteran who wheezed his way through the day as he coped with the pathology induced by inhalation of poisoned gas from the trenches of the First World War. He was a good, firm teacher with whom I felt very comfortable, and I sat at my desk absentmindedly dipping my nib in the inkwell on hot days while the cicadas droned their rasping lazy song in the trees outside, wishing I could join them.

On Fridays Mum gave us a penny pocket money, which I carefully placed on top of the inkwell. I gazed at it longingly all day, waiting for the bell to ring so I could go to the dairy and buy a red iceblock.

Every morning, each class lined up on rows of white dots painted on the black asphalt of the playground and marched into school, to the beat of a couple of kids playing the drums. On Mondays we sang 'God Save the King' and saluted the flag. And on Anzac Day, 25 April, we had a special ceremony. Nobody bothered to teach us the significance of this day. Nevertheless, we dutifully brought wreaths and floral crosses to school as instructed and placed them reverently on a designated spot on the black asphalt. I tried hard to make my floral tributes as perfect as those of the other girls, but I never could—my flowers always dropped off and were dying before I got to the school gate.

I wished that Mum would help me like the other mothers helped their children, but she never did. She read her books or listened to the ever-running radio serial called *Blue Hills*, which came on just as we had to rush back after our awful 'nutritious' Kraft cheese and brown bread lunch she made us eat, but she never seemed interested in what we were doing or what happened at school. She always arrived late, if at all, for sports days or Mother's Day events. We were just not a high priority.

I was a skinny girl with brown plaits and I desperately wanted to be pretty, coveting the dresses, lacy flowery hats and black patent leather shoes the other girls in my class wore to school. But Mum said that those dresses were common—I was a schoolgirl and therefore, she said, I must wear a uniform. She dressed me in checked dresses with white collars that she made and ugly brown socks and brown shoes. Every year when we lined up for the annual school photo, I tried to look prettier by undoing my plaits; to no avail, because my hair hung dankly in kinky strands around my shoulders.

So I looked different and was different. I never seemed to fit into the social pattern at school, and I didn't understand why. In retrospect, I can see that I had no social graces, I tended to say exactly what I thought, and then, as now, I was eminently teasable. I was almost always alone, although I did have two friends intermittently over that six year period, Valerie Russ and Margaret Haines, who for some strange reason seemed to like me. When I topped grade five and was about to receive a prize at the end-of-the-year ceremony, I was chased around the school yard by some kids who taunted me, saying that I would never get the prize. I did, but really only because my friend Margaret, the best student in the class, had been sick during the class tests.

I must have been a somewhat strange child. I remember being called precocious by a next-door neighbour when I was about five; I knew he was admonishing me, but I didn't have a clue what it meant. I was always attracted to the conversation of adults; it was much more interesting to me than the idle chatter of my female peer group at school, and I used to hang around at home when Mum and Dad had guests, listening to their fascinating discussions.

But this was not always safe, because of Mum. I was wary of her, mainly because I never knew from one day to the next how she would treat me. Some days when I came home from school, she was engrossed in a book and hardly noticed my existence; on other days she would meet me on the doorstep and say, 'I have a bone to pick with you,' and lash out at me. The loss of a hair ribbon or other inconsequential item was almost always a trigger that could precipitate a towering rage. She used to hit me with a coat-hanger or a wooden spoon, even kicking me as I cowered on the kitchen floor trying to avoid the blows. She attacked Susan and Richard, too, but not so often because, I think, being the oldest, I was the chief target. So I copped her greatest fury.

These onslaughts left me guilty and frightened, crying alone in my room for what seemed to be hours with no comfort. Oddly enough, I never felt angry with her; in a funny way I seemed to understand her. Dad may have known she hit us, but he was at work when it happened, so perhaps he didn't. He never said anything. His temper was quick, too, and he could be irascible, suddenly slapping us or kicking us under the table for holding our knife and fork the wrong way, but his anger never lasted long.

Mum's moods grew really bad from the time I was about six, and I didn't understand why until years later. She suffered from a chronically fissured tongue, which hurt when she ate pineapple, which she loved, or anything acidic, so her local general practitioner took a biopsy and performed a Wasserman test. When the test results turned out to be positive, he referred her to a specialist who told her she had syphilis and that she was a wicked woman. She staggered home from town, fell into Dad's arms at the front door and said, 'I've got syphilis'. He never believed the diagnosis; he cared for her even more, and their lovemaking was as passionate as ever. Only when Dad was on his deathbed did Mum tell me this story, to illustrate what a noble man my father had been.

Sometimes the actions of my colleagues are reprehensible. In those days a Wasserman test was thought to be a definitive test for syphilis, but it was later discovered to be a non-specific indicator for chronic inflammatory disease. As well as her sore tongue, Mum was also developing acute arthritis, later diagnosed as rheumatoid arthritis.

Syphilis is a ghastly disease. It can be inherited, but is usually transmitted by sexual contact, and the infecting organism can cross the placenta. It has three phases: acute, subacute and chronic. In the end it can induce insanity, called general paralysis of the insane, and it can mimic almost any other disease. Consequently, Dad had to be tested, and Mum also collected me from school and took us all to the doctor for a blood test. Nothing was said, but I could feel that something was terribly wrong. Her brothers were all dragged into the saga to be tested as well. So her whole family knew, and the ignominy was severe. Because we all tested negative, there was only one person from whom she could have caught the disease, and that was the brother of Mary Holdsworth, a pilot with whom she had had an affair before he was killed in the Second World War.

Mum's rages at this time became even more unpredictable, and being the eldest child, I felt responsible for her every mood, until one day when I walked into the kitchen, she suddenly burst into tears. For the first time in my life I knew I wasn't responsible, and I felt a huge sense of relief as I ran into the backyard to get Dad, who tenderly scooped Mum up in his arms and carried her into the bedroom. She told me later that if it hadn't been for us kids, she would have put her head in a gas oven that year.

It wasn't until we moved to Adelaide ten years later that she was finally relieved of the dreadful burden. A specialist physician, Dr West, one of my teachers in medical school, said to her 'Don't be ridiculous, you haven't got syphilis, you've got acute rheumatoid arthritis', as if the ravages of acute arthritis were not bad enough.

Even though she suffered so greatly during my childhood, Mum never succumbed to self pity. When I was about seven, she decided to study interior design at Swinburne Technical College. She loved the course, and discovered that she had a real flair for design. But she never took the final exam, which seems to fit the previous pattern of her abortive stay at the university. For a woman so outwardly self confident and intelligent, she was surprisingly insecure in the areas of academic pursuit.

Before she took the tram in to Melbourne each day, Mum would peel the potatoes and leave the uncooked Irish stew in the pressure cooker. It was my job to finish cooking the dinner when I got home from school. I didn't mind; I often had to finish making the icecream out of vanilla junket, and I always took more than several spoonfuls as I whipped it with a hand beater prior to refreezing. Every night after dinner Dad piled us into the car to collect Mum. Those were particularly happy times because he would muse about the origins of the universe and why some street lamps were orange and some were green while we plied him with questions. He was always intensely curious despite his lack of formal education.

Mum was settling down, Dad was working, life was pretty stable. In many ways, the life we led as children was free and aimless. One of our favourite amusements was playing in the rubbish tip opposite Wattle Park (a large piece of relatively natural bush located at the terminus of a tram route, owned by the Tramways Department), trying to derail trams by putting rocks on the tracks as they came hurtling down the hill.

In those days refuse was relatively safe; there were few if any toxic chemicals and the rubbish consisted mainly of old rotting household garbage, pieces of tin and other curiously cut metal fragments from factories. Hanging around the rubbish tip was fun. We watched with fascination as the bush rats ran in and out of their burrows, and we often found interesting items such as old sheets of corrugated iron, from which we fashioned cubbyhouses. Huge blackberry bushes grew next to the tip; when the fruit was ripe, I would gingerly balance on strips of corrugated iron, eating the beautiful berries while the wine red juice ran down my chin.

Every Guy Fawkes Day, on 5 November, the neighbourhood had a huge bonfire. Weeks before the great night kids carted tree limbs, old car tyres, wooden fences and anything flammable to the empty paddock, and gradually the pile became enormous. Then we would put a scarecrow of Guy Fawkes on the top and set it alight. What heat and what fun—firecrackers, catherine wheels, rockets, bungers, you name it. Then we settled down on the damp grass and ate the delicious carbonised spuds swathed in butter that we'd thrown in the fire.

Sometimes on Sunday mornings a Salvation Army band wearing navy blue and maroon uniforms appeared on the street corner, pumping out hymns. In our woollen pyjamas, we followed them for miles as they collected a gaggle of similar kids, almost like the Pied Piper of Hamelin. We returned home only when our stomachs got the better of us.

The outer Melbourne suburb of Surrey Hills was initially built among empty paddocks. Our white timber house with picket fence designed by Mum and Dad was very pretty. As a young child I spent hours playing in the surrounding paddocks, picking and smelling wildflowers like the 'harbinger of spring', and making intense studies of ants as they scurried around collecting food. But gradually suburbia expanded over the empty paddocks, as new roads and new houses were built. We explored every nook and cranny of the half-built houses, walking barefoot across second-floor joists placed 60 centimetres apart and 6 metres above the ground. Sometimes we slipped, skinning the inside of our legs all the way up to the crutch, and the pain was excruciating. But we seemed to have no sense of danger at all and could easily have killed ourselves. I don't know what Mum thought we were doing; she never asked where we'd been, but there was a certain sense of freedom in this.

The new roads were smooth and black, made of bitumen,

and we spent days drawing steam engines and boxes for hopscotch up and down the road, using the chalky clay we surreptitiously stole from just inside the front gate of our neighbour Mrs Miller. The motor car was not yet the noisy and insistent presence it later became, and the milkman, the iceman and the baker delivered their wares in horses and carts instead of trucks. Sometimes the horses left manure on our artwork, which was disconcerting, but Dad was always pleased, because he collected it in a bucket for his vegetable garden.

I was a tomboy, much preferring the company of the neighbourhood boys to the girls. I climbed trees, learned to drop kick a football, built cubby houses and rode my bike like a demon. But I was also a very maternal little girl and spent hours playing with my dolls, sometimes with my erstwhile friend Judith Wiggerham. I was waiting for the day when I could be a real mother and life could begin. I dressed my cat Pinkle in dolls' clothes, complete with bonnet, and wheeled him around the neighbourhood in my beautiful white dolls' pram until he got sick of it and leapt out, leaving a trail of clothes behind him. I dearly loved my doll Margaret Rose, named after Princess Margaret, with her china head and real hair that smelled of perfume, and I longed for her to be a real baby who could suck from my non-existent breasts.

Because Mum was always so busy or distracted, I was lonely, so after school I went to the neighbours' houses. Mrs Blythe next door fascinated me because she always had a baby at the breast, and I sat for hours watching her feed it. Every day she made sponge cakes; she taught me how to bake too, and told me I had a light touch. Mrs Neale down the road had a fairytale garden full of delicate pink prunus blossom, ranunculus and poppies, and her lawn was covered with English daisies. Pictures of fairies adorned the walls of the Neales' house, and Rosemary, their daughter, delighted us by making us tiny steam engines out of matchboxes and cotton wool. Mrs Neale, who had a refined Adelaide accent, was very proper. Mr

Neale, on the other hand, was a gruff man who ate tomato sauce sandwiches, which he said made the hair grow on his chest, and he opened his shirt to prove it. He put lit matches into his mouth, much to our delight and fear.

Before Mum began her interior design course, Dad would arrive home from work shortly after five in the evening, methodically hang up his suit, take off his shoes and don some comfortable clothes; dinner was served soon after. Life was generally harmonious, although my parents' relationship was not always placid. Both were quick-tempered, and they sometimes had blazing rows, which often ended with Mum giving Dad the silent treatment for hours or days. He couldn't bear that, so he always pursued her until there was peace. I can still see my 188 centimetre father bending over Mum, who was at least thirty centimetres shorter, hugging her protectively with great affection. Mum had difficult straight, fine hair that had to be 'set' at the hairdressers every week in the approved styles of the 1940s and 1950s, and Dad fondly called her Fluffynut. Another of his nicknames for her was Trotters, because she had thick ankles—she loved that. When I was little, Mum told me that intercourse was the most wonderful feeling in the world—how right she was. Later she told me that they had a passionate and fulfilling sex life.

After dinner we would sit by the fire listening to the radio or talking. When I was small, I often sat on Dad's lap while he read us Kipling's *Just So Stories* or the Greek myths and legends. The mysterious and majestic image of the white winged horse Pegasus has never left me. One of my earliest memories was lying in bed beside Dad as he told the tale of Henny Penny, the chook who got a fright when she heard a loud noise and set off to tell the king the sky was falling down. It is because of her that my family nickname became Hen. And interestingly, I've spent half my life telling the world that the sky was about to fall.

On the weekends we would climb into Mum and Dad's bed in the mornings, where we laughed and played while Dad told us jokes and stories. He told another cautionary tale about a mouse who ate some tablets out of the medicine cabinet and then set off on his bicycle to find and eat a giant. We also learned a joke alphabet, culled from an English music hall act, that started off: 'A for horses . . .' and finished 'Z for breezes' (you had to say it aloud to get the full effect). He talked in Cockney slang—'He put on his bag of fruit [suit] and his almond rocks [socks] and caught the bread and jam [tram] to work.' He was a very funny man.

I was besotted by books and loved reading, like Mum—I read for hours in bed at night. In the window of the second-hand bookshop next to our local pie shop (which sold hot meat pies dripping in tomato sauce that Mum frowned upon because she said pies were bad for us) was a copy of *The Adventures of Robin Hood.* For months that faded green book stayed in the window; for months I longed to read it. I finally persuaded Dad to give it to me for my ninth birthday. It almost became my bible. I read it over and over every lunch-time as I forced down the gluey Kraft cheese and brown bread while my school colleagues wolfed down their aroma-rich pies. Robin Hood, stealing from the rich and giving to the poor, became my hero. His band of merry men adored him, and he was at the same time unassuming and brave.

Meanwhile, Dad continued working at Kempthorne for several years, and when I was about nine, he left to become a salesman for the Lusteroid Lacquers paint company. Both he and Mum were determined to give us a good education, and they worked hard and fiercely for us. For a while Mum took a job in a biscuit factory to help support the family. The broken chocolate-covered biscuits she brought home for us melted in our mouths.

One weekend when we were on our customary Sunday drive, Mum and Dad discovered a new subdivision among the sandhills of Seaford, a seaside town on Port Phillip Bay. They bought two blocks of land that were pretty cheap at the time, and Dad decided to build two houses as an investment. He intended to let them out to holidaymakers, and the rent would help pay for our education at private schools. The houses were typical Australian weekenders, mostly constructed of asbestos; we had no idea of its dangers at the time. Several nights during the week, after he had finished work, Dad loaded up the trailer behind our Austin Seven with asbestos sheeting, wooden joists and stumps and drove more than thirty kilometres there and back with the heavy trailer swaying along behind the little car.

When he reached the block, he stored the construction materials under the tea-tree bushes, ready to begin building on the weekends. An irritable old ex-soldier named Frank taught him how to build the houses and I came down with Dad to give him a hand. I held the fragile asbestos sheets while he sawed them, covering us both with dust. I spent hours holding the sheets onto the rafters of the ceiling with a broom, while he hammered nails into them. If the broom slipped, the sheet cracked and broke, and the air would turn blue with Dad's swearing. I helped Dad put the stumps into the holes, adjust the joists and uprights, and hold the rafters in place while he hammered in the nails. I became so knowledgeable about building houses that I knew I could easily do it myself.

They crowned the Queen the day after I decided to ride my bicycle down to Seaford—more than sixty kilometres altogether. As I trudged, exhausted, pushing my bike up the last hill at dusk, I saw the headlines—'Hillary Conquers Everest'; I was so excited and proud. What a gift to the new young monarch. These were days of endless hope and heady excitement. Like most Australians at that time, I adored Elizabeth, having spent half my life lying on the floor reading tales of the royal family in the ubiquitous *Australian Women's Weekly*.

When I was small, I wanted to be a teacher, partly because of one of my own teachers, Mrs Clarke. She was the mother of

John Clarke, who was in my class and was my first love. We walked around the school yard for several days with our arms around each other, sharing chewing gum. But I also loved his mother. She was kind, gentle and understanding, and one day after school I actually discovered where she lived and went to see her. She was a little surprised, I think, when her vacuuming was interrupted by this child appearing at her door.

But my plans to be a teacher changed one Sunday morning when I was eleven and I suddenly knew what I really wanted to do with my life. I climbed into bed with Mum and said, 'I'm going to be a doctor.' When she asked why, I said, 'Because I can help more people as a doctor than I can if I'm a teacher.'

I can't remember Mum's reaction to this, but she seemed vaguely interested. I don't remember if Dad even commented. So this was my idea, my own destiny, not influenced by my parents at any stage. I was determined to be a healer. My decision was probably influenced by several things. One of the first stories I heard at Sunday school was about the Good Samaritan, and it affected me greatly. Then there was Robin Hood, and then there was my brush with death as an infant. Maybe if I understood the process of disease, I would have more control over my own life and the lives of others. Also I had always loved the disinfectant smells of hospitals and doctors' surgeries. There had never been a doctor in my family.

At about the same time, I made another decision. Hearing Dais play the violin had nurtured my innate love for classical music, and now I wanted to learn more about it. I had studied the piano for a year when I was ten, but Richard had been taught the violin from the age of six and was a member of the Victorian Junior Symphony Orchestra. I decided to learn the clarinet and join the orchestra, too. I don't remember why I chose the clarinet.

Initially Dad refused point-blank, saying he couldn't afford to pay for more than a year's tuition. I persisted, nagging him so much that he finally said, 'All right, but if you don't get into the orchestra within a year, the lessons stop.' He probably thought that was the end of the matter, but he was wrong. I never missed a lesson and practised like mad, trying to master the difficult reed. The family all hated the squeaky sounds I made, and Dad threatened, tongue in cheek, to banish me to the wattle tree in the backyard, out of earshot, but he never did.

Within a year I was accepted into the orchestra as second clarinettist. The auditioners said they put me in not because I was a brilliant player but because of my enthusiasm. I loved being part of the orchestra, supporting gifted soloists, playing wonderful music. Mendelssohn's Violin Concerto became one of my favourite pieces, and we played many other famous works, including Beethoven's *Egmont* Overture and his Piano Concerto No. 3. The melodies one hears as a member of an orchestra are more precise and individual than the mixed but still beautiful sound you hear in a concert hall or on a record.

Music has always been an important part of my life. I remained a member of the orchestra for four years, and when we moved to Adelaide, I joined the Adelaide Conservatorium Orchestra. I eventually abandoned the clarinet for medical studies, but years later, while studying paediatrics at the age of thirty-one, I joined a chamber music group for a brief period. I'm ashamed to say, though, that I have given up and become too rusty to take pleasure in the sounds I make these days. Even so, music continues to feed my soul. The first thing I do when I walk in my front door is switch on classical FM radio or put on one of my records or CDs. Brahms is particularly important.

Around age eleven I was becoming more confident, more *myself*; I started to accept Mum's attitude that women could do anything. When I first menstruated, she told me proudly, 'You're a woman now,' and I felt very pleased. For the first time she acknowledged that I was worthwhile, no longer telling me that I was a gangling, gauche child who walked like a duck with out-turned feet and who would never be able to wear high heels.

As I moved into adolescence, I longed for true love. I was convinced that soon a man would come into my life, sweep me off my feet and adore me forever. The *True Romance* and other love comics I devoured as I lay on my bed assured me that this was the way life would be. But I was very worried, because at the age of eleven, my chest was as flat as an ironing board. All the other girls at school developed breasts before I did. What sort of life was I doomed to have? How would I feed my babies?

It never occurred to me to express my fears to the other girls, and I wasn't the sort of girl who 'told' things anyway. And even with our newfound understanding, I didn't talk to Mum; I think I didn't trust our relationship yet and didn't want to push things too far. Besides, she was, as always, fairly inaccessible.

The only person I told was Dad. He was wonderfully sympathetic and understanding. Night after night when he finished work, we walked round the garden together while he assured me I was normal, and that I would certainly develop—I was just taking my time. Sweet Dad. In due course a small breast bud appeared, then another, and I was on my way.

CHAPTER 3

Mum decided that I should go to an exclusive private school called Fintona in Balwyn when I completed my primary education at Surrey Hills State. After investigating the private schools, she chose this one because Miss Cunningham, the headmistress, was in all senses of the word a remarkable woman who subsequently became one of my mentors.

Mum was excited about Fintona, and for the first time almost since infancy, she began taking an active interest in me. It was as if I had graduated from invisible childhood into the age of significance.

A scholarship was offered to prospective students, so one hot afternoon late in November, in my last year at primary school, I went to Fintona to sit for an exam, which in essence was an IQ test. Now I may have come from an interesting, non-conformist family, but I was ill equipped to answer many of the questions that day. I guess I'd never posted a letter, so

I had no idea about the price of stamps, and I also didn't know the name of the current prime minister of Australia. It seems we lived a somewhat sheltered existence as children and were not exposed to the practicalities of everyday life, although I have no idea why I couldn't identify the prime minister. IQ tests are all very well and good, but they seemed to assess not innate intelligence but rather the environment from whence the children came. I failed to win the scholarship.

Fintona was set in elegant grounds in Balwyn Road. The main building, an old Victorian brick mansion with a slate-covered round tower and stained glass windows, was graced by a curved drive lined with statuesque elms that arched around to the front door. On clear days during recess and lunch hour, the domed, bouncy lawns of buffalo grass were littered with girls in tan uniforms sunning their legs, much to the discomfort of Val the gardener. We wore brown felt hats, brown blazers and brown shoes, and I don't like brown. Once a week we had to undergo a uniform inspection when the school bursar checked the height of our hems and made sure our underpants were the standard brown!

Miss Cunningham was a woman of means and owned the school herself. Unlike other private schools in Melbourne, it was non-sectarian, although we used the Presbyterian hymn book during morning assembly. Margaret Cunningham, in her mid-fifties, didn't resemble a typical headmistress, being five foot (152 centimetres) tall with a very big bosom and a red, bulbous nose. The shape of her face and her kind, intelligent, wise eyes reminded me of my grandmother, Nanny, and also reminded me now, in retrospect, of Margaret Mead. Unusual for a woman in those days, she was a chain smoker, and her frontal lock of greying hair was stained brown by nicotine.

She collected a talented and sometimes quite eccentric group of teachers, all women and most of them single. Our teacher, Miss Boyd, wore the same hand-knitted pink sweater every day over her quite handsome breasts. She used to charge up and down the classroom when she was exercised by our lack of knowledge. Occasionally when a girl completely dumbfounded her, we would hear a loud bang and would turn to see Miss Boyd lying flat on her back in the aisle. We called her Basher Boyd.

Miss Cunningham herself taught religious instruction; she would enter our classroom carrying a Bible in one hand and a box of matches and cigarettes in the other. The discussion often took a right turn and became a fascinating conversation about sex or the latest issues in politics.

She was a woman of enormous integrity and made no concessions to parents' expectations, no matter how wealthy, or how important they were to the school. In her address during one annual speech night, she told the parents that a girl had been caught by a teacher cleaning the blackboard with a glove. When the teacher scolded her, the girl said, 'It's all right, Dad will buy another pair.' Fixing the parents with a stern gaze, Miss Cunningham told them that girls develop their values from their homes, and castigated them for their lack of respect for decent values and for spoiling their daughters. She raked the audience with her eyes and asked, 'Have you ever pulled strings? Have you ever committed graft? Have you ever lied in your business affairs?'

You could have heard a pin drop when she finished speaking. It was as if the parents were also her pupils. Uncle Bob, Dad's brother and the father of my cousin Dorothy May, who was also at the school, stood up at the end and said with a snort, 'She's a communist.'

Despite Miss Cunningham's direct, no-holds-barred relationship with parents, Fintona attracted girls from some of the wealthiest and most established families in Melbourne. It never occurred to Dad that he should tell me that our family was relatively poor, so I naturally considered myself to be the samc as the other girls.

'Can I have a horse?' I asked one day.

Dad: 'No.'

'But all the other girls have horses,' I whined, at which point Dad became angry and forced me to look at all the monthly bills he had to pay. I hated looking at the bills, I was confused and felt guilty, but I got the message loud and clear.

I loved Fintona. It was a school that emphasised the arts. Every year we had Shakespeare Day, when we dressed up and performed acts from the plays in the quadrangle. I developed a love for his verse that has never left me.

We also had a hobbies day, during which we competed for points for the particular 'house' to which we belonged. Mine was called Ower, named after a former teacher. There was great excitement when we arrived early that Spring morning to arrange bowls of magnolia blossoms and other flowers, to hang the art we'd just completed and to set up our plates of scones, sponge cakes and pastries. I never did very well, except once when I unexpectedly won first prize for a rather primitive painting of a picnic. There was also a musical hobbies day, when we competed by singing and playing musical instruments. Although it was serious, we had a lot of fun. My bloody classmates sat in the front row sucking lemons the year I performed the slow movement from Mozart's Clarinet Concerto, the buggers.

Every Thursday morning the school rang with the celestial beauty of ancient English madrigals as Miss Baker, the sweet, gifted, white-haired music teacher, led the group. I couldn't wait to be part of it, but it was not until I was fifteen that I became eligible, and even then my voice was quite mediocre. Another activity I enjoyed was the debating class. We were taught how to develop a case even if it was the antithesis of our belief and how to sway others to our viewpoint. I had been given an important skill that would stand me in good stead for the rest of my life.

I had a natural aptitude for biology and always seemed to score 100 per cent without ever studying. I drove the poor teacher, Miss Rowe, crazy by asking too many questions. I loved learning about botany and photosynthesis and was fascinated by embryonic development, spending hours studying the preserved foetuses in the museum cabinets. Maths also came easily, as did physics and chemistry, but I had no gift for languages, and English was just so-so, despite the fact that I loved reading. I discovered the Scarlet Pimpernel books by Madam d'Orczy in the library when I was twelve and devoured them. He was such a hero, always courageous, supporting the poor against the rich during the French Revolution, I suppose a little like Robin Hood.

Probably the most important factor in my future development was Miss Cunningham. In retrospect, she was a crucial mentor. She was a courageous, independent thinker who never gave a damn about social convention and seemed to need no overt approval for her actions. If people didn't like her school and her policies, they could take their children elsewhere, but the stronger and more independent she was, the longer the waiting list. In a certain sense that is the way I have lived my political life.

It took me a couple of years to settle down at school, although I did make a close friend called Helen McGrath. She reminded me on our first day that we'd gone to Strathcona kindergarten together, although I'd forgotten her. We became fast friends, and I took her on an exciting family holiday to an old gold mining ghost town called Walhalla, where the village store, run by an Addams family woman with dank hair and long green teeth, leaned precipitously at an angle over the creek. We panned for gold and hiked for hours through dense bush, exploring old gold mines.

Gradually, over a couple of years, I noticed that people started to like me and to treat me with some deference, but I never really knew why. I suppose I had metamorphosed from an ugly duckling to a swan, but so had we all. The girls were more interested in what I had to say and somehow I seemed to be a person worth knowing and even a bit of a leader. I was more confident, and certainly felt part of the general scene. I continued to do quite well, although I never studied and my report cards were variations on 'Could do better'. I received credits instead of distinctions, which annoyed me, because I knew that I was bright enough to win top prizes. It never occurred to me, however, that a bit of work might be necessary to achieve this. It all came so easily.

❧

My adolescence crept up on me, and gradually I discovered that I had become physically attractive to the opposite sex. This became overtly apparent when I went to a holiday music camp at Geelong Grammar School at about the age of fourteen. A young trumpet player named Clarrie, who had slicked-down, oiled hair, started hanging around me. I was flattered but confused. One night when we went for a walk, he pulled me down onto the ground and started kissing me and feeling my breasts. I had been kissed only once in my life—at dancing class when I was thirteen—and I let Clarrie go on for a while because it felt so good. Then when he became more urgent, I grew uneasy and stopped him.

When I told Mum what Clarrie had done, she seemed not to be upset and offered no advice or guidance. She was noncommittal, which I found strange. Though she had given us all the information we needed to know about the mechanics of sex, she said little else, and I was left to discover the emotional intricacies alone.

In the summer of my fifteenth year, we went on a family holiday to Lake Tyers, about 160 kilometres north-east of Melbourne, and we stayed in an abandoned guesthouse and slept on the dusty wooden floorboards in sleeping bags. Dad used to stay here in his youth, and he took us here, I think, to recapture those times of former glory. During the day we sat on the sagging wooden front steps overlooking a grove of old, dark pines, listening to the radio as Lew Hoad and Ken Rosewall won the Davis Cup for Australia. Dad was very involved and excited. But the holiday was difficult for me. I was a typical morose teenager, bored silly with the stupid and uninteresting antics of my family, removed from my newfound friends at Fintona, with nobody of my own age and nothing to do, and I was consumed with adolescent angst and loneliness.

Camping nearby were several older people, including a twenty-one-year-old man, who took a fancy to me. Because I was bored, I played along, and when we got home after the holiday, he asked me out. I am astonished now that I was permitted to see him. It was totally inappropriate for a naive fifteen-year-old to be consorting with a twenty-one-year-old man. Furthermore, since I had reached menarche Mum and Dad had stressed the importance of virginity before marriage, so what on earth did they think we could be getting up to?

He was much more experienced than me, and for a short while I thought I may have fallen in love with him. But as the weeks went by, I saw that it was really about sex, which at that age assumed a biological imperative. We spent a lot of our time together on the ground in Wattle Park, near our house. Although we didn't actually have sex, we got pretty close to it. This had two consequences. First, my grades dropped dramatically because I couldn't concentrate on my school work, and secondly, I realised that he and I did not have much in common. He was much older, with adult expectations, and we had little to talk about. Though he continued to be interested in me, I started to feel uncomfortable. However, I had no idea how to extricate myself from the situation.

The linked problems of grades and my friend were solved when Dad announced that he had been promoted from a travelling paint salesman to manager of the Lusteroid Lacquers factory in Adelaide. Getting rid of my erstwhile lover paled into insignificance in the face of a much greater calamity. I would have to leave Fintona after four years, the school I loved, where I finally felt I belonged. I was devastated. How could this school ever be replaced?

I was not the only member of the family to feel dismayed.

After Mum completed her interior design course, she established a little shop called Bretts, where she sold Featherstone chairs and beautifully designed fabrics for curtains and upholstery. The clientele was increasing; her interior design practice was starting to thrive. On the other hand, she was pleased about Dad's promotion and enthusiastic about the prospect of a new life. Richard was dragged out of his school, Carey Baptist Grammar, and Susan from Fintona, where she had just begun.

Dad sold the house, packed our furniture and carpets into a removal van and drove us to Essendon airport. One of the compensations for our upheaval was the excitement of flying for the first time. We boarded a noisy old DC3 propeller-driven plane, and during the flight we were served what we kids thought was absolutely delicious food.

After Melbourne's solid nineteenth-century prosperity, its parks and gardens and cool, rainy English-type climate, Adelaide was strange. It was hot, flat and dry, and to our eyes it appeared to be a large, over-organised country town. Its central business district was an orderly chequerboard; there seemed few tall buildings, and the whole was bordered by a square mile of parched, brownish parkland. It was surrounded on three sides by low-lying hills. This city, I later realised, would be a perfect target for an atomic bomb because the radiation would be reflected back into the city by the hills.

Until we could find a place to buy, we rented a house in one of Adelaide's flat, dry suburbs, a working-class district known as Enfield. The house had lino floors and a great deal of dust, and its only saving grace was a navel orange tree in the backyard with huge, sweet fruit. I developed appalling hay fever, perpetually suffering from streaming eyes, sneezing and a totally obstructed nose; my worried mother took me to a doctor who gave me desensitising injections that proved completely useless. I was cured only when we moved out of this awful joint six months later.

Mum and Dad found a beautiful, elegant house on the eastern side of the city, cradled by low hills. It had a long verandah, fronted with white, wisteria-covered columns, high ceilings, a large garden with flowering orange trees, and room for a tennis court at the back. After our houses in Melbourne and Enfield, this was luxury, and we could hardly believe our good fortune.

On the recommendation of Miss Cunningham, Mum and Dad sent me to a school called Wilderness, run by the three old Misses Brown. They wore their hair pulled back into buns, high-collared blouses fastened by cameo brooches, and long, brown skirts. Though this was the early 1950s, they could have stepped out of a Henry James novel.

Wilderness was aptly named. The school grounds were a jungle, the classes chaotic. The girls came from a social group similar to those at Fintona, but they were totally undisciplined. In jammy Adelaide accents they swore at Miss Wait, the deaf French teacher, which I found horrifying, and when her back was turned they threw orange peel at me because I was the strange new girl. They were the rudest mob of people I had ever encountered.

Although I was still determined to do medicine when I left school, I was beginning to learn that my lazy academic existence would not get me very far. I would have to work. The South Australian education system was six months in advance of Victoria's, and because of all that time spent with my boyfriend, I was starting to fail or just scrape through tests in calculus, chemistry and physics. During the weekends I would lock myself away in my dusty room while the rest of the family went off on picnics or attended to social life. For the university entrance exam I worked harder than I had ever done in my life. I passed four subjects with one credit and failed French—not good enough to get me into medical school.

To get better results, I needed to repeat my final school year, but not at Wilderness. Despite the pleadings of the new headmistress, who promised to make me a prefect if I stayed,

I fled to a state school, Unley High. This turned out to be an excellent decision. The teachers were highly professional. There was music as well; our music teacher, Duncan McKay, wrote an opera that we performed called *The Black Tulip*, set in Holland about a man who cultured a rare pure black tulip. He also conducted the whole school in a performance of the *Messiah* at Christmas. It was exhilarating. Mr McKay was a lovely, enthusiastic man who had a plethoric complexion and who, sadly, died at an early age of hypertension.

It was fun attending a co-educational school for the first time since I had become an adolescent. I fell in love with one of my teachers, who was handsome, introspective and brilliant, dreaming of him day and night. He rode a powerful blue Triumph motorbike, which I thought was very sexy. For the school social one year, the girls were told to wear high-necked dresses. Defiantly I made a grey cotton blouse with a plunging neckline. My reward was a lift home on the back of the Triumph. He wrote my phone number on the back of a matchbox. Dad had strictly forbidden me to have anything to do with motorbikes, so it was extraordinarily exciting.

After the dance he asked me to his home for dinner. He was an only child and his mother prepared a cold salad and meat for a meal; it all felt somewhat surreal. He seemed so old, although he was only twenty-one. He was handsomely pensive and looked a little like Lord Byron. He began writing me love poems. Then he sent me a complex six-page letter that puzzled me for a long time. On the fifth reading I suddenly understood that in a poetic way he was asking me to sleep with him. Shocked, I wrote back and refused, so he dropped me. I was acutely miserable and mourned him for months.

Mum, on the other hand, was happy with her life. She had found a job as an extension officer for the state Department of Agriculture, which meant driving to various centres in

South Australia and talking to rural women about decorating and extending their houses. She really enjoyed it, but was even happier when she started her own private interior design consultation once again. One of the interiors she did was for the new Queen Elizabeth Hospital. She was photographed for the paper with the new curtains, and we were all very proud of her.

I believe that this period—when we children ceased to be a burden or a drudge, and when she was doing a job she loved—was one of the happiest times in Mum's life. Thanks to Dr West and his enlightened medical diagnosis, she no longer had to suffer the stigma of syphilis, her arthritis was much less painful, her general health was better, and she and Dad were very happy.

Susan, Richard and I were all teenagers, and life seemed full of exciting and satisfying possibilities. We led our own lives for the most part and got on well. In Adelaide we settled into a series of family routines. On Sunday mornings Dad usually mowed the lawns, and midday dinner consisted of roast beef with Yorkshire pudding or lamb and mint sauce, with our favourite chocolate 'delicious' pudding to follow. To this day the smell of freshly cut grass and orange blossom, combined with roast dinner, always recalls these happy times.

We played silly dinner-table games. Often, when Mum got up to get something from the kitchen, Dad would put her dinner plate on her chair. We held our breaths, waiting to see whether she would fall for the trick, but she never sat down on her meal. Once he told us all to leave the table and hide when Mum was in the kitchen. She came back, saw the empty table, and burst into tears, so we crept back, feeling rather sheepish. After Dad came home from golf and a few too many beers some Sundays, he would move the piano around without saying a word just to tease Mum, much to her feigned annoyance.

Joint family projects were another highlight of our lives. We cleared the backyard and made a tennis court. Dad took us down to the sandhills in the beach suburb of Glenelg, where we dug out mounds of couch grass and planted it on the prepared earth at home. Before long we had our own grass court, and we held tennis parties most weekends. Between sets Mum served homemade scones and jam and cream, or delicious hot chocolate squares with coffee.

Weekends were times for our friends to join us, and our house was always full. At school and later at university our friends brought their guitars and played and sang, often until three in the morning, fuelled by Dad's sherry and Mum's good food. As a family we sometimes played chamber music to our assembled guests: Mum the piano, Richard the violin, Susan the cello, and me the clarinet. Dad sat back beaming with pride.

The house often rang to the sound of passionate arguments about politics, philosophy or history. This was unusual: at the time, political debate was hardly a feature of Australian family life. Television, which has done so much to increase popular awareness of world issues, did not even reach Adelaide until 1960. Mum, however, was always well read and well informed, and she did not hesitate to challenge us and our friends, who frequently left our house with their heads buzzing with new insights into issues they had scarcely considered before.

CHAPTER 4

In January 1955, when I was seventeen, I was on holidays in Melbourne when I discovered that I had been accepted to study medicine at the University of Adelaide. Being accepted was exciting enough, but even better was the knowledge that my fees would not be a drain on the family budget. My final examination results had been good enough for me to be awarded a Commonwealth Scholarship, which meant that the federal government paid all tuition fees for the six years necessary to complete my medical degree.

In March I took my place as a first-year medical student at the University of Adelaide. This was a tiny campus, dating from the 1870s, its elegant old stone buildings set among tall poplars and green lawns fringing the River Torrens, on which ducks placidly cruised. It looked like the English institutions of higher learning on which it had been modelled, and I could hardly wait to embark on life.

I discovered that I was one of only thirteen women in a

first-year intake of 150. Having lots of boys to flirt and work with was my idea of paradise. As time went on, I became close to the men in my year, rather than to my female colleagues. However, I did have one close woman friend in medical school, Rena Zimmet, who had been at Wilderness with me. We worked and studied together, and we liked similar clothes and similar boys (particularly the so-called Perth boys, a bunch of roguish, charming blokes who studied with us for our first three years until the medical school was established in Perth). Rena is Jewish, and I was honoured when she asked me to play my clarinet at her synagogue one night. This was the first time I had had any contact at all with Jewish people, whose customs and religion I found fascinating and exotic.

I had acquired a boyfriend in the holidays before I entered medical school. He was a second-year medical student named Brenton Mollison, a sweet guy who was fond of me and whom I also liked a great deal. Brenton was about five feet eleven inches (180 centimetres) tall, with straight blond hair and blue eyes. He belonged to the university army corps, which because of my pacifist leanings I didn't like much, but this never became an issue between us.

After about eighteen months Brenton was replaced by another boyfriend. In fact, for a lot of the time I was at medical school I was either in the middle of an intense and meaningful love affair, planning to buy the engagement ring, or else in the depths of despair, having broken up with somebody or been dumped myself. I went to all the university balls, which were held in the refectory, usually in a dress I had made myself. I loved the sensuality and smell of new materials—taffeta, silk, satin. One of my first ball gowns was a beautiful opalescent blue georgette sprigged with white flowers.

I made my dresses on our old Singer pedal sewing machine using *Vogue* designer patterns. (Years later I was shocked to discover that the Singer company was involved in the nuclear arms race.) Usually when a boy picked me up for a date, I was frantically putting the finishing touches to a new dress, feeling sick with excitement, sewing up the hem or putting tabs on the shoulder straps to hold my brassiere straps in place. At these dances, the boys wore black dinner suits and brought us flowers. Towards the end of the night, when things became hot and heavy, we moved to a smaller hall and danced with the lights off. It felt very daring, and who's to say what happened in the cars on the way home?

In first year we studied basic science subjects: physics, chemistry and biology. They were not very exciting, but I worked like a demon, determined to do well. While I was studying, my proud parents crept respectfully around the house, knocking on my door when they wanted to speak to me and bringing me cups of coffee and sprigs of fragrant daphne to keep me happy.

During our lunch hours we lay on the lawns at the back of the refectory, munching our sandwiches and talking about everything. The air shimmered with excitement, sexuality and the freedom of new ideas, and I loved every minute of it.

However, I soon realised that my fellow students' receptivity to new ideas was limited if they were not comfortable with them. During the mid-1950s Britain, America and Russia were going hell for leather testing nuclear weapons in the atmosphere. Having been taught by a brilliant genetics teacher, Dr Peter Martin, about Müller's radiation experiments with the fruit fly, and understanding that radiation induces mutations, I was greatly alarmed to discover that there was a high fallout of strontium 90 and other radioisotopes in the northern hemisphere. I tried to draw my fellow students' attention to it by speaking at lunchtime in the refectory hall. But the boys were far more interested in their perennial poker games, and they looked up with disdain in their eyes—who was this madwoman interrupting them?—so I desisted. Their reaction was intensely frustrating, but at that stage I unquestioningly accepted their rude behaviour, which I now see was sexist in a typically Australian way.

In December of my first year the final exam results were

posted in the cavernous grey stone front office of the university. I walked up on leaden feet, afraid that I had failed. On the way I met Brenton, who greeted me with a big grin and said, 'Guess what? You came eighth in the year!' I was overjoyed.

During the long university vacation I always worked to supplement my keep at home. Crouched down behind the counter, I wrapped axe handles and pounds of nails in Woolworths, and the hours dragged interminably.

Later I worked in the Friendly Society chemist shop in King William Street, one of the main streets of Adelaide. I loved mixing lotions, ointments and medicines and making suppositories and pills. I especially liked the smells. But the job did have a few problems. Initially I was put in the front part of the shop behind the counter to serve the customers and the woman in charge refused to give me any responsibility, always putting me down and treating me like a kid. I was only seventeen, but I knew I was smart enough to handle any shop problems that may have arisen. Fortunately, I was moved into the dispensary, where I worked with a smiling young man named Trevor, a friend of Brenton's who was training to be a chemist.

In second year I started bona fide medical subjects: histology, anatomy and biochemistry. I felt like a real medical student because we were now introduced to the dissecting room on the second floor of the school. I had never seen a dead body before and I was both morbidly fascinated and terrified. But when the stiff, fat-soaked sheet of canvas was lifted, the corpse was so soaked in formaldehyde and so grey that it looked as though it had never lived.

Six students were assigned to dissect each corpse. Our body was so riddled with cancer that finding some anatomical landmarks was difficult, if not impossible. Nevertheless, we soon became accustomed to dissecting out the nerves and blood vessels and sitting around the bodies in anatomy seminars. Before long we ceased thinking of them as people and gave them nicknames and made jokes about them. We would nonchalantly eat our sandwiches as we dissected, and sometimes the formalin-soaked fragments mixed with our food.

I drank in the information like a thirsty horse and studied hard. In second year, I came second. 'Who came first?' asked Dad teasingly. He wasn't putting me down, just expressing enormous pride that I had done so well.

Because of my results somebody suggested that I apply for a scholarship to St Anne's, a residential women's college. To my amazement, I won it—the first time I had been given a real scholarship (the Commonwealth scholarship wasn't significant because if you made a good pass in your final year exams, the government automatically granted you free university education). The college was in North Adelaide, a couple of kilometres from the university through beautiful parklands, between the Adelaide Children's Hospital and Lincoln, the men's residential college. I lived there for the whole of third year.

This was my first experience of living away from home—it was exciting and somewhat lonely at the same time. My roommate was Margaret Dwyer, a physiotherapy student and devout Catholic who went to Mass every morning. I had never known a Catholic before and her devotion amazed me. Margaret and I became dear friends, and I once made her a dark green velvet dress. We cooked toast on our bar radiator at night and drank black instant coffee, and it all felt very grown up. Not being accustomed to housework and also as an act of rebellion and freedom, I didn't wash my bedsheets for six months until they became so grey that Margie couldn't stand them any longer and took them away to wash them herself.

Life felt joyous and free. We would come down to dinner dressed in our academic gowns with pretty clothes underneath, ready to go out on an exciting date. We flirted outrageously with the boys who lived across the park, at St Mark's College as well as at Lincoln. On Tuesday nights the solemn sound of the bellringers rehearsing floated across from nearby St Peter's cathedral to my window while I studied cardiac function and the causes of hypertension. The exotic fragrance of pittosporum blossom also drifted through the window, the perfume that permeated the air each spring when I always fell in love.

Flirting was a pastime I adopted with great enthusiasm, and sometimes I used my sexuality to advantage. For the viva voce (oral) exam in third year physiology I made a red woollen dress with a wide, white bertha collar that was somewhat revealing. The professor asked me some difficult questions: 'Miss Broinowski, what colour is a patient who has carbon monoxide poisoning?' I stumbled over the reply, so I was surprised to discover that I came top in that subject. The difficult questions were to test the depth of my knowledge because I did well in the written exam, but I'm sure the dress was not a hindrance.

In fourth year we entered the wards and had to deal with live patients for the first time. This was exciting but traumatic: here, literally, was blood-and-guts reality. First thing in the morning we attended post-mortems, to which we were rostered in groups. I never knew what human tragedy would greet me on these visits to the mortuary.

It was difficult not to become emotionally involved with the patient, impossible not to say: 'There but for the grace of God go I.' Deeply upsetting was the body of a young, lactating woman riddled with breast cancer: when a lactating woman develops cancer, it spreads like wildfire because of her high circulating levels of hormones. That forlorn, lonely, heartbreaking image stayed with me for years—a dead mother and a motherless baby. Another day we confronted the marble-grey body of a young man, as perfect as Michelangelo's *David*, lying on the slab without a mark to be seen, his brainstem severed the night before in a motorbike accident.

One morning just after breakfast we were watching a particularly grisly post-mortem: a man had died of peritonitis and the pathologist was using a soup ladle to scoop pus out of the abdominal cavity. We were only just keeping our breakfast down when Borrie Hewitson, one of our group, started vigorously smacking his lips, as if he were about to savour a really good meal. Borrie, with darting black eyes and a full black beard, was older than the rest of us, and we loved him. He always made us crack up in difficult situations.

In fourth year, life was fairly easy-going. Dressed in our stiffly starched white coats (bum huggers for medical students, longer for qualified doctors), we took part in morning medical and surgical ward rounds, then departed for the hospital canteen where we devoured hot scones, apricot jam and tea prepared by women volunteers. We ambled back for more rounds, then lunch at the refectory, followed by a postprandial lecture in the Verco Theatre in the Medical and Veterinary Institute behind the Royal Adelaide Hospital. Our tummies were full, the room was warm and about half the class fell asleep at some stage of the lecture, whether the subject was gastric ulcers, renal disease or liver function.

I often ate dinner alone at the refectory and studied at the university's Barr Smith Library until ten p.m., when I wandered through the empty streets of Adelaide to catch the bus home, after buying delicious dark nut chocolate from the Haigh's Chocolate shop at the Beehive corner next to the bus stop.

During the afternoons we took case histories, examined patients, read the case notes and recommended treatment. Though we were not primarily responsible for the care of our patients, I grew to love some of them. A very pretty middle-aged woman with a chronically painful hip hadn't been diagnosed properly by several doctors, and had been pushed from pillar to post until finally an X-ray and biopsy revealed cancer, a secondary malignant deposit. Her husband and family seemed to have abandoned her.

I lost touch with her until, six months later, when I walked down the centre aisle of a surgical ward, I heard somebody call my name. I went over to the bed, and there she was. I hardly recognised her, she was so wasted away, with the yellow-grey look that cancer patients get. She said she had spent the last few months in a ward for terminally ill patients. She was still pretty, but so sad, so forgotten. I hugged her, lay on her bed, and cried with her. She died soon afterwards.

Ward rounds took place twice a week. They were conducted by the consultant honorary physician or surgeon (honoraries were not paid either for teaching or for treating public patients; it was considered a contribution to society), who questioned us closely about our allotted patients. Some of our teachers were outstanding, including Professor Norrie Robson, a Scot and a gentleman, who was tall and thin with a patrician nose and intelligent blue eyes. Thirty-five years ago he was predicting that as medical care improved, so the population of Australia would be burdened with old people unable to contribute to the economy. He was seriously concerned about this trend, which has now come to pass.

Another memorable doctor was Syd Krantz, a short, stocky surgeon who had been a doctor on the Burma railway. He had been so short of instruments that he operated on patients with can openers and knives. His gruelling and terrible experiences had made him less than considerate when handling patients. Accompanied on ward rounds by a retinue of sisters, nurses and medical students, he would march up to a patient seated on a chair and announce in his loud, raucous Australian accent: 'You've got a cancer and we'll cut it out tomorrow.' Whereupon the patient would collapse on the floor and a puzzled Syd would turn to the sister and ask, 'Sister, what's the matter with that patient?'

Later poor old Syd was hospitalised with a heart attack. He was known at the time to be the most difficult, fractious patient that the doctors and nurses had ever had to deal with. Strange how some doctors don't really learn the art of healing until they themselves have truly suffered.

In fourth year I was attached to a surgical clinic consisting of two long wards, male and female, each containing about twenty patients. There I met a surgical registrar, who was about six foot three inches (190 centimetres) tall, with a bushy black moustache and brown eyes. He looked very handsome in his dark suits, shiny black shoes and white coat, and I was instantly smitten. One afternoon as we were scrubbing up together for an operation, he asked me out. I was flattered and quite overwhelmed.

He picked me up in a big, black American Dodge, and we went to dinner. I was dazzled, thinking all my birthdays had come at once. When he took me home, I was trembling. 'What's wrong?' Mum and Dad asked, after I staggered in and sat on their bed at two in the morning.

'I don't know,' I told them. But I did. I was deeply in love.

Every third night when the surgical registrar, Tom, was on duty, I came into the hospital and assisted him in the operating room; we spent much of our time there. It was a tender, loving romance that was destined not to become permanent. I was broken hearted when it came to an end five months later.

About a year later I went out with a medical student who was a reckless driver. Not far out of town he went through a red light and hit another car. I regained consciousness in the smashed car to discover that he had disappeared from the scene. Someone called an ambulance, and I was taken to the Royal Adelaide Hospital. My nose was broken, squashed sideways onto my face; I looked terrible. And who should walk into the X-ray department as the registrar on duty but Tom. Although we were no longer going out together, my heart leapt when I saw him. After administering pethidine, he pushed my nose back into shape. But it never looked quite the same again.

But I recovered from the heartbreak and in 1960, with one more year to go before I graduated, life was rich and full.

Mum and Dad had built a holiday house in Sellick's Beach, about eighty kilometres from Adelaide, where they spent a lot of time, Dad revelling in his passion for fishing and Mum catching up on her reading. At last they were able to relax; Richard had almost finished a law degree and Susan was in nursing school, so all of us were doing well. On 30 November I gave them a big party at our house in Adelaide to celebrate their twenty-fifth wedding anniversary. It was a wonderful evening, full of fun and laughter. The card I wrote said that if after twenty-five years of marriage Richard, Susan and I were as happy as our parents, it would be because of their example.

Just before Christmas I attended the wedding of some dear friends, Brian and Jennie Elliott, and afterwards Richard and I drove down to Sellick's Beach. It was summer, the fields of wheat shone silver under the moon, and I was full of peace and happiness. Mum and Dad were waiting for us in the pretty little house overlooking the Southern Ocean.

The next day I was driving with Dad when he suddenly said, 'When I press in the pit of my stomach, it feels as if I've been kicked in the solar plexus.'

My blood suddenly ran cold. Dad was looking at me anxiously, so I said as lightly as possible: 'I have the same feeling when I press in my stomach.' But I knew all was not well.

I tried to dismiss our conversation from my mind. Dad was obviously lacking in energy. He had always been so strong and reliable, but suddenly everything was an effort. He couldn't pull his fishing boat up onto the trailer without sweating profusely. On the way home from the holiday we persuaded Dad to see a local doctor, who found nothing on physical examination. He later consulted Dr West (Mum's doctor), but he too was unable to find anything.

Dad grew weaker and weaker until he could no longer go to work and had to stay in bed. This was quite uncharacteristic because he had rarely missed a day's work in his life. It was January, a hot, dry time in Adelaide, and as he lay on top of the bedcovers, the house reverberated to the music of the new records he had received for his anniversary—Dvorak's Cello Concerto and Brahms' First Symphony, which Dad called 'bittersweet music'. Mum bought him a heap of paperbacks, but he really wasn't in the mood to read.

I returned to medical school early in January for my obstetrics and gynaecology term at the Queen Victoria Maternity Hospital. Our group of five was living in a separate section of the nurses' quarters set aside for medical students. One day the four men were playing cards in our sitting room and I was pottering around. I remember I was wearing a pair of black and white shorts with bows at the side and a matching top with white bobbles just reaching my waist. I rang home to see how Dad was, and he told me he was in such agony that he had to crawl down the hall to the lavatory on his hands and knees. Immediately I phoned Dr West, who arranged for him to be admitted to Calvary Hospital as one of his private patients.

Dad was already on painkillers, but he insisted on driving if it was the last thing he did. He and Mum had a big fight about it, but she eventually yielded. They picked me up on the way, and Dad was admitted to a room with a balcony on the second floor of Calvary, overlooking the North Adelaide golf course.

The weather continued to be hot and Dad was uncomfortable. Fortunately, his nurse was Sister Katherine, a devoted nun with kind eyes who wore a black habit and bib and a starched white vamp across her chest, which Dad would flick playfully when she bent over him. She loved his naughtiness and she prayed for him every morning in chapel.

The doctors examined Dad's stomach with a barium meal, his colon with a barium enema, and his gall bladder with a cholecystogram and did blood tests, all to no avail. He grew weaker and weaker. After a couple of weeks they had to put a brace over his bed so he could pull himself up, and he could only shower sitting on a plastic chair. I went to see him most days, as we all did, and he was inevitably his cheery, reassuring self to all of us. He and I alone knew that something was deeply wrong; none of the rest of the family had any idea.

After three weeks he developed bruising in his navel. 'My navel's got a black eye,' he said jokingly. Later I learned that this is Cullen's sign, indicating bleeding in the peritoneum.

Dr West decided to operate, to look inside Dad's belly. I was shocked to learn Dad's haemoglobin level was so low that he needed a transfusion before they could touch him. I was still hoping for the best, but I was full of dread.

On the morning of the operation Richard, Mum and I went to see Dr West. We met in a tiny room on the second floor of the hospital, surrounded by wards full of patients.

'Well, what did you find?' I asked.

'Nothing much,' he said, 'except his liver was full of white masses.'

Part of me died. My very worst fears were confirmed. 'He's got cancer,' I said quietly.

'Yes,' said Dr West.

Then Mum started to scream. 'No, no, no,' she kept saying, 'I had no idea . . . no . . .' It was dreadful. Richard and I were too numb to do or say much to her, and Dr West just stood there. We eventually bundled her out to the car and drove up to Magill hospital in the Adelaide foothills, where Susan was a student nurse. Richard went into the ward where she was dispensing tablets in her nurse's cap and apron, and she was delighted to see him. When she came out to the car and we told her the news, her face collapsed. She wanted to come back with us to see Dad, but the battle-axe of a sister refused to give her time off. Susan was only eighteen, and she didn't have the confidence to stand up to the woman and leave.

Back we drove to Calvary, where Dad had just recovered from the anaesthetic. The day was very hot and he was sitting up in bed on his balcony, a wet washcloth on his forehead, his chest bare and a bandage on his stomach. We were very nervous about seeing him: what should we say? What *could* we say?

His first words as we walked in were, 'I'm sorry to do this to you all.' He knew the diagnosis. Before the operation he had made Dr West promise to tell him the truth. But even *in extremis* he put us first. Later when we asked the surgeon how much longer Dad would live, he said, 'Maybe a week or two.' We were stunned.

The next day Dad grew very excited, insisting that he had to get out of hospital as soon as possible and book an airline ticket. He had never travelled, and he insisted that he must see Paris before he died. I could hardly bear to listen. He had worked so hard all his life to educate and care for us. Now I was about to enter final-year medicine, Richard final-year law and Susan would soon be a nurse. We were almost independent; this was the crowning point of his life, and now he would never be free to explore the world. The knowledge of this was so bitter.

The next night, on the way to the hospital, we bought him an icecream, one of the few things he could eat. Dad was still just able to walk, and when we arrived he pulled Mum behind the door and gave her a passionate kiss, their first real one since their argument about driving to hospital. The desperate kiss of a dying man, Mum said.

Over the next few days Dad was in so much pain that they had to drug him with pethidine and chlorpromazine. Sister Katherine said he was most lucid in the early morning, before he needed drugs, and he wanted me to be with him. We had always been close—more than ever now—and I had to be there. So the next morning I got up early and put on the blue pleated silk dress I had just made, but I didn't leave immediately. I had promised to make Dad an egg flip and I dawdled as I whipped the egg whites. I don't know why, probably because I couldn't bear to see him so ill, to face the fact that he was dying.

I travelled the sixteen kilometres to Calvary on the tram, and Sister Katherine met me in the hall. 'You're too late, we had to medicate him,' she said.

I went into his room where he was deeply asleep. I could only just wake him to tell him I was there. Sitting beside him for hours reading copy after copy of the *Women's Weekly*, I felt sick: why had I been so slow? But Dad knew I was there and he seemed comforted.

That day I had arranged to meet Mum in town on some errand, and I felt a confusion of divided loyalties. I wanted to stay with Dad, but I knew Mum needed my support and she was expecting me. I don't think she could admit to herself that Dad was about to die, and she was desperate. Eventually I told Dad I had to go. He begged me to stay with him, but I left. I made the wrong decision. I never saw him conscious again.

That night he became delirious, but somehow he found the strength to get out of bed and stagger around the room. He must have been frantic. Then he slipped into a coma. They rang us early the following morning—1 February 1961—to tell us he was dying and that we should come to the hospital.

With trepidation Mum, Richard, Susan and I entered his room to see our lovely, strong, reliable father, now with his eyes rolled up in his head and oxygen prongs up his nose. Because of the effort breathing cost him, his mouth was deformed and his short, panting breaths whistled through his bottom teeth. We stayed with him for only about ten minutes, then the nuns gently took us into a sitting room and gave us cups of tea. We were so stunned that we were moving like zombies. 'We don't know how long it will be,' they said. 'You'd better go home.'

So we did. We didn't know we needed to sit with Dad and hold his hands, to comfort him and help him die. None of the classic work on grief (such as that of Elisabeth Kübler-Ross) had been done in 1961.

Within half an hour the phone rang from the hospital. Dad was dead.

I wanted to see his body, to make his death real, to say goodbye. So I dragged the whole family into Calvary, including Dais, then in her eighties and crippled with osteoarthritis in her hips. Poor Dais was almost dumb with shock and grief. 'Why him?' she kept saying. 'Why him and not me?' But the body lying in the bed was not Dad. He wasn't there. His face had shrunk away to only half the size it had been in life, and his ears seemed enormous. I kissed his cool cheek, we all did, then we left.

The doctors wanted to do a post-mortem, but I knew that they stuff the eviscerated corpses with old rubber gloves and newspaper. I couldn't bear that happening to my beloved father, so I refused. I didn't want to know the exact cause of death. He was my father, not a patient.

Even though I had kept things under control during Dad's illness, Mum decided that Richard should be beside her when she made the funeral arrangements. This hurt. I had been Dad's partner in many ways: we had built the holiday houses together; he had given me the reassurance I needed when I was entering the difficult years of adolescence; he had encouraged me in my study and been proud of me; and I had comforted him in his last illness as best I could. But my place was now being usurped by my brother. Mum needed a man to lean on, and now Dad had gone, her only son filled the gap. Though she was an innate feminist, she respected men more than women, as did so many women of her generation.

Shortly after we arrived home from the hospital, the doorbell rang. It was Uncle Bob, Dad's brother, who had driven nearly a thousand kilometres from Gippsland in Victoria to see him. I said, 'You're too late, Dad's dead.' Hugging Uncle Bob was surreal. He had the same voice, the same feet, he even felt like Dad. Was Dad really dead?

The next day was the funeral and I cleaned and vacuumed

the house almost obsessively just for Dad. When we arrived at the crematorium, there was a large group of people standing around; I said to Mum, 'These must be from the last funeral.' But they weren't, they were there for Dad. He would have been thrilled to know how many people cared for him. Mum's four brothers and their wives drove over from Melbourne; we had never had so many family members together at one time. Some of my dear friends from medical school also came, and several of them carried the coffin.

The Reverend Arthur Jackson, the Methodist minister who performed the ceremony, said that although Dad had always claimed to be an agnostic, he was the most Christian man Arthur had ever known. Ironically, Dad had been christened in St Patrick's Cathedral, Melbourne, and he died in a Catholic hospital: the full extent of his contact with formal religion.

We all got through the ceremony intact and were just walking out of the crematorium when Susie's friend Mick Best put on the last movement of Brahms' First Symphony. As the strains of this glorious music filled the place, Mum stopped at the door and said loudly, 'I want to hear this.' The bittersweet music Dad had loved so much destroyed our feigned composure, and we all wept.

That night we held a wake for him. It was Dad's party, he was there; we told his jokes and laughed ourselves silly. But the next morning we woke up to emptiness as the sickening, brutal reality hit.

Sometime afterwards Mum set down her own feelings in words.

> Grief is so different from what I imagined. One commiserates with someone on their loss without having any conception of what it means.
>
> Grief has a taste and a smell. It is a physical lack of a physical presence, a deprivation of a voice, a laugh, a wit, an attitude of mind. A loss of a sturdy independence. A complete irreverence, a flashpoint temper, a warm understanding, an unassuming

shyness. A loss of a reliance, complete in its absolute steadiness and predictability.

Grief hides in music, in a tone of voice, a footstep down the passage—a loneliness in preparation of the evening meal. It surrounds the double bed and flourishes in the quietness of the night. It is a realisation of the solitariness of each human, alone at birth, alone at death. And the worst of all is its utter and final ending of a life while the mind still holds the image of a personality. It is this fight between life in the mind and death in the body that makes adjustment so impossible.

Grief is not a beautiful thing, never let them tell you this. It's a ragged, tearing bitter thing—a sickness of the mind from which the patient might recover but most likely will finish life less complete, less normal than before.

After Dad's death Susie was so distraught that she seriously considered leaping off the balcony of the nursing home. Richard remembers caring for Mum and sorting out Dad's will and business affairs. He was working full time as an articled clerk at the time. But he was distressed, and I remember him occasionally driving the family car through the hills at great speed.

I was in a state of shock, but I felt surprisingly stable, probably because I had not come to terms with what had happened. I barely cried, and I was obviously in denial. In a way, too, I felt that psychologically I had stepped into Dad's shoes and, by becoming him, was reliable and dependable; I didn't need to grieve. I became the main support for Mum and would arrive home from medical school to find her in his wardrobe crying among his clothes. She was heartbroken and never really recovered.

As a memorial to Dad, I decided to come top in final year. He had always been so proud of me, and in his absence I would do him proud. I worked like a Trojan, but though I won prizes for anatomy and clinical medicine, I failed to make the grade and came only second. Graduation day felt meaningless. Mum was there in her best hat and clothes, but Dad wasn't. In a subtle way much of my life has felt like that ever since, a certain emotional void that will never again be filled.

On the night we graduated, everyone in the year came to our house for a party. We felt a huge sense of relief that six years of study had ended, and incredibly, we were doctors at last. We danced on the tramlines in Goodwood Road until dawn.

CHAPTER 5

Being an intern was no fun. I had been a pampered and respected student, able to enjoy myself and sure of my place in the world of medicine. Now that I had entered the wards as a responsible doctor, I found myself at the bottom of the hospital pecking order.

Interns (known as 'housies' or house surgeons) are little more than glorified ward clerks, inordinately busy attending to patients, filling in forms and being bullied by nursing sisters. We worked eighty hours a week for very little pay and little gratification. Sometimes I was so tired, having been up all night, I hardly knew what I was doing. And to make matters worse, I found myself working with a medical registrar who seemed to know little more than I did.

I felt empty inside. I was lonely and my life seemed flat and purposeless, an endless round of menial drudgery. All my props had disappeared. I no longer had the security of a father who loved me, I wasn't a star of medical school anymore. I couldn't confide my feelings to Mum. She had her own problems, and in any case I always knew that Dad understood me and she really didn't. I was alone.

I was also involved in an anxious on-again, off-again relationship with a medical student named Bill Caldicott. I had met Bill several years earlier. He was a friend of Richard's. They were in the University Air Squadron together, and Bill often played tennis at our house. (This had family echoes: my parents had met because Dad played tennis with Uncle Terence, Mum's brother.) About five foot eleven inches (180 centimetres) tall, Bill was lean, with a friendly face, beautiful blue eyes and blond hair. He was a year behind me in medical school and several months younger. I was always aware of when Bill was around. He was bright and curious, and we liked talking together. We became good friends: when I broke up with my surgeon lover, Bill was very kind and supportive and I appreciated his friendship.

Bill was the most successful and career-oriented member of his family. His father, George, was a fruit farmer, his elder sister, Judith, was a homebody like her mother, and younger brother, John, had no academic interests. He was his family's golden-haired boy: as far as his mother, Dot, was concerned, he could do no wrong.

Bill and I gradually became closer, but he often complained that I didn't regard him with the same degree of devotion that I had given to the surgical registrar, who was eleven years my senior. He was right. Bill and I had a great deal in common, but I had always intended to marry an older man. Possibly because he was jealous, Bill told me that he thought it was bad for older men to become involved with younger women, and was insistent that we should share similar experiences and grow up together.

Bill also saw me as a challenge. He appreciated the fact that I was clever and did well in medical school, and that I was popular with other medical students, who considered me to be somewhat glamorous. But I was never sure whether Bill was the right man for me, and I kept breaking off our relationship because I didn't want to become too deeply involved and hurt him. Yet each time I did, I grew lonely, missing his lively mind, and we would get back together. We were always great friends.

I had broken off with him yet again just before commencing my internship. Although I had gone out with other men whom I found attractive, I also found them relatively boring. For this reason, as well as my general dissatisfaction with this stage of my medical career, I was feeling lonely and restless. My feelings came to a head one day after an arrogant surgical registrar admonished me for failing to test the urine of a patient who was about to go to surgery. This wasn't my fault: incredible as it seems, we had never been taught how to properly prepare a patient for surgery—much of our training as doctors was excellent, some left much to be desired. But I felt worthless and depressed.

I was slouching along the corridor in the surgical building when I looked up and saw Bill coming towards me with his long, youthful strides. I was really pleased to see him. We went up to my room, where I poured out my unhappiness. He listened sympathetically, as he always had, happy to see me, as I was him, after six months.

A few nights later we went to a party. Being back with Bill was a relief. I was lonely and had missed him terribly.

We had a good time that evening and felt very close to each other. That night marked the turning point in our relationship. Some days later we went to see the film *Kind Hearts and Coronets,* but half way through we looked at each other and decided to leave. In the car Bill asked me to marry him. I accepted.

The family were pleased. Mum liked Bill very much. Richard was tickled that I was marrying his old mate, and for her part Susan thought he was very attractive. Yet I was uneasy at some level. I used to sit for hours on my bed at night in the residents' quarters, capturing the light in my sapphire and diamond engagement ring, mesmerised as it flashed on the ceiling. I was trying hard to maintain the elation and relief I had felt the night of the party, but I couldn't. For although I cared for Bill very much, in truth I was flirting with depression.

Looking back I can see that several influences impelled me to marry. Most important, I was still deeply affected by the death of my father. I wasn't even aware of what we now know as the grieving process. At medical school we had been taught nothing about grief, or human emotions in general. The loss of Dad was immense, but instead of facing it head on, I chose to marry, replacing him with a husband.

Second, I was heavily influenced by social pressure. Early marriage was the norm in my circle at that time. It seems strange now, but in the early 1960s, a woman who was not married by the age of twenty-three was considered a failure and an old maid. I, who had always been so popular with men, found the thought of being 'on the shelf' galling, especially since all my friends were either engaged or married.

I loved Bill, but the romantic passion I had dreamt of as an adolescent was absent. On the other hand, he had a fascinating mind and a keen sense of humour, and he was much more interesting to talk to than the other men I had been out with. He was steady, he loved me, and despite my unease I felt that we could build a good marriage.

Several months after the engagement I discovered to my dismay that I was pregnant.

This was devastating news, particularly in 1963. Girls were supposed to be virgins when they married. Mum and Dad not only bought into this societal ethic, but they were forever giving me little pep talks about the lack of reliability of contraceptives. I don't know why virginity was so important to my parents, but I suspect Mum became pregnant by another man (the pilot who was killed in the Second World War, perhaps) and had an abortion. Or maybe Mum aborted Dad's baby before they married. In fact, I never used contraception until I married, because I never consciously intended to sleep with anyone.

Naturally I had to tell Bill. I piled into my little Morris Minor and drove down to Mum's house at Sellick's Beach, where he and two friends were studying for their final medical exams. Bill was shocked by my news. 'You wouldn't do this to me!' was the first thing he said, as if I had deliberately become pregnant just before his final exams. Although he was more accepting of my news later in the evening, his first remark was all I heard.

With his words ringing in my ears, I thought, 'That's it, I have to terminate the pregnancy'. I drove back to the hospital and next day gave myself an injection of ergometrine to induce an abortion. I vomited all over my bedroom floor, but the drug induced no uterine contractions. In truth I was secretly relieved that the abortion attempt was a failure and in retrospect I realise I made the attempt to comply with the admonitions of my parents. Susan knocked on my door just after I had cleaned up the mess, but I didn't tell her that I was pregnant, that I had just tried to abort the foetus, or that I was extremely depressed.

My guilt and depression led to increasing isolation. I had nobody to talk to. At the time I had no close woman friends. Dad, my chief confidant, had gone, and nobody could fill his shoes—though now, in view of his attitude, I wonder what his reaction would have been. I never had confided in Susan, and Richard, too, knew very little about my life? Though we lived side by side and were fond of each other, we were not close in this way.

When I eventually told Mum, her words were 'This is the first time you've let me down.' I was stunned. Was she really aware that all those times she had punished me with physical abuse I had done nothing wrong? If so, she never admitted her duplicity. Did she really know that I'd actually been quite a good girl all my life? And if, in fact, she herself had conceived an extramarital pregnancy, how could she possibly castigate me, her daughter?

During the early days of my pregnancy I was rostered on the urology clinic, working for two gung-ho macho surgeons. I suffered greatly from morning sickness, and my job was not pleasant. I had to catheterise old men's penises, asking them questions about their patterns of urination: Did they have to wait for their stream to begin? Was their stream slow, and did they dribble at the end? Several times when I assisted at surgery, I almost vomited into my mask and had to flee the operating room. I think my superiors suspected I was pregnant, but they were very sweet about it.

Bill and I moved our wedding date up several months so I wouldn't look pregnant. 'This may be second best,' I thought, 'but at least I'll be a bride.' I had wanted this ever since I was ten when a friend of the family had given me her wedding bouquet of gardenias, which I kept in the laundry sink for a week, watching the flowers darken and go brown but never lose their haunting perfume. I went to a big department store and bought some beautiful French braided lace, which I had made into a simple, flawless dress with a wide boat neckline and a train, and I ordered a bouquet of gardenias.

When the wedding day dawned, I was anxious, hoping everything would magically come right. But the occasion felt a little like my graduation. Part of my bridal dream had involved floating down the aisle on Dad's arm, but without Dad the day had little meaning for me. Mum didn't help by saying, in an irritated voice, 'Helen, pull your stomach in,' while the dressmaker was zipping me up. I nearly died—how could she embarrass me so in front of a stranger? Richard was the obvious substitute for Dad, but when I was dressed in my finery ready to go to the church, he was nowhere to be found. I discovered him asleep on his bed in his dirty clothes; the poor bloke had just mown all the lawns and had put his head down for a short rest.

Arthur Jackson, the minister who had buried Dad, chose a modern, not very attractive Methodist church in the seaside suburb of Glenelg for the ceremony. There were about seventy-five guests: Bill's parents and family, my family, and our friends. I had never really clicked with Bill's family; we had little in common. And his mother, particularly, felt that I was not the appropriate person to be marrying her beloved son. To prove the point, she went to the wedding of Bill's former girlfriend, whom she had liked a great deal, several hours before she arrived at ours.

Mum, who looked very pretty in a coffee-coloured lace dress, coat and hat, was fifteen minutes late for the wedding because she got lost on the way; so I had to sit outside the church cooling my heels waiting for her to arrive before I could enter. I felt annoyed with her: was this a subliminal sign that she was uneasy about the union?

Tony Corbet, a mad, intense doctor friend of ours known as Corb, was a jocular best man, and Susan, wearing a dress of jacaranda blue, was my bridesmaid. I myself still harboured some anxiety as I approached the altar on Richard's arm, when Bill turned and looked at me and suddenly my doubts dissolved—I knew everything would be all right. At the end of the service as the wedding party signed the legal documents, Richard and his lanky friend John Lawton played the lovely slow movement from Bach's Double Violin Concerto.

The reception was held on the long, columned verandah of our house at Goodwood Road, and it was great fun. When Bill referred to Mum as 'Mary' during his speech, the loud voice of my uncle Terence insisted: 'You mean Mona!'—her family name.

We drove up the east coast as far as Palm Beach on our honeymoon, but we were both too tense to enjoy ourselves. Bill seemed resentful, I was suffering morning sickness, and there was little passion between us. However, I do remember one peaceful, delightful day when we lay on the bed together in a Canberra hotel room, listening to the rain splash outside our open window. The weather had been very hot, and the smell of the fresh air was delicious as water soaked the trees outside. Bill's father had taught him to appreciate the beauty and tranquillity of rain, and Bill taught me.

We returned after two weeks. Bill took a job as a locum tenens (a substitute doctor) for a little while, and I worked in the casualty department of Royal Adelaide Hospital to complete my internship. At about three one morning after a long hard day, I lay in bed and suddenly felt a slight fluttering at the base of my stomach as the baby moved for the first time. I was filled with deep delight, and from that moment I thanked God that my attempted abortion had failed.

Bill and I decided that we should return to Canberra for the first year of our marriage, mainly because I was embarrassed about the pregnancy, but also because we wanted to escape from the influence of our families. Bill was employed as an intern in the Canberra Community Hospital. We rented a nice little brick house in the suburb of Dixon from some family friends who were in the diplomatic corps, and we settled down, ready to get to know each other and wait for our baby.

In the 1960s reminders of Canberra's origins as a sheep station were never far away—in many places the rows of neat, new houses with green lawns, small trees and standard rose bushes backed onto brown, dry paddocks, and most of the roads were new. I settled down, content to be a wife, enjoying my swelling pregnancy, making babies' clothes and knitting, devouring books that I had missed reading while studying, and cooking meals for Bill. But I did wonder at the time whether I should bring a new life into this nuclear world with its uncertain future.

Bill's job paid a small salary and money was tight; we lived on cheap cuts of meat and vegetables and I became an inventive cook, making exotic meals from very little. On Sunday afternoons we would go for a drive together, and when the petrol gauge hit half-full, we would turn around for home. Nevertheless, we felt very grown up and sophisticated, drinking our evening sherry from our new crystal decanter—one glass each—and Bill smoking a pipe.

But true intimacy evaded us. We didn't know how to express and communicate our real feelings. Instead, the unresolved tensions of love and resentment often became quarrels. One day I spent hours lovingly cooking a special dinner for Bill, then drove in to the hospital to meet him after work. He wasn't there, so I waited expectantly for about an hour before driving home. We had missed each other; Bill walked the several kilometres home furious with me in a quiet, resentful way. I tried to tell him of my expectations and disappointment, but he would not accept it; I think he felt I'd missed him on purpose. This episode, typically, was never resolved, because Bill refused to discuss it. I was often lonely that year.

On 9 July 1963 at about three a.m., during a bitterly cold Canberra night, we were sleeping in the sitting room in front of the fire to keep warm, when I awoke to dragging period-type pains. I roused Bill and told him I was in labour. He tried to pretend it wasn't happening and went back to sleep, but there was no escaping the inevitable, so he finally drove me to the hospital.

The first thing the nurses did was give me an enema and lead me to the shower recess—normal procedure in those days. I had to cope simultaneously with a huge contracting uterus and large bowel contractions while standing upright under a shower. This inhumane practice is now out of vogue. The labour was long. I had practised my breathing exercises, which helped me cope initially, but towards the end I started to drown in the pain and was given pethidine.

Eventually, at seven that evening, the obstetrician, who was impatient because he had to leave for a skiing holiday, gave me an anaesthetic and extracted the baby with forceps. Bill was unnerved when I lost consciousness, and he later told me of his fears that he might lose both me and the baby. I came out of a haze of drugs to see, briefly, a tiny being that I was told was a boy. The nurses wheeled me off to my bedroom to sleep and isolated the wee creature in the nursery for twenty-four hours, so I spent the first day of my child's life hardly being aware that I had given birth. These days nurses and doctors are wiser: they put the child on the breast immediately after birth so it can bond with the mother and suck the nutritious colostrum, and the child never leaves its mother's side unless the mother requests it.

When the nurses finally wheeled in the little bassinet, I took one look at our son and was besotted. He was the most beautiful thing I had ever seen. My heart went out to all the other mothers when I visited the nursery, because their babies were so ugly compared with mine. On 10 July, when our son was a day old, I looked out of my window and saw snow on the distant Brindabella Ranges. The first snow of winter, the celebration of a new life. I felt wonderful. My breasts swelled with milk, and to my surprise I discovered that my breast tissue extended into my armpits and reached just below the clavicle. This was something they had never taught us in medical school.

Bill came to visit every night and seemed thrilled about the baby. He suggested we call him Philip, after Dad, and I decided the second name would be John, after Pope John XXIII, who was dying as Philip was being born. I had cried during my pregnancy when I heard the old man's farewell words: 'I'm ready, I've got my bags packed.' Put in only as a caretaker pope because he was so old, he had revolutionised the Catholic Church. A simple man, kind and exceedingly wise, he used to get lonely rattling round in the Vatican by himself, so he would invite the gardener to lunch. I felt he was the only pope in recent history who truly walked in the 'shoes of the fisherman', to quote Morris West. It may seem strange that I should be so entranced by John XXIII, but I had always been on the lookout for godliness in the true sense of the word since childhood. He fitted the bill, but his stay was all too brief!

We decided to circumcise Philip: this was the done thing in 1963. But the pain of waiting in my room while this poor little boy had his foreskin clipped off by bone forceps without anaesthetic was almost too much for me. I was beside myself when they laid him in my arms again, his eyes red and filled with tears after the first trauma in his life imposed by his ignorant mother.

I went home from the hospital after ten days, and every morning when I picked Philip up from his bassinet, the sky was bluer and more luminous than it had been the day before. I was so full of love for him that I developed a stiff neck watching his face as he sucked milk from my breast, and the sound of warm milk gurgling down his hungry throat was the most fulfilling I had ever heard. One day as we drove across a rickety temporary bridge spanning Canberra's new Lake Burley Griffin, I suddenly realised that I would willingly drown to save my baby. I had never felt like this about another human being before. In fact, I suddenly realised I was now an adult. No longer could I expect other people to make the world safe. I had to accept that the responsibility for the safety of my child, for his future—for that of all children in this nuclear age—was now mine. This was a profound turning point for me, a rite of passage from childhood to maturity.

At Christmas we drove 2400 kilometres on a round trip to Adelaide to show Philip off to Mum and to Bill's parents, all of whom thought he was beautiful. On the drive back to Canberra, across the flat plains of the wheat country, the temperature reached 40 degrees Celsius, and Bill booked us into an air-conditioned motel for a day or two to recover. Oddly, my milk supply was not keeping up with demand, a serious thing for a baby in this hot weather, so we were forced to buy a bottle for supplementary feeds.

Not long afterwards I discovered the reason for my lack of

milk: I was pregnant again, and the hormones produced by the placenta were inhibiting my milk production. On most occasions lactation provides protection against pregnancy, but not this time. Though the pregnancy had not been planned, Bill and I were delighted. If having one baby was so wonderful, what would life be like with two?

Our year in Canberra was over, and we returned to Adelaide, where Bill decided to train as a radiologist. We bought a small cottage with a huge walnut tree spreading over the back terrace in Medindie, a leafy, upper-class suburb north of the city centre. Our neighbours were an old Lutheran pastor and his wife and their timorous middle-aged daughter; just up the street lived Dr Earle Hackett, a charming Irish pathologist, with his wife Eileen and three children. We spent many delightful Sunday afternoons with them.

We also renewed our friendship with Tony Corbet, the best man at our wedding. Every Thursday after work Bill and Corb would go drinking in the pub, then drive home at great speed, sozzled, to a delicious dinner I had worked on all day. Then the three of us would sit on the sitting-room floor in front of the fire talking politics and philosophy until the early hours of the morning. We had a ball together, forming what amounted to a platonic ménage à trois. Corb adored little Philip, soon known as Pip, and he carried him everywhere, even to the pub, where he would sit the baby on the bar. One night he even took Pip aged sixteen months, and dressed in a mask, cap and gown, to watch a Caesarean section from the visitors' gallery.

Bill, Corb and our friends were happily involved in the world of medicine. Oddly enough, I did not feel envious, nor did I miss working as a doctor. In the back of my mind, I vaguely planned to return to my career, but I was totally content at this stage of my life having my babies. However, when one of my teachers advised me to become a pathologist because it was a nine-to-five job and therefore suitable for a married woman, my hackles rose. How dare he suggest that just because I was a woman I should train for a nine-to-five profession? And he had been one of my brightest teachers and my most important mentor in medical school. I knew he would never suggest a similar course of action to one of my male colleagues. Attitudes then were fundamentally very sexist.

But these feelings were short-lived; with one small child and another on the way, I was deeply content. Pip was very cute; his little round face, button nose and engaging sweetness captivated everybody. At nine months he was walking and began to speak lucidly. When we went to the beach, he often wandered off alone on an expedition, usually returning with an adoring adult in tow, sucking an icecream or a lolly.

Except for morning sickness in the first trimester, my second pregnancy was a breeze. Just as I left for the hospital, Pip said to me, 'Keep your mouth open, Mummy, and don't bite the baby.' I had expected my second labour to be much shorter than the first, but no such luck. Once more I did the breathing exercises, following what we called the 'childless painbirth method', while Bill sat beside me meticulously cleaning my engagement ring. Finally, when I pushed out our second child, he exclaimed with joy, 'It's a bird!' And it was. A funny little girl with a huge tongue, fat tummy, long arms and legs, and a big head with not a skerrick of hair. When we came home, I placed her in thirteen-month-old Philip's lap and said, 'Here's your baby.' From that moment they bonded, as they have ever since.

She was a funny little thing. She had no name for about two weeks, then we decided to call her Penelope after the faithful wife of Ulysses, and Mary after Mum. Pen was a slow developer, quite different from Philip. She rarely crawled, and showed no inclination to roll over until she was seven months old. Her limbs were flaccid, with little muscular tone, and her large tongue and protuberant belly made me feel uneasy about the possibility of retardation. Until she was twelve months old, she was totally bald, without eyelashes or eyebrows, but she eventually grew white-blonde hair.

She continued her slow development until one day, at fourteen months, she began to articulate a strange Penny-type language—*I fuck my fumb, Maamy, my noo red shooes*—and she never looked back. She is now a general practitioner and smart as a whip. We still quote her baby phrases within the family, though.

I loved having a baby girl to dress up and make beautiful, and Pen was so feminine and soft. I made her brown and blue velvet dresses with lace collars, Liberty lawn smocked dresses and lacy nightgowns. In the mornings I would dress Pip and Pen and put them in the sandpit at the back of the yard, where they played with old pots and pans for hours. I took photos of them with my old box Brownie camera, hardly able to wait until the film was developed so I could look at my beautiful babies in black and white.

I was so hooked on the process of conception and childbirth that if I had had my way I would have had a baby every year until menopause. In fact, if my life had turned out differently, I would have been perfectly happy to stay at home, bake cakes, work in the garden and look after my babies. Now, when the world is already so crowded with human beings and we are in danger of destroying other species, it shocks me to realise how strong and exhilarating is the physiological drive towards reproduction. But I certainly didn't understand the overpopulation problem when our children were young, although I did wonder whether I should bring a child into this nuclear world when I was pregnant with Philip.

When Penny was about six months old, I decided I should do a little medicine simply to keep my hand in, so I worked in an allergy practice. Mum's neighbour, a dear Latvian woman named Irene Berzins who cleaned her house once a week, came by bus to care for the babies.

Bill decided to specialise in paediatric radiology and he commenced training at the Adelaide Children's Hospital under the tutelage of Dr Bill McCoy. I was a good and supportive wife, driving into the hospital at night to pick him up with the babies in the back seat of the car, singing nursery rhymes and lullabies over and over again while we waited for him to appear. He studied for the first part of his degree in Pip's bedroom; Pip often appeared dressed only in his nappy with his teddy bear under his arm, and Bill's heart would melt. He loved our babies as much as I did.

Life was stable. Bill was doing well, we had two beautiful children and a pretty house, and we were all healthy. There was no reason at all why we shouldn't have been happy with out lot—yet, instinctively, Bill and I felt there was something missing from our relationship. And when I conceived again, our problems became clearer.

CHAPTER 6

When Penny was fifteen months old, I became pregnant again with our third child. Once again I was delighted and couldn't wait to see what the random combination of our genes would produce this time. Bill also seemed pleased. But the equanimity of our life was shattered when my brother Richard, who had joined the Department of Foreign Affairs, was posted to Japan as Third Secretary in the Australian Embassy.

Bill occasionally said that he felt trapped by marriage and babies at the age of twenty-six, before he had really had time to travel and experience life. Despite these feelings, he seemed relatively content with his lot. But Richard's departure upset the emotional applecart and triggered an intense desire in Bill to travel.

He didn't tell me how he felt, but I sensed a distance between us, and I would find him sitting on the old fruit tree in the back garden gazing up at the planes as they flew overhead. At the time, he was paving the terrace at the back of the house beneath the walnut tree. He dug furiously in the soil for days, using the end of his spirit level to make holes for the bricks, and in his frustration he wore more than a centimetre off the end of his metal tool.

We still were not good communicators; I was at odds to know how to help him, and I felt lonely and depressed myself. Several months later Bill McCoy suggested that Bill apply for a fellowship in radiology at Harvard Medical School. He leapt at the opportunity and cheered up immediately, and I was so relieved by his change of mood that I agreed. He was accepted, and so we made our plans. I would stay with Mum for the last two months of my pregnancy, have the baby, and three months later take the children and Mum to Boston. Mum was delighted. Since Dad's death four years ago she had lived alone, and she was hungry for company. Bill was thrilled, not only because of the career opportunity the fellowship represented, but also because he could travel.

I wasn't sure how I felt about it. Trained and accustomed to placing the needs of my husband before my own, I sat in front of the fire after dinner night after night preparing his clothes for departure, even sewing name tags on his socks. But as Bill's anticipation mounted, I became more disturbed. I think subconsciously I knew that I was about to shoulder a huge burden—the delivery of a new baby, caring for three small children plus my lonely and ailing mother—alone. I suppressed my fears because I didn't want to stand in Bill's way, and I couldn't confide in Mum because she was so looking forward to us coming to stay with her. I became quite upset, and developed nominal aphasia—difficulty remembering the names of people and things—obviously a symptom of my anxiety.

After weeks of preparation we rented our house to friends, Bill packed his bags, and we moved the babies and all out stuff to Mum's house. The night before Bill left, we slept in

Mum's double bed at the front of the house, bathed in the perfume of wisteria blossom, while a bird sang like a nightingale all night. I lay awake, nestled in Bill's arms, dreading his departure.

On the way back from the airport after seeing him off, we were so anxious that Mum and I had a terrible fight in the car. I can't remember what it was about, but I later realised that she was as worried as I was about the new situation. Both of us were shaken by the intensity of our anger, and we agreed to have no more fights and to live in peace for the next five months. We had a big job ahead of us.

When we got home, I sat on Mum's empty double bed, and reality hit me like a ton of bricks. Here I was, seven months pregnant, alone and unsupported, with two small children and a lonely mother, all of whom depended on me to be strong and secure. I had let my most important reliable support disappear from my life, and I would miss him terribly. I sat on the bed, and for the first time I was able to cry. Mum discovered me in the bedroom sobbing in despair, and she hugged me; but still the load remained on my shoulders.

Some days later I received a letter from Bill, written on the plane between Adelaide and Sydney, telling me he loved me and thanking me. But I don't think he fully understood the awful situation I was in. He was happy to be free. I was glad for him, but how would I cope?

Mum and I quickly settled into a daily routine, which seldom varied. We got up early, I bathed and fed the babies, while Mum, who was still working as an extension officer for the South Australian Department of Agriculture, showered and dressed for work. After she caught her bus to the city, I spent most of the day doing housework, washing, cleaning, ironing and taking care of the children. In the evening I would drive with them into the city to meet Mum, having already prepared the dinner. The kids and I watched *Mr Ed*, then I put them to bed and Mum and I watched news and current affairs shows while we ate dinner.

She and I thoroughly enjoyed each other's company. In the two months before the new baby was born, we established a closer and more supportive relationship than ever before, perhaps because we were both caring for the children and were united in our love for them. Mum was as supportive as Bill had been, perhaps more. I developed the bond with her that I had always longed for; I think she could now give me some of the love she had been incapable of giving me as a child, because as grandmothers are wont to do, she loved these babies without reserve. There is a quantifiable difference between a mother's love and the love of grandparents—I think this is because mothers are so caught up in the everyday practicalities of life that they don't really have the time or luxury to revel in the beauty and perfection of their babies.

Mum particularly adored three-year-old Philip, who slept beside her bed in a little wooden cot. Because of her arthritis, she kept a bucket by the bed so he could urinate in the morning without her having to trundle him down to the bathroom at the back of the house. She rarely mentioned her own feelings, but it was clear that she had never really recovered from Dad's death. The signs of her despair were there: when she drove to country centres in South Australia to help rural women redecorate their houses, she refused to wear a seat belt, and she drove around corners in neutral gear. She was normally a good driver, and I think she took these risks because she didn't really care whether she lived or died. She also started smoking again. The joy she experienced in living with me and the children, however, gave her a new raison d'être.

As time went on, her physical health gave me increasing concern. Sometimes her arthritis was so debilitating that she had difficulty even holding a knife and fork, and she could not eat unless I cut up her food for her. At night she was in constant pain, taking anti-inflammatory drugs that gave her indigestion and peptic ulcer pains. She was also increasingly short of breath, though she never complained and was quietly brave.

Mum's close friend Jo, who was big, fat and caring, scolded me because I often wanted to talk to Mum when she got home from work. 'Your mother is tired, she needs her sleep,' said Jo. 'You should leave her alone.' Jo knew Mum was very ill, and she tried to force me to acknowledge this. But I was proprietorial about my mother and felt Jo had no right to interfere with our relationship or the way we lived together.

I should have understood that my mother had significant health problems. But there was another dynamic at work—if she was really sick, I didn't want to know. Losing Dad had been bad enough; I couldn't face the thought that I could lose Mum as well, especially now, when I was feeling so alone and fragile. Denial is a very powerful mechanism: looking back, I see what a huge part it played in my emotional reality at this stage of my life and probably always had.

Perhaps, too, I didn't want to upset the newly harmonious relationship Mum and I were enjoying. We had established our own routine, I had settled down to accept Bill's absence and I no longer felt as lonely as I had done at first. I lived for Bill's letters from Boston, which arrived every three or four days. He seemed to be having a good time, and wrote about his job at Harvard and the respect he felt for his renowned boss Ed Newhauser and equally renowned colleague Dick Wittenborg. He made new friends, whose photos he sent, as well as photos of his new abode (a small room in the Judge Baker Building at the Children's Hospital Medical Center) and copies of the children's pictures he had framed and placed on his desk. He said he couldn't wait for us to arrive, and I felt the same way. So the last two months of my pregnancy were not difficult, and I began to relax and to feel relatively calm and confident.

When labour began at an ungodly hour on the morning of 17 August, Mum drove me to hospital and left me there; she had to go to work that day. This was the first time I had laboured alone, without Bill, but I felt strong and managed to keep on top of the pain using my breathing exercises. The labour lasted fifteen hours. During the second stage, however, when the agony was unbearable, I grabbed the nitrous oxide mask, inhaling with such desperation that I knocked myself out. I came out of the soporific haze to hear the doctor telling the nurses that I had been stupid to lose consciousness. I had sufficient presence of mind to tell them, 'I heard every word you said,' and they apologised.

I gave birth to a fierce-looking little boy whom I named William after his father and George after Bill's father. I was still being sewn up, my legs in the air, when Tony Corbet, who was the paediatric registrar, strode in to inspect the new infant. It was great to see Corb, though I did feel I was not in the best position to receive guests. However, considering what close friends we had been, it was almost as good as having Bill there.

Mum came rushing in, took one look and delightedly announced that the baby looked exactly like Dad. I was thrilled, too, though I experienced the usual post-natal depression two or three days after delivery. When I discovered a rock-hard painless lump in my left breast just below the clavicle, I was convinced I had breast cancer and persuaded my poor obstetrician, Les Poidevan, to give up his Sunday tennis game to check it out. But it was only milk engorgement.

While Mum was at work during the day and I was in hospital, Penny and Philip were cared for by Mum's next-door neighbour Irene. After eight days in hospital I returned to a house of chaos. Penny was very quiet and withdrawn; Philip looked lost and confused and had cut his hair diagonally across his fringe, ending up at his hairline on the right side. He had also discovered the laundry bleach, and little white hand marks now decorated his dark blue corduroy trousers. Poor Mum—she simply hadn't been able to cope on her own with two lively toddlers. I was shocked to see how exhausted she was. She could hardly walk without gasping for breath, and in the mornings after she got up, she would sit on the yellow plastic stool in the kitchen and cough and cough until she lost her breath. I'd never heard or seen anything like it before.

At some level I knew she was irreversibly sick, but I was frantically trying to handle two children under the age of three plus a new baby, and I couldn't face the truth. In any case, what could I do? I saw that she might not be well enough to come with me to Boston as arranged. I was aching to see Bill, but I couldn't possibly leave her behind. It was very difficult, and I had nobody to consult; Richard was overseas and Susan was living in Montreal with her architect husband, John Ballinger. For the first time in my life, I had painful decisions to make and nobody to turn to. I was terrified.

It all started to get to me. Some mornings I was so tired after feeding the baby during the night that I could hardly get out of bed to bathe and feed the children, let alone gather enough strength to drag ourselves into town for the passport photos, visas and so on for our trip to Boston. Three children and a sick mother were just too much of a load for me to handle, and I began to lose my temper with Philip and Penny, screaming at them, sometimes even slapping them in sheer frustration. Philip grew bewildered, Pen very quiet. I was like a madwoman, taking out my rage and fear on my beautiful babies. And it's interesting: as I did so, a tape played in the back of my head: 'That's right, Mum did it'—the mark of Cain handed on from generation to generation. Meanwhile the baby slept like a dream all day. He liked to socialise at night; Mum and I were exhausted, but he was not to be ignored. If we left him alone, he screamed blue murder until one of us—whoever was less tired—went to his basket in the dining room and gathered him into her arms. Several hours later when his social requirements were satisfied, he slept.

I remember lying in bed one morning, eyeing a huge

mound of nappies and children's clothes, unable to move, let alone decide what clothes to pack for the trip, when Bill's sister Judith Miller arrived and selectively packed them for me. Judith was very comforting; like me, she cared intensely about her family, though we had little else in common. She was a staunch friend, particularly then, and I remain eternally grateful for her help.

Gradually Mum's health improved enough to make the trip. I bought two white leather harnesses so I could keep hold of Penny and Philip, and we all set off for the airport. The baby was now three months old and was still totally breastfed. This was convenient in one way, but also tiring because the body uses a lot of nutrients to produce enough milk for a thriving, growing baby.

We kissed relatives and friends goodbye, and off we flew to Tokyo, where we were to stay for ten days with Richard and his wife Alison, who was also in Foreign Affairs. I was apprehensive before I boarded the plane: my post-natal hormones were still causing me to be extremely sensitive to the baby, and every fibre of my being was geared to protect him. I gave a sedative antihistamine, Phenergan, to Penny and Philip on the plane to quieten them. But they didn't respond: quite the reverse. They screamed up and down the aisles for nine hours like a pair of monkeys, almost tearing the plane apart. Just as we were about to land, they lapsed into a deep coma. So Mum and I staggered off the plane carrying two unconscious children, a baby and all the accompanying baggage. I later discovered that Phenergan, which is still used as a paediatric sedative, can paradoxically also be a stimulant.

Richard and Alison lived in the suburb of Aoyama, fifteen minutes from the centre of Tokyo, in a house leased by the Australian Embassy. It was spacious by Japanese standards, managing to accommodate two extra adults and three children with the minimum of inconvenience. We saw comparatively little of Richard, who was investigating the crash of an aircraft with Australians aboard into Tokyo Bay.

I found Japan fascinating, and so did Mum. Ali showed us around, and she and Richard took us on a car trip to Mt Fuji and around the beautiful Japanese countryside, every square centimetre of which was cultivated. In 1966 there were still neighbourhood bathhouses, and in the evenings the streets were full of people in their kimonos and wooden sandals (gettas) carrying their soap and towels to the baths. Mum loved the simplicity of the Japanese lifestyle and the architecture.

One day I went to the hairdresser, who covered my head with a warm cloth, gently and sensuously massaging my ears. I came out of a reverie fifteen minutes later to see Penny with her white-blonde hair braided Japanese style and tied with red ribbons. What kind, sweet people the Japanese were, I thought. My blond children fascinated them, but they love all small children. They give their own extraordinary adoration until the age of five, when children are kicked out of the nest and expected to perform at school, and their lives become a lot tougher.

Ali had found the Australian diplomatic service to be even more sexist than I had found the medical establishment. In the 1960s university degrees were the springboard to careers for men, though not for women. In Canberra, where the Department of Foreign Affairs was based, women public servants received 20 per cent less pay than men for the same work. When they married, they had to resign and become 'temporary' without superannuation or annual leave, and the department was reluctant to recruit or train women or to give them responsible work. Alison was just as well qualified as Richard, but when she married him and they went to Japan, she had to give up any thought of a diplomatic career. (This situation did not change for women in Foreign Affairs until the Whitlam government came to power at the end of 1972. Two years later Ali, who had been studying Japanese and making her name as a broadcaster and writer, rejoined the foreign service, now with equal pay and permission to work in the same post as her husband, provided he was not an ambassador.)

When the time came for us to fly on to the United States, I grew worried about the flight again. Richard had told us about the kinds of injuries the passengers had sustained in the Tokyo Bay crash, making my fear of flying ten times worse. I was so anxious that I had difficulty sleeping those ten nights before we left. Eventually we boarded a TWA plane for Seattle. The last part of the trip was very rough. Each time the plane slammed about as we dropped altitude, Mum said, 'We're landing now,' but in fact we were not. I was so terrified that I nearly leapt out of the plane. But we landed safely, got the luggage and the children to a hotel, and fell into a deep sleep for fourteen hours.

When I ordered breakfast the next morning, a trolley arrived covered with perforated rubber matting and laden with jugs of orange juice, huge quantities of toast, cereal, butter, jam and eggs. My first meal in the USA! I was shocked by the quantities of food, far more than we could ever eat.

Delighted that we had finally made it—even if we were on the other side of the continent—I sent Bill a telegram. He didn't reply, which surprised me a little, and we flew on to Boston. When we got off the plane, there he was waiting outside as we descended the steps, holding two red roses, one for Mum and one for me. The moment I set eyes on him I knew how much I had missed him, and I could hardly wait to be held in his arms. Bill greeted the children with tremendous love, but I had to wait for about ten minutes before my turn came and then his embrace was short.

Bill drove us to an apartment he had rented that day. It was on the second floor of an old white wooden house in Jamaica Plain, across the road from a beautiful lake called Jamaica Pond. There was no bed for Mum. Bill said he hadn't had time to find one. I suppose he wanted us to himself, and I don't think he realised how sick Mum had been, or what she had done for us. Unwell, jet-lagged and exhausted, she had to go to the home of Oscelio Cartaxo, a Brazilian colleague of Bill's, to spend the night. I felt terrible.

My worst fears about her health were confirmed when I showed Bill her chest X-rays. His face turned ashen. 'They're the worst X-rays I've ever seen,' he said quietly. Mum's shortness of breath was caused by severe pulmonary fibrosis, a rare complication of rheumatoid arthritis, and she had obviously suffered right heart failure. We both knew there was no treatment for this, and the prognosis was grim. We didn't discuss the subject any further; I still preferred not to face reality. Not after Dad. Not so soon.

What were my initial impressions of America? I never expected to really like it, because of the propaganda and films we had seen in Australia depicting ugly streets littered with neon signs and advertisements, with guns and violence at every street corner. I was quite unprepared for the beauty of New England. Bill took us for drives in Vermont and New Hampshire, where the scenery resembled postcard pictures or Norman Rockwell paintings on the covers of the *Saturday Evening Post.* So people in America really lived in houses like that, I thought, it was not just some lovely fantasy. Mind you, I was absolutely overwhelmed when I entered a supermarket. I had never in my life seen such an array and variety of food; it seemed almost decadent.

Soon after we arrived in Boston, Mum flew up to Montreal to stay for a few weeks with Susan, who was expecting a baby. For the first time in five months Bill, the kids and I could be together as a family unit. I felt as if an enormous load had been lifted from my shoulders, and Bill was also very happy.

Years later he told me something that quite shocked me: when he left Australia, he was troubled, thinking our marriage was in difficulties and that a separation might help. Now that we were together in the States, we were much more comfortable and relaxed with each other, so he must have felt that his theory had been vindicated. He was very sweet and grateful for everything and set about getting to know his children again, including his new baby. We soon became closer than we had ever been, sleeping in a state of marital bliss with our baby in a string crib at the foot of our four-poster bed.

This peace and harmony lasted only five days. One afternoon when the babies and I were taking an afternoon nap, I heard a car door slam downstairs. It was Mum. To my dismay, she had returned early, apparently missing, as she said, 'my babies'. I think she felt that Philip, Penny and William were hers.

Thus began five months of purgatory. Bill understandably felt threatened by Mum's proprietorial attitude towards the children, and every night when he came home from work, he and she would fight. Almost anything would set them off—politics, history, the treatment of the children. Either she baited him with a provocative remark, or something he said irritated her.

Bill's difficulty with Mum had more complicated causes than just jealousy over the children. She challenged him even more than I did, and that could not have been easy for him. She was an older woman like his mother, yet she did not give him the kind of uncritical love that emanated from Dot. This was all the more difficult for him because initially he had been attracted to Mum's intelligence and charm. In fact, he told me half jokingly that he had fallen in love with her almost before he knew I was around.

I was the emotional meat in the sandwich, loving them both, but having no idea how to handle the situation. If Bill thought I sided with Mum in any way, he refused to speak to me. I felt miserable and guilty. On the other hand, the thought of being rejected by Mum made me just as unhappy, if not more so. I needed love and closeness so badly that I felt I would do almost anything to gain approval, and so I ricocheted between the two, often being rejected by both. I should have told both of them to take a running jump at themselves and grow up, but I was not sufficiently strong or emotionally mature to stand up to such powerful personalities.

I became increasingly distant from Bill, and I also pulled away from Mum. In the end I sided with Bill against Mum. In a strange way I felt that she would understand my decision; after all, she had always told me that if her own mother had lived with them and caused any difficulties, Dad would have asked his mother-in-law to leave the house without hesitation. But making this decision did not mean that my guilt was any less, of course.

Mum planned to travel on to Europe, but she had to rest for several months until she grew stronger. We moved her into an apartment around the corner so we could be alone. Even though she was delighted to have her own TV set, enabling her to follow American politics, which she found fascinating, she was terribly lonely. I saw her enormous confidence begin to disappear. Five years earlier she had lost Dad; now she must have felt she was losing her daughter and grandchildren.

Indeed, I stopped sharing my feelings with her, and I no longer confided in her about the children. She felt so alienated when I pulled away from her that she was even tentative about coming around to our apartment during the day, presenting herself at the door with a peace offering such as a bunch of bananas for the children. But I wasn't free to tell her how I felt and why I had pushed her away, because I thought it would mean being disloyal to Bill.

Our time together was painful, our newfound intimacy and love dwindling into stilted little conversations on walks around Jamaica Pond. Things came to such a pass between us that when Mum asked me to deliver her case down to the Boston docks for shipment to Australia, I did so reluctantly and with resentment. After all she had done for me!

But during these same months Bill and I were unable to sustain our hard-won new intimacy, and it gradually slipped away. As it ebbed, I saw that I had lost out on both sides and was alone.

Mum was growing thin, but she was still determined to go to Europe. Her courage was extraodinary. She intended to join a tour group—people she had never met in her life before—and travel with them all over the continent, including eastern Europe. Just before she left, a riot took place in the Roxbury area of Boston between the police and the black population. The next day Mum boarded a bus that headed straight into the middle of it. She questioned everybody she could find and returned with a wonderfully detailed account of the whole event, much to the astonishment and admiration of our Boston friends. This was Mum at her best—unafraid, gutsy and unquenchably curious.

On the day of her departure, I delivered her to the Greyhound Bus terminal, for the trip to New York and the flight to Europe. I felt relieved and glad that she was going and this difficult period was over. I kissed her soft cheek goodbye. As I walked to the door, I looked back to see her face collapse, her little body shrunken inside her purple and blue print dress. I never saw her again.

That night Bill and I opened a bottle of champagne to celebrate our freedom, but I couldn't drink it with enthusiasm. And for Bill and me, Mum's departure changed nothing. We might still have been half a world apart.

CHAPTER 7

After Mum left, I became desperately homesick. I hadn't realised that homesickness is a real disease, with a taste and an emptiness that leaves one feeling desolate and unconnected. I waited each day for the mail van, recognising the sound of its engine before it appeared, hoping for a letter from Mum or one of my friends. The children were as beautiful as ever, but living twenty-four hours a day with infantile talk can drive any mother a little bats. Sometimes I wondered if I would ever enter intelligent adult society again.

I decided to resume my medical career, but only on a part-time basis. Bill agreed with this decision—perhaps because he understood that my brain needed stimulation—so I asked him to find me a part-time job at the Children's Hospital Medical Center at Harvard, where he worked. Not long afterwards he came home very excited and told me that he had run into Harry Schwachman, who had agreed to employ me part time. Harry was a pioneer in the treatment of cystic fibrosis. I was very pleased and began to read to prepare for my apprenticeship.

Cystic fibrosis is the most common fatal disease of children; in 1967 its treatment was not as sophisticated as it is now. (The gene for CF has now been identified, as has the physiological defect that causes it.) In a Caucasian population, the disease occurs once in every 1600 live births, with varying degrees of intensity. Children suffering from CF produce thick mucus that is secreted by the lungs and the digestive tract, particularly the pancreatic ducts. The pancreas is the organ that produces most of the powerful digestive enzymes, and the excretory ducts are blocked by this thick mucus. Eventually the glands of the pancreas are digested and destroyed because the enzymatic secretions they produce are dammed back by the obstructive mucus and cannot escape. Consequently, children with cystic fibrosis are as hungry as horses and eat huge amounts of food, but they digest very little.

In severe cases, mucus quickly builds up in the lungs and children with a severe expression of the disease develop pneumonia and bronchitis. Eventually their airways fill with pus, and they die of respiratory failure. Treatment consists of antibiotics for the lungs, frequent physiotherapy to help expectorate the mucus, and doses of pancreatic enzyme before and after meals to assist in the digestion of food.

I returned to medicine with relief and gratitude. But in order to practise in the United States, I had to sit an exam for foreign medical graduates. I was nervous about this; it had been five years since I had read any medicine, and I was afraid that I might have forgotten everything I knew.

During the exam we were given a rather surreal English test. The woman examiner would ask: 'What is a sheep? Is it an animal or is it something you put on your bed?' and questions of similar difficulty. At the back of the examination room were six Latin American guys, all wearing dark glasses.

After every question, one would mutter the answer to the others: 'An animal', and the answer would pass down the line: 'An animal, an animal, an animal ...' I suppose they made the grade, although their cheating was clearly audible.

I did, and was employed as a research fellow in the nutrition clinic at the Children's Hospital, seeing patients in the CF clinic three times a week. I also learned to perform duodenal biopsies and helped with research, as well as attending clinic meeings. Harry Schwachman was an irascible man of about sixty, with a case of severe psoriasis, which mottled his face with bright red scaling patches of skin. He was obsessed by his work on CF, was utterly devoted to his patients and their families, and always seemed to be writing four or five papers at once. He beetled at great speed along the hospital corridors sideways like a dog and when he grew angry, as he frequently did, scales of skin would shower down all over his collar, a sign that we should stay away. Yet he was an excellent teacher, and I soon developed great affection for him.

Working at Harvard proved to be one of the most fascinating and rewarding experiences of my life. For the first time my perpetual curiosity was accepted as a gift, not a handicap. In Adelaide the medical system had been strongly based on the English model; the senior doctors were often rather old-fashioned and insular, relatively ignorant about current literature, and clung to their jobs by a process of intimidation. Seniority and therefore mediocrity reigned supreme, and if you challenged your teachers, your job could be threatened.

At Harvard I discovered that the pursuit of knowledge was considered sacred, and students challenged some of the greatest medical minds in the world. This left me breathless. Once the mighty pathologist Dr Sydney Farber made a statement at his weekly medical meeting, and a student immediately said, 'You're wrong.' Just that, no 'Excuse me, sir'. When Farber asked why, the student quoted an article that contradicted what Farber had said, and Farber capitulated. End of story. Students were treated as equals, and I had never seen such grace and humility exhibited by the great medical minds who wrote our textbooks. Grand rounds—the name given to the weekly medical meeting held in a lecture theatre during the lunch hour, attended by medical staff from the most junior to the most senior and the current crop of medical students—left me feeling euphoric and stimulated, as though I had spent an afternoon in the Louvre, viewing some of the greatest paintings in the world.

I started work at eight a.m. five mornings a week; like many allegedly part-time jobs this one soon expanded. I didn't mind the heavy workload; I loved the excitement, but my life soon became extraordinarily busy. Before eight in the morning I had to bathe and feed three children and deliver them to our babysitter, a Jehovah's Witness named Mrs Weisbergs, collect them at the end of my working day and then do all the usual tasks: feed them, put them to bed while at the same time cooking the evening meal, clean the apartment once a week, and do a huge wash at some nearby Laundromat. I would stagger up the stairs to our apartment carrying huge bags of laundered clothes as well as carloads of food from the supermarket, with children in tow.

Torn between medicine and trying to fulfill the emotional requirements of my children, I felt I had to do everything; nothing could be compromised. Like so many mothers who have faced the same conflicts, I became a prisoner of what has recently been dubbed the Superwoman syndrome, although thirty years ago I knew no one who was in a similar position. It was unthinkable at Harvard during those years that mothers should be treated any differently from other doctors, who were mostly male. No allowances were made for women in my position. Typical of most men of his generation, Bill, who had encouraged me to go back to work in the first place, did not often help. He still felt very angry with Mum, even though she was not with us. Further, he continued to be withdrawn, and I felt very lonely.

At about this time I became fond of a woman doctor from

Belgium who worked with me in the CF clinic. She had a lively, intelligent mind, like Mum's. We began work at the clinic at the same time and there was an immediate and unusual rapport between us of warmth and communication. One day I found myself imagining what it would be like to lie in bed and hug her. I did not connect these feelings—which I never allowed myself to express—to lesbianism, something with which, even though I was twenty-nine and a physician, I was barely familiar. Now I realise that there was an emotional void in my life and I was in love with her.

After eighteen months at Harvard I became physically and mentally exhausted and developed ulcer pains. These symptoms forced me to face the fact that I couldn't possibly operate as an adequate mother and a clever Harvard doctor at the same time. Something had to give, and it couldn't be my children, so with great reluctance I left work. It was sad, but at the time I had no other choice, because my body was giving clear signals. Strange how we often don't consciously recognise the reality of our situation until psychosomatic symptoms force us to.

As our two years in Boston came to an end, Bill decided to stay for a third year to engage in research and to work on hypertension with a brilliant doctor named Norm Hollenberg. I wrote to Mum, who was now back in Australia after her European sojourn, telling her that we would not be coming home. Her reply: 'How dare you stay another year!'

I know now that she was sad, lonely and progressively incapacitated, and was almost certainly relying on me to come home after two years. But why on earth didn't she tell me the truth instead of lashing out at me with anger? My automatic reaction to Mum had always been to please her and capitulate to her demands because I was scared of her anger; this had been a familiar pattern since childhood. But for the first time in my life I was furious about her dictatorial attitude, and sick of being pushed around. I vowed I wouldn't let her manipulate me again. It had happened so often, and I always gave in. When Dais died, for example, shortly before we left for the States, she left half her money to me and half to Dad's brother Bob. Mum insisted that I share my inheritance with the rest of the family, and instead of keeping her at arm's length and thinking about my position, I gave in almost immediately. I kept one-third and split the remainder between Mum—who hated Dais—Susan and Richard. My primal need to placate Mum was paramount.

But now finally I took her on frontally, without fear. I wrote and told her that my place was with my husband, not with her. Furthermore, I said, I objected to the way she talked about Bill behind his back, telling other members of the family that my husband was selfish and egocentric and that he never helped me. I wrote this letter in the cold certainty that I was right, and when I finished I showed it to my Belgian friend.

'Are you sure you want to post it?' she asked. But I was determined, and on a cold, snowy Boston night I slipped it into the letter box. About two weeks later, back came the following: 'Helen, I never thought I would be estranged from my eldest daughter. Mum.'

I was stunned and, not knowing how to react, I tried to pretend that nothing had happened. I should have written back: 'Don't be stupid, I still love you. Why are you reacting like this?' But I never explored my feelings with her, confining my letters from then on to superficial discussions about the children. She took her cue from me and responded in kind.

After I left work, the children and I spent the summer of our second American year at a tiny fisherman's cottage, called an El, attached at one end to a charming old wooden house on Cape Anne, about eighty kilometres north of Boston. Bill lived in Boston and worked at the hospital during the week, visiting us on weekends. Smaller than Cape Cod, Cape Anne is even more charming, covered in trees, with small inlets and harbours full of sailing boats. We all slept upstairs in an airy room surrounded by lacy locust trees and a garden full of irises, tiger lilies and lilacs. The days were languorous, lazy and hot, and I took the children across the green lawns, the warm bitumen and sandy streets to the beach each morning, where I shocked the New England locals by wearing the latest in tiny French bikinis.

While the children swam, I pursued a new enthusiasm—landscape painting, inspired by the beauty of the beach and a nearby lighthouse. Afterwards we staggered home in the noonday heat, took off all our clothes and ate tuna sandwiches in the cool, dark sitting room. Then I carried the children's soft little bodies up the winding staircase and gently laid them down for our afternoon sleep.

Cape Anne was just what I needed. I loved the old wooden houses, the gardens and above all the kind, reserved people. I joined a book club and discovered *Portnoy's Complaint* by Philip Roth, laughing out loud at its audacious and refreshing Jewish humour. As well as painting, I developed an interest in local craft, and I bought quantities of woollen fabric and a braiding stand to make a round cottage rug.

After this summer interlude our apartment in Boston seemed unsatisfactory. I had developed a difficult relationship with our landlady, a woman of Irish ancestory who lived below us with her six children. She strongly supported segregated schooling in Boston and it was the first time in my life that I had confronted overt racism. The children and I missed the peace and solitude of Cape Anne, so Bill found us a converted stable at the back of the Old Corner Inn in Manchester-by-the-Sea on the Cape. Manchester was a small community of old New England houses and large leafy trees, facing a beautiful harbour, and we lived here for the last nine months of our time in the United States.

After the drama and tension of the previous couple of years, we settled down to a steady, quiet life. Bill commuted to work each day and I looked after the children. Life was fairly humdrum, but our neighbours Tom and Mary Baker and Irene Slater quickly became dear and lasting friends. Tom, a shortish sturdy man with a broad snub nose and roguish blue eyes, was a reprobate whose family had lived in Manchester for generations. He was a gifted artist who liked a drop of alcohol. His wife, Mary, a beautiful woman about five feet two (157 centimetres) with white waving hair and twinkling blue eyes, was a charming, cultured Irish woman who had fallen in love with this funny, outrageous man. Irene, a slim woman with cropped brown hair who dressed in elegant male-style clothes, had five children. She lived across the road from me and was always in a frantic frenzy caring for her offspring. We shared the child care. I remember one night having five Slaters strewn across my sitting room floor while Irene recovered from pneumonia.

Although I enjoyed these days of domesticity, I was keenly aware that my intellectual nerve ends would soon need to be nourished. One day as I was making the beds upstairs in the 'stable', out of the blue I suddenly knew that when we returned to Australia, I wanted to sit for the membership examination of the Royal Australasian College of Physicians.

Meanwhile, other problems started to impinge upon my reality. One of our dear friends, Doc Clarkson, a gangling six foot three inch (190 centimetres) footballer and renal specialist who had graduated in Bill's year and who worked in Adelaide, came to stay for a few days. He was a close friend of Mum's, and he told me gently that because of her lung disease she had been put on steroids, which I knew was the treatment of last resort. The implications were simply too horrific for me to contemplate. I can think clearly about it now, twenty-five years later, though at the time I consciously denied it. But at another level I really understood, because I found myself doing deals with God: 'If I hang the shirt on the line this way, everything will be all right.' I couldn't bear to face what I meant by 'everything'. One of the stages of grief, I later discovered, is bargaining with the Almighty.

If I had felt that Bill was more amenable, I think I could

have talked through my dilemma with him. In my distress I retreated further into myself and found that I was thinking obsessively about my old flame, the surgical registrar. He was on my mind day and night. I lacked the courage to face reality and was beginning to lose control of my thinking. Sleep eluded me, and I dared not read the papers in case I saw any word or phrase that reminded me of him. Some nights I was so overwrought that I left the house and ran miles to a distant beach, hoping that physical exhaustion would dissipate my obsession. Nothing worked.

On 29 April, about three weeks before we were due to return to Adelaide, I bought artichoke hearts and fillet steak at the supermarket and cooked a special dinner for our friends Roy Strand, a radiologist, and his English wife, Pat, who came from Boston for the evening. As we sat down to eat, the phone rang. Bill answered it and handed the phone to me; 'It's Richard,' he said.

I knew my brother had returned from Japan and was in Adelaide, but I took the receiver with no sense of foreboding. The voice said: 'Mum's dead.' I dropped the phone and my legs crumbled. When I picked up the receiver, I heard Richard say: 'Her heart stopped. They started it, but it stopped again. She died an hour ago.' After he hung up, I returned to the table in a trance. We finished dinner. I made the right noises, but nothing seemed real anymore.

Feeling as if my world had collapsed, I visited Mary Baker the following morning. As she opened the door, I said, 'Mum's dead,' and stood there on the front doorstep, unable even to weep. Mary had been about to go to church, but she quietly put down her Bible, took off her hat and gloves, and made me a cup of tea. I told her everything, and she was warmly sympathetic, but I felt as if I were reciting lines from a play. This couldn't be true—the first stage of grief—shock and disbelief.

I decided to take the baby, William (now known as Nookles), and fly home for the funeral. But my friends said it wasn't a good idea because Mum was already dead and my only family was now with me in Boston. We were returning in three weeks anyway, there was so much to do, I couldn't help Mum now, they said. Bill agreed and was in fact strongly opposed to my returning for the funeral. I let myself be persuaded, a decision I was to regret for the rest of my life.

It was a terrible mistake. Years later, after my emotional numbness passed, I understood how much I had needed to hold Mum's small body in my arms, to say goodbye. This would at least have given me some sense of reality, forcing me out of my fugue state. Friends try to be caring, and they are, but nobody who hasn't done so can ever understand how it feels to lose a baby, a husband or a mother.

My withdrawal from our marriage now equalled Bill's. Terrified, I could not tell him of my terror; lonely, I could not speak of my loneliness. Yet I could see that he too was lonely and unhappy, and that only increased my own despair. I was frightened that he would discover my obsession with Tom, the surgical registrar, of whom he had once been so jealous. Divorce would surely follow, and then what would happen to me? I had no mother, I would have no husband. What about the children? Was I going mad? But then I would think, 'I can't be mad, I'm a doctor.'

Only days after Mum died, a neighbour invited us to sail on his yacht in the Atlantic. I went through the motions of normality, dressing the children, preparing breakfast for Bill and our house guests, driving to the mooring. But once on board, my overwhelming desire was to leap into the freezing Atlantic. I couldn't cope with any more reality, and I wanted to die.

I had lost all feelings of emotional safety, and during the next three weeks before we left for home, life became almost unbearable. My obsession with Tom grew even worse, my hair fell out, I couldn't force food down my throat, and I lost six kilos. Sleep was impossible. I could relax only when Mary

Baker took me on drives around Cape Anne or out to lunch with friends, when I would fall asleep in the middle of the meal. It was early June and the narrow roads and lanes were smothered in perfumed lilac blossoms that dripped with recent summer rains. I will always associate the scent of lilac with this time in my life.

A week after Richard's telephone call I received a letter from Mum, written the day before she died. Seeing the familiar handwriting was surreal. The letter began:

> *My dear Helen,*
>
> *You can't possibly be angry with me. I kept on thinking how I would feel if my poor old Mum had been so sick. I know that we haven't been communicating honestly for the last year, but Susie* [my sister Susan had returned from Montreal heavily pregnant with her second child] *and I miss your loving support and we can't wait until you get home.*

In this letter Mum poured her heart out for the first time. She described how sick she had been, how she used to make the bed and fall unconscious on it, how she crawled breathless on her hands and knees down the passage to the bathroom, just as Dad had done. And now she too was dead, and I, her eldest daughter, a doctor to whom my father had entrusted her care, had failed her. If only she had lived for another month, if only she had waited until I got home . . . such was my guilt that I felt she had died just before I got home to punish me for rejecting her.

Throughout the weeks after she died I shed not one tear for her, and all my emotional energy went into my obsession. A classic case of displacement activity, I later discovered. If something is too horrible to contemplate, the mind grabs onto something easier to think about.

During our final two weeks in the United States, I was only just hanging on; I was depressed and inactive and our house was covered in dust. Bill, who must have resented this, arranged everything for our return trip to Australia and did all the packing. We did not discuss the situation. I recalled our trip to the States three years before and the terror I had felt that the plane would crash, taking Mum and the children with it. Now, as we boarded the Qantas jet for home, I wished it would.

Will suffered the most. He was a strong and stubborn child, needing equal amounts of discipline and love, but I had the strength to offer neither. We spent the transit night in a hotel on Hawaii, and the following day I took the children to a toy store where, paralysed by grief and fatigue, I watched my youngest son tear the place apart.

We were lost, all of us: the children, Bill and me, the adults unable to care for each other. My parents were now both dead, and Bill's mother had died several years earlier. We were in a sense orphans at the tender age of twenty-nine, still in a way children ourselves and we had Philip, Penny and Will to look after. God help me. I loved them more than life itself and I had nothing to give them.

When we finally got back to Adelaide, Bill took up his new appointment of director of paediatric radiology at the Adelaide Children's Hospital. He was given tenure and was thrilled and challenged by his new position. Meanwhile, I went straight to Mum's house, hoping to find some trace of her. From room to room I wandered, recognising the dark bedroom with the green eiderdown and the red and chartreuse curtains, the big grey kitchen with blue, red and yellow cupboard doors. All was still and quiet. Mum had gone, and I found nothing. Death is so final, so empty.

Mum's friend Jo, who had been admitted to the Royal Adelaide Hospital, told me that the day after Mum died, she saw her walking down a hospital corridor towards her. 'Don't worry, dear, I'm all right,' Mum said. I felt betrayed. Why had

Mum appeared to a friend and not to me, her daughter? Or was it just Jo's vivid imagination?

Interestingly, as soon as I returned, I began wearing her clothes and jewellery and found myself using her expressions and mannerisms—if I became her, I wouldn't lose her. Bill objected to this strange behaviour, so I stopped it.

To save my sanity, I went to work as a clinical fellow in the renal transplant unit at the Queen Elizabeth Hospital, where Mum had died. Perhaps unconsciously I thought I might make some sort of connection. I went to the autopsy room and tried to imagine her small, arthritic body lying on the table. The pathologist told me he had her lungs in a bottle. They were the most interesting he had ever seen, he said, but he wouldn't let me look at them because it wouldn't be good for me. I'm sure he meant well, but in retrospect I think I should have challenged his paternalism. I walked away from him feeling lost, weak and pathetic.

I worked only part time and found a day care centre for Penny and Nookles, while Philip started at the local primary school. In Boston I had spent months teaching him to read so he could catch up to his age group at home because the United States was one year behind Australia. But I couldn't feel any excitement about his first day at school, and I didn't even enjoy choosing the little blue corduroy pants and viyella shirt he wore. The day care centre was utilitarian at best, and little Pen and Nookles seemed to subsist on red jelly and icecream, which they were served every day. Pen told me later that Nooks used to cry when I left, and the staff would put him under the table in the hall as punishment, poor little boy. After work I used to sit in the car outside the centre until I had summoned the emotional strength to go inside and collect my babies. My basket of love was empty, I had absolutely nothing to give.

I was also agoraphobic; I couldn't stand being in large shopping centres, where a pall of depression would descend and I would hardly be able to open my eyes. I was so sad, I would have to leave. One day the house was bereft of food. Bill's father was staying with us, so I went to the supermarket, but couldn't raise my hand to gather food from the shelves. I slunk out and sat in the car for about half an hour, unable to move.

I was only just surviving, going through the motions of medicine at work in the renal clinic, but not really involved. One day, less than a month after starting work, I pricked my finger while taking blood from a female dialysis patient. Over the next three weeks I watched, rather concerned, as she gradually turned yellow, became comatose and died. Three months later to the day I started to feel nauseated. I developed a deep, aching pain in the upper right side of my abdomen and sickening discomfort when I tried to lie on my stomach. I rang the head of the renal unit, and he told me to come in for blood tests. I had hapatitis B. I had not been told when I started work that many of the dialysis patients were infected with this virus and that some of the medical staff, including the surgeons, had developed acute hapatitis.

I was admitted to the Queen Elizabeth on a hot November day, and a sweet nursing sister put me to bed in a room that—ironically—had been decorated by my mother ten years before. There I lay for three weeks, vomiting day and night. The nausea was intensely unpleasant, similar to the morning sickness of pregnancy. My skin and the whites of my eyes turned bright yellow, and my stools were bright white because the bile ducts in the liver were totally blocked. The doctors were secretive about the results of my blood tests, so I persuaded the junior nurses to show me my chart. It was bad.

I was barrier nursed (in isolation) and visitors and staff had to don gowns and masks when they entered the room. The children stood outside the door looking in through the glass. I couldn't even touch them, let alone give them reassuring hugs. They were farmed out to various relatives, and Penny later said she was aware that something dreadful was happening and she was terribly unhappy.

I grew worse, became precomatose and began to die. My liver enlarged from its natural position under the right side of the rib cage to fill the entire abdomen. One day I was so sleepy I couldn't wake up, even though I was vaguely aware that somebody was moving around in the room. It was quite pleasant slipping into a coma after the acute discomfort of the illness, but I didn't see any tunnels or lights typical of a near-death experience. After about half an hour I opened my eyes, and there was Bill. We were still emotionally estranged, but he came to see me three times that day.

The head of the renal unit was in charge of my case. In desperation, he dusted off a sample bottle of a new type of concentrated sugar solution called Xylitol and ran it full blast into my arm. After fifteen minutes I thought my head would explode. Even though I was extremely sick, I knew the Xylitol was the problem and screamed: 'Turn it off, turn it off!' and they slowed the drip. The superconcentrated sugar solution had temporarily caused my brain to shrink at a time when my liver disease had reduced the blood-clotting time to 17 per cent of normal. As the brain shrank, a small connecting vessel in my head could have torn, and I would have bled to death. I almost died in the same hospital five months after my mother.

The next day I woke up craving soup. Miraculously, I was beginning to recover. Had the Xylitol kick-started my immune system so that it killed the hepatitis B virus, or was the timing serendipity? I didn't know. Gradually my strength returned, but I was so weak and thin that the nurses had to wash my hair while I lay down because I couldn't sit up.

With recovery came the return of intense loneliness. I would stand in the doorway of my hospital room, wearing a green negligee (and green eyeshadow that neatly matched the colour of the 'whites' of my eyes), using all my seductive powers to see how long I could engage people in conversation before they walked away. I was hungry to read and my doctor supplied me with heaps of books, which I devoured, including

Gunter Grass's wonderful *The Tin Drum* and novels by Iris Murdoch. Sometimes I read almost two a day.

When Bill finally took me home after five weeks, I looked like a Belsen survivor. The summer days of December and January in Adelaide were hot, long and empty, and I lay in our white bed, so lonely that I felt like a satellite swirling around in space with no earthly or physical contact. I was distant from the children, and I felt my marriage to Bill was at an emotional end.

Yet in the midst of this desolation I gained some important insights. I recovered enough to return to work as a locum tenens, filling in for other general practitioners, and I found that my brush with death and my experience of depression had made me a more understanding doctor, better able to feel empathy with my patients. More importantly, however, I knew that I had been saved for a reason. My life, in a strange way, almost didn't belong to me anymore. I felt that I would be called upon to act in service, not to myself or even my family but to something greater.

Part 2

Liberation

CHAPTER 8

The next two years, 1970 and 1971, were to be a watershed time. As I gradually recovered from both hepatitis and the depression and entered the angry stage of grief, I read a book that affected me profoundly—Germaine Greer's *The Female Eunuch.* She urged women to recognise and own their *own* thoughts, rather than saying the 'right' things to conform to the dictates of a male-dominated society. It was OK to *say* those things out loud and to *be* the person I really was. Wow, what a sense of liberation. It wasn't until I read that book that I realised I had never really stopped to consider what *I* thought about things, let alone to expose the real person beneath my inhibitory layers of 'niceness'.

Suddenly I didn't care what other people thought about me, and I started to feel my oats. I developed a white hot certainty that left no room for compromise. The depression lifted at last, and I had no compunction about speaking my mind at dinner parties, political meetings and other social settings, much to other people's discomfort. One evening we were invited to a rather social dinner party given by one of Adelaide's most influential and well-connected radiologists. Somehow the conversation turned to the delicate subject of relationships, whereupon I mentioned the word 'orgasm' and the ceiling metaphorically crashed onto the table. Of course, there was a certain sense of wickedness that accompanied my sometimes wild remarks.

My energy level was high and I was eager to explore and experiment. I took painting lessons at the local technical college, and after my one and only class in portraiture I rushed home and drew the faces of Bill, all three children and Bill's father, George; they weren't bad, and I had them framed. I also took lessons in sculpting and pottery. Even more importantly, I was awakened sexually by reading the feminist literature, which did wonders to improve our ailing marriage. The children became more secure also.

During 1971 my political activities began when I challenged the Australian government and the French to halt atmospheric nuclear testing in the Pacific. But it wasn't just the big guys I took on; I blasted local council workers in North Adelaide for heavily pruning the trees in our street, and I took on a prominent businessman to save a local historic pub just around the corner from our house.

Then I discovered the three volumes of Bertrand Russell's autobiography, and he became my next mentor. His thoughts about moral societies and his leadership against nuclear weapons perfectly matched my own newly emerging sense of righteousness. A highly intelligent, compassionate man, he articulated his truth loudly and clearly with no reservations, and if he was proven wrong, he would acknowledge his mistake, recant and continue preaching the new truth. I liked that.

I discovered for the first time who I really was, the real person hidden beneath the layers of intense societal and parental conditioning. I ceased to be a puppet and became me. Difficult, contentious, lively, irascible, with enormous amounts of energy and an irrefutable certainty about the truth as I saw it, I was not an easy person to live with, I'm sure.

While we were in the States, I had been intoxicated by the energy of the burgeoning movements in the late 1960s, particularly the civil rights and anti-Vietnam War movements and the strong push towards anti-authoritarianism. I observed the progress of these momentous political events from the sidelines, but I learned how a democracy can be used to achieve political ends, and I began to put this newfound knowledge into practice.

But now to backtrack a little in the chronology of this momentous year. After I recovered from hepatitis, we moved into a two storey townhouse set in a row of terraces fronting onto Gover Street in North Adelaide, one of the trendier parts of the city, not far from the hospital. Our house had a pretty, north-facing wrought-iron balcony that trapped the winter sun, and I used to sit there on Sunday afternoons luxuriating in the warmth and reading while Bill played golf and the children were off with friends.

To make matters interesting and to my delight, we rapidly found that our neighbours were intelligent, argumentative people with definite opinions on a wide range of subjects. Some of them were also slightly crazy. For instance, one morning as we sat on our back terrace, a young man appeared dressed only in a pair of shorts and flying boots, with a bottle of beer tucked under each arm. 'I'm Bill Balmain,' he said. 'I come with your house.' Bill, who had been friendly with the house's previous owners, was a pilot who flew the outback prospecting for minerals, including uranium. His eyesight was so bad that he memorised the reading chart so he could fake his annual flying test, but he never crashed. Once he took Nookles for a flight without my permission because he knew how much I hated flying. Nooks came home delighted and announced: 'I've been flying upside down with Bill Balmain.' I was very annoyed, but it didn't inhibit our friendship. Syd Feldheim, a delightful reprobate with a broad Australian accent you could cut with a knife, was someone else who came with the house. He was always broke and he would walk unannounced through the front door muttering to himself: 'How can I be Jewish and so unsuccessful?'

Then there was Doc. We ran into him in the crowd as we left a performance of *Jesus Christ Superstar* one night and became inseparable friends. He was in his early thirties, about five foot nine (175 centimetres); his hair framed his head in a fifteen centimetre thick black curly mass and his eyes sparkled above a thick black beard. His nickname was a legacy from his musician father, Doc, who was also not a medico. The kids adored him because he was eccentric, funny and completely unpredictable. A keen amateur musician, he would wander into our kitchen at some ungodly hour of the night and open the fridge door searching for the remains of my latest chocolate cake. One night he materialised in our bedroom after we'd been woken by his activities in the kitchen, removed his violin from the case, and serenaded us at three in the morning. Another late night companion was my medical mate Borrie Hewitson, who once appeared in our bedroom brandishing a bottle of whisky. After Bill and I had pried our eyes open, the three of us would hang out discussing life and philosophy. Our bedroom came to be the neighbourhood meeting place.

These were wild days. It was the beginning of the 1970s, and liberation was in the air, sexual and otherwise. Although I remained faithful, we certainly kicked over the traces from time to time. Every Christmas I gave a party and invited all the interesting people I'd met that year; the butcher, federal politicians, medical colleagues, the local dry cleaner, Doc, Syd, Bill Balmain, all the neighbours and lots of others. I crammed them all into our small sitting room, and filled their tummies with baked ham, homemade bread, lashings of fresh strawberries and whipped cream, and large quantities of ethyl alcohol. We had a ball. Various nefarious activities took place on our back lawn—or so I'm told.

We had lots of dinner parties, mainly because I loved cooking and entertaining. I'd spend all day in the kitchen concocting complex gourmet meals while Philip, then ten years old, watched, but I would never let him eat anything until after the party. He is now an excellent cook and attributes his prowess to the gustatory titivation he received as a child. Our dinner guests were always lively, as was the conversation. How exciting and stimulating it was to talk about subjects previously verboten in polite society, like sex, intimate relationships, and our newly emerging philosophies of life.

We also bought a wooden fisherman's cottage in a tiny town called Goolwa, situated on the mouth of the Murray River. It was so old that the dried seaweed used for insulation seeped out through the expanding cracks between the internal clapboards. We drove eighty kilometres from Adelaide each weekend to relax from the tensions of the week. The kids, dressed in their coloured tracksuits, fished, fell in the river and rode their bikes; at the end of the day they took long, steaming baths. Bill amused himself by hammering and building, while I lay on the rush matting in front of the fire sleeping and dreaming deeply for hours. Often, on Sunday nights, while the ocean wind howled in a gale outside and rain beat on the tin roof, our cosiness was completed by eating scrambled eggs on toast with Vegemite.

Against this background of frivolity and family intimacy my medical and political careers were emerging. I visited the Adelaide Children's Hospital and, to my horror, found that children with cystic fibrosis were virtually untreated, the attitude being that if they had inherited a fatal disease, the sooner they died the better. I tentatively suggested that I knew how to treat these patients, but to no avail. I was not trained as a paediatrician, I was told, and I had no right to work in that hospital until I had earned the appropriate degree.

Right, I said. I'll bloody well go back and train as a paediatric intern working eighty hours a week, and then when I complete the arduous training and pass the exam for the royal Australasian College of Physicians, I'll establish a CF clinic. I had an implicit agreement with the hospital hierarchy that I would then be given the clinic.

Bill was somewhat reluctant to go along with my new decision, but when I pointed out that he had done his post-graduate training with my support and it was now my turn, he agreed to swap roles and be the primary caretaker for the family. Besides, I had already employed a housekeeper to look after the children and do the housework. I started at the hospital in January 1972, working all night one night in three. Bill was very supportive.

In 1971, before I got to the hospital, our marriage went through some stormy times. At a certain point I decided to leave Bill because our relationship was so strained; I would take our children to Sydney and live with my sister Susan and her husband. Stupidly, or perhaps not, I told my next-door neighbour, who told Bill. The next thing I knew, all hell broke loose, and he said, 'You're not leaving, they're my children, too.'

But this episode broke the ice. Bill and I really started to talk for the first time in years. We were hesitant at first, not being used to such honesty, but our intimacy gradually increased. With trepidation I told him my great secret—my two-year obsession with the surgical registrar. To my surprise, Bill was sweet and understanding. I was so grateful that I went no further with my plans to leave.

We decided to attend marriage guidance counselling, where we resolved some of our outstanding difficulties. Once we began, we found we could communicate easily, and we started really telling each other many secrets. We lay awake all night talking about ourselves, sharing experiences: the naughty things we had done as children, the most embarrassing things about our adolescence. Frequently, we were still awake when the milkman clinked the bottles on the front steps of the verandah.

As the marriage improved, several interesting political opportunities presented themselves. One Sunday afternoon in 1972 during a party, I was standing in the front room of our neighbour Ushi, arguing vociferously with a Scotsman who had just been appointed by the state government of South Australia to supervise among other things the national parks in the state. He seemed to enjoy the provocative nature of the discussion. Before I knew it, I'd been invited to become a member of the National Parks and Wildlife Council of South Australia, not that I was an expert on flora or fauna, but I learned a lot and participated in some lively discussions.

I also teamed up with an enthusiastic man named Laurie Bryan, who persuaded me to join the Aboriginal Education Foundation, an organisation devoted to the preschool education of Aboriginal children living in Adelaide. Like most Australians brought up in cities, my knowledge of the country's original inhabitants was sketchy. Certainly I believed that society should do everything to help them, but my understanding was purely theoretical. Now I was confronted by the human face of the Aboriginal problem, and I was appalled. These were fringe dwellers, living in shanties and hovels, with virtually no education or medical care. Many girls were pregnant by the age of thirteen. For the first time in my life I saw a race of people who had been deprived of their culture, their dignity and their land by the invading white settlers, and now lacked the rudiments of self respect. I had become aware for the first time during those years in the United States that we had a racist society in Australia when I was arguing with a man during a Boston dinner party about the black/white problems in Boston. He turned to me and said, 'What about your Aborigines?' and I was shocked into silence.

How could we, an affluent society, have allowed this to

happen? I couldn't understand it. At that time most white Australians cared little about the plight of the Aborigines. National and international mining companies exploited them because the outback land is often rich in minerals and pastoralists had exploited them since European settlement, both for slave labour and for their land. Aborigines, generally a shy people who often take years to make decisions by consensus, were not used to demanding their rights in white society. Since the early 1970s they have become much more vocal and effective.

I also joined the Australian Labor Party and began attending meetings. This was an exciting time to become a member of the ALP. In Australian politics, the winds of change were beginning to blow. For over twenty years, the Liberal government had been in power, presided over by a sycophantic Anglophile, Sir Robert Menzies, and his successors. But a new generation of Australians was rebelling against them, rejecting their slavish allegiance to the British crown. They demanded independence for Australia in other ways; Australian troops had been backing American forces in Vietnam since 1965, and the groundswell of opposition to Australia's involvement in a foreign war was strong. Real change and enlightenment, spearheaded by a Labor government, seemed close.

In some ways South Australia was ahead of the rest of the country. In 1970 the voters had chosen a state Labor government led by Don Dunstan, a lawyer who grew up in Fiji and then attended St Peter's College, Adelaide's most prestigious private school. In his late thirties when he was elected premier, Dunstan shocked the Adelaide establishment by wearing pink shorts and long socks to Parliament one hot day. Meanwhile, he liberalised industrial relations in South Australia and instigated Aboriginal land rights, while strongly supporting the arts and literature, building a Festival Centre and establishing the internationally known Adelaide Festival of Arts.

One quiet Sunday morning I left our house for an ALP meeting at the University of Adelaide. Penny, Phil and Nookles had climbed ladders up into the branches of a large tree in our street and were sitting there happily eating their cereal; I left then in Bill's care. I returned to a strange silence several hours later; an empty street, cornflakes scattered over the footpath and a deserted house. Panicking, I rushed next door, to be told by David Bright, 'Don't worry, Nookles just fell out of a tree. He's unconscious and Bill's taken him to hospital.' My blood turned cold.

I rushed to the hospital. On the table in the X-ray department lay Will, ashen faced and unconscious, with a lacerated forehead. I swept him into my arms and paced around the radiology room, kissing him all over. He woke briefly and said, 'Mummy' and I was so relieved. Bill and the technician told me not to hold him, so I put him back on the cold table.

David Bright had walked down the street to say hello to the kids; Nookles had turned, lost his balance and fallen three metres head first onto the concrete gutter. David carried his limp body around to Bill, who was mowing the back lawn. Nookles' pupils were dilated and he had ceased to breathe. Leaving Penny and Philip with David, Bill put him into the car where he started showing some signs of life on the way to the hospital.

Nookles had the classic symptoms of concussion, though—thank God—there was no indication of internal bleeding. He was taken to the surgical ward, where he stayed for a week. For two months after the accident I was haunted by the thought, will he be normal? Has his brain or IQ been damaged by the injury? He did exhibit several lingering neurological signs, indicating that there had been some damage.

During the agonising weeks it took for these questions to be resolved, I kept thinking what a fascinating child Nooks was. When he was small, he refused to be parted from an old baby's quilt, which he called his 'ra-ra', short for rag, which it came to resemble. When it grew too grubby and disgusting to contemplate, our housekeeper at the time made a unilateral decision and sent it to the tip. All hell broke loose. None of us would be able to sleep again until we drove in the dark to the tip to retrieve it, and Nookles was made happy again.

When we were living in the States, I took him into the Harvard Co-op one afternoon, where a big, fat Boston cop with a gun on his hip confronted this barefoot, blond, cherubic little boy dressed in a blue and white checked gingham sunsuit. 'What's your name, little boy?' he asked. Our youngest child stuck his chin out, looked up, and said aggressively, 'Called Nookles.'

On another occasion I drove the three kids, freshly bathed and in their pyjamas, to collect the babysitter before Bill and I went out for the evening. I parked the car in the college parking lot and we went in to get her. When we returned, the car wasn't there. It was like a nightmare. I knew I'd parked it in a certain spot, and it had disappeared. I finally found it resting against another car at the bottom of a short hill near a busy highway with Nookles standing on the front seat, still turning the steering wheel with tremendous zeal, while Philip and Pen cowered in the back sobbing, 'Nookles drove the car.' By some mysterious means he had managed to get the car out of gear, allowing it to roll down the hill. When we filled out an insurance claim, under the heading 'Driver', we wrote: 'William Caldicott, aged 18 months'. The claim was duly honoured.

To my everlasting relief, Will was discharged from hospital without permanent brain damage. However, the accident badly affected the family for some time. Phil disappeared into his room and buried himself in books; Penny developed such severe abdominal pain that I thought she had appendicitis, though tests proved nothing was organically wrong. They had seen their brother fall, and it must have shocked the hell out of them. I must admit that I didn't give them enough attention at the time because I was so preoccupied with Nooks.

This reaction is common in a family with a sick child. The healthy siblings are ignored to their detriment, and the sick child receives all the attention.

I blamed myself for what had happened, as most mothers probably would have done. My despair, however, took a long time to fade, and Bill grew impatient with me. In retrospect, I think I was still suffering from unresolved guilt over Mum's death. It was all my fault; the thought never occurred to me that I had actually left the children in Bill's care, although I was aware that they were in the tree eating their breakfast before I left.

I was so terrified that Will would hurt his head again that for a year I insisted he wear a cycling helmet every time he ventured outside. This increased the friction between us, for he was a very strong-willed little boy. He became hyperactive, and the more hyperactive he grew, the more fearful I was, so it became a vicious circle. I found myself resenting him, and I even sought psychiatric help and counselling to come to terms with our relationship, but it wasn't very helpful. Not for years was I able to understand the grief and confusion I felt at this time.

I was also hypochondriacal about my children. Being a doctor, I knew hundreds of potential diagnoses that would fit their complaints when they were sick and I always chose the disease with the worst prognosis. This was an extension of my own hypochondria, which had plagued me all my life, probably related to my brush with death as a baby. It was comfortable to choose cystic fibrosis as my specialty because I knew my children would never get it.

There were other dynamics that led to the decision to pursue my profession aggressively: (a) I was bored with life. (b) I needed the intellectual challenge. (c) I wanted to establish a cystic fibrosis clinic. (d) I needed to channel the energy of my emerging anger and liberation into something constructive. (e) I needed to remove my projected neuroses from my children. (f) I had to be an individual in my own right and not the wife of Bill Caldicott, mother of three children. (g) Last but not least, I had been badly bruised by the trauma of our marital relationship during Mum's death and I needed some space, even though Bill and I were now more comfortable with each other.

CHAPTER 9

One day late in 1971 I was surprised to get a phone call from the vicar of one of Adelaide's poshest churches, Holy Trinity; he was a man who prided himself on being up to date with the newest trends. 'We'd like you to come and talk to our congregation one night about women's liberation,' he said.

I was obviously becoming known as a ball of fire outside our immediate circle, somebody with firm and somewhat controversial opinions. Nevertheless, it was hard to believe that such a conservative church group would appreciate what I had to say.

'Do you really want me to say what I think?' I asked.

'Of course,' he replied.

So a week later I found myself standing before a group of well-bred Adelaide ladies and gentlemen, giving them the gospel according to Germaine Greer. I said that women in Australian society were less confident than men because they rarely had orgasms, which I discovered from surveying my patients in general practice. I also said that venereal disease was not inherently evil but a product of intimacy, like measles, chicken pox or tuberculosis.

None of this sounds radical now, but in those days my words created a sensation. Halfway through my speech, a woman rose, fixed me with a stony look and ostentatiously walked out, slamming the door behind her. When I finished and the vicar called for questions, one of my co-speakers, a female gynaecologist with her hair in a stiffly starched beehive, stood up and said in a strained tone that I was wrong because venereal disease makes people go mad and become sterile.

This should have prepared me for the scene when we retired to the rectory for coffee. You could have cut the air with a knife. I stood awkwardly holding my cup and saucer, chatting to a visibly uncomfortable vicar, while the audience and my fellow speakers kept as far away from me as possible. In no way could my talk be considered a success.

I drove home feeling embarrassed and uncertain and walked into our warm sitting room. Bill looked up and asked, 'How did it go?'

'I think I've done a terible thing,' I said, and described the scene I had just left.

He responded: 'No, you haven't. I think that's one of the best things you've ever done.'

This was one of the nice things about Bill. If he agreed with my activities, he would support me to the hilt. His reaction encouraged me to go on, to continue speaking the truth. I think he was partly fascinated by this unpredictable new creature he had on his hands and partly horrified.

Shortly after this episode, I discovered that since 1966 the French government had been exploding nuclear weapons over the Pacific atoll of Mururoa, and since 1968 they had consistently been violating the International Test Ban Treaty newly negotiated by the superpowers, which banned atmospheric testing. Prevailing winds from Mururoa blew over

Australia, so our cities were at risk from dangerous radioactive fallout. Then someone handed me a leaked government document indicating that Adelaide, which uses rainwater for domestic use because it has such a dry climate, had been exposed to particularly high levels of fallout. This radioactive rain fell after a drought when the collecting tanks were relatively empty, hence there was no unpolluted water to dilute the radioactivity.

As a doctor I knew that radiation could induce genetic disease as well as cancer and leukemia, particularly in children, who are ten to twenty times more radiosensitive than adults. I brooded about this a great deal. All the anxiety I had felt since reading *On the Beach* years ago returned, increased by new information as well as anger. How *dare* the French test nuclear weapons so close to Australia? If testing was as safe as they assured us, why weren't they exploding their bombs closer to home, in the Mediterranean? I was enraged and decided that I must inform the public about the medical dangers posed by these tests.

I wrote a letter to the local paper, the Adelaide *Advertiser*, pointing out the medical dangers of radioactive isotopes in human breast milk. After several days I rang the editor.

'Where's my letter?' I demanded.

In a patronising tone he replied, 'Madam, we receive many letters each day.'

'Yes,' I retorted, 'but *mine's* important.' I patiently explained the reasons why, and the next morning my letter was published.

When I think of all the things that stemmed from that letter, and so quickly, I can see that I must have been a godsend to the media, especially in Adelaide, where few newsworthy events took place. Here I was, not only a mother of three but a doctor, so my warnings about the dangers of radioactivity to young children had real authority. The media responded with alacrity. On the evening of the day the letter was published, I appeared on the ABC-TV current affairs program *This Day Tonight*, where I was questioned by a sceptical reporter named Clive Hale. I must have acquitted myself quite well.

Soon afterwards I gave my first public speech about the nuclear issue in the YWCA hall in North Adelaide. I spoke with passion about radiation, genetic disease and the medical ramifications of the French nuclear tests. My audience was six little old ladies who placidly knitted as I spoke, and ate their lunch out of brown paper bags.

I could have given up in despair, but something interesting was happening. Radio programs, letters to the editor, and comments among people I knew indicated that Australians were beginning to feel uneasy about the French tests. Like me, they were beginning to wonder: if nuclear testing was as safe as the French said it was, why weren't they doing it close to France? Because I had the facts and figures to make sense of this anxiety, and also because I was a doctor, people wanted to hear what I had to say. Before long it seemed that every time the French exploded a nuclear bomb in the Pacific, as they frequently did in the early 1970s, I was on television talking about the medical consequences of radioactive fallout. At first my appearances were limited to ABC-TV in Adelaide, but before long the ABC flew the tapes to Sydney and I appeared all over Australia.

Not being a nuclear physicist, I made occasional errors, and I was sometimes attacked by physicists who supported the nuclear industry as well as by other doctors. The Adelaide *Advertiser* published an article by Stewart Cockburn in which Dr Peter Ronai, the head of nuclear medicine at the Royal Adelaide Hospital, accused me of being hysterical and said some of my information was wrong. I felt demeaned and acutely embarrassed when I was publicly criticised, but I also knew that fundamentally I was speaking the truth.

Actually, attacks from the press and other forums proved to be useful. Not only did they draw attention to what I was saying, but each one motivated me to learn more, to read everything I could get my hands on, to hone my arguments, to back up my words with more precise information.

After several months the Union of Australian Women in Adelaide decided to present me with a certificate of recognition for my anti-nuclear work. I had never heard of this group, but they seemed very supportive. The meeting turned out to be a dinner dance, attended by more than two hundred people. This was the biggest gathering of this sort I had yet attended, and Bill, who was nervous on my behalf, said I should prepare a written speech. I thought this was a good idea and sweated over it, filling it with facts and figures.

I was standing at the microphone in the 'Homing Pigeons Hall' in Adelaide delivering this manifesto when I became conscious that everybody's eyes were glazing over. This was the first time I'd had this reaction, and I couldn't understand why. I had done my homework, I was presenting good material; what had gone wrong?

Later in the evening while I was dancing with a union official, he gave me some valuable advice. 'Never read a speech again,' he said. 'You must keep speaking spontaneously; you're so effective on television because you are forceful and speak from the heart.' It was a lesson I never forgot. I had never considered the mode of presentation, thinking it was enough simply to give people the relevant information. This union official really changed the course of my life. Since that time I have almost never read a speech. I learned that you must engage an audience with passion, humour, wit and intelligence or you lose them and they fade away. It is an insult to give a second-rate speech to people who have given up their evening to be stimulated and inspired.

It was exciting to see that throughout Australia anti-French feeling was steadily growing. People stopped buying French perfume, postal workers refused to deliver mail to and from France, waterside workers stopped loading French ships. A psychiatrist friend of ours whose child had just been diagnosed with leukemia was so furious with the French that he decided to drive his Citroën into the centre of the city and blow it up, although the disease was clearly unrelated to the fallout, because it takes several years after exposure to radiation for such a situation to develop. In the end he didn't carry out his plan.

One Saturday morning early in 1972, soon after I started work as a paediatric intern at the Adelaide Children's Hospital, I finished rounds and walked into the city. I was vaguely aware that a march had been planned to protest against the French, but I'll never forget the feeling I experienced when I got to North Terrace and it was chockablock with people as far as the eye could see. I ran along beside them, unable to believe that so many people cared. Fathers marched carrying their babies on their shoulders, with placards around their necks reading 'I don't want to die of leukemia from French tests'. There were men, women and children of all ages from all walks of life. Most of them had never made a public protest about anything in their lives before.

During the first half of 1972 thousands joined anti-nuclear marches in the streets of other Australian cities. The media coverage was phenomenal. Whole pages of newspapers were devoted to angry letters about the French tests, and editorial opinions abounded. Seldom had Australia seen such a unified display of indignation. The anti-nuclear protests were at least as big as the anti-Vietnam War protest marches of several years before and had a much more widespread community base. And what made the anti-French demonstrations even more extraordinary was that they were spontaneous in origin, not having been organised by any official body.

I was making speeches and appearing on television more and more frequently. Rupert Murdoch's *Australian* newspaper featured me in a front-page editorial. I was delighted with the coverage, but before long I found my public life was as demanding as my work as a paediatric intern. I would insert an intravenous drip into the scalp vein of a child with meningitis, run up to my tiny bedroom in the hospital's residential quarters, take off my white coat, and sit in a chair to be interviewed for national ABC television. And outside in the hall a man wearing a Commonwealth cap emblazoned with a crown would be waiting to whisk the tape off to Sydney for national broadcast that evening.

At that time I was working eighty hours a week at the hospital, I had a young family, and I was spearheading a national anti-nuclear campaign. And I handled it all. This is why I am often irritated when after one of my anti-nuclear or environmental lectures people who have been moved will say to me: 'I care, but I haven't got time to do anything.' There is *always* time when you feel passion about the earth and all living creatures.

The anger that had been provoked by my emerging sense of liberation was a primary source of energy for me, then and for many years after. I see now that I was rebelling, not just against my relative powerlessness as a woman within the patriarchal Australian society, but also against my parents. They were the most powerful people I had ever known. I was never game to act out the normal adolescent rebellion because I was scared of them. They supported me during medical school, when I lived at home and was financially dependent on them. The veiled threat if I misbehaved was that I would be kicked out with no means of support, and I couldn't contemplate the thought of not finishing medical school.

In a way, my depression and subsequent anger, all part of the grieving reaction after Mum's death, gave me the impetus to engage in a delayed rebellion, to discover my real strengths and beliefs. I chose to take on people who were even more powerful than my parents had been—the politicians who were arrogantly promoting nuclear policies endangering the future of our children. Perhaps, too, because I had been so unprotected as a child, I needed to protect the world's children as a compensatory mechanism.

The hospital switchboard was taking more calls about the

French tests than about patients, and one afternoon I was called into the office of Dr Bill McCoy, the hospital's medical superintendent. He didn't invite me to sit down so I stood in front of his desk, feeling very uncomfortable. Then he told me that the consultants' wives had complained about the amount of publicity I was receiving. 'If you don't stop this public campaigning,' he said, 'we may not be able to appoint you as medical registrar next year.'

This was very intimidating; I had to have this appointment in order to sit for my membership exams. 'Has my work suffered?' I asked as evenly as I could. 'Have you received any complaints about my medical practice?'

'No,' he replied.

I waited for him to continue, but he calmly reached for some papers on his desk and began to read, taking no further notice of me. I was amazed by his rudeness. 'Does this mean I can leave now?' I asked.

'Yes,' he said, and I stumbled out of his office.

What had I done wrong? It seemed perfectly logical that I, a paediatric intern, should be making people aware that nuclear testing meant their children were in danger of developing cancer and leukemia. And how did the wives of the medical staff come into this? Were they instrumental in formulating hospital policy? Were they jealous of me?

When I got home, I poured out the whole story to Bill. He had trained with McCoy and was close to him. I don't know whether I expected Bill to side with his old mate, but he didn't. So furious was he that he leapt into the car and sped to the hospital, taking the corners on two wheels, to have it out with McCoy.

The medical superintendent had left for the day, but Bill made an appointment to see him the following morning. During their discussion, Bill told him that his behaviour was outrageous and that he would not treat a ward maid as he had treated me. McCoy finally admitted in a rather shamefaced way that his behaviour had been totally inappropriate and he later wrote me a letter of apology at Bill's insistence. That was the last I heard of the matter for some months.

It's interesting to me now that although I was confident enough then to tilt at global windmills, I was still somewhat emotionally insecure. At times such as these Bill came to my rescue.

Not long after this I had a strange dream in which I was on a plane to Paris. The dream remained with me when I woke the next morning, but it seemed to have no relevance. Three days later I received a phone call asking me to join a delegation of Australians to Tahiti to protest against the French tests. The delegation included unionists, students, church people and politicians. I was very excited, and even though Bill wasn't overjoyed at the idea, he agreed it was a great opportunity. The next step was getting permission for a ten-day leave of absence from the hospital, which meant another confrontation with Bill McCoy. Once again I climbed the creaking old wooden stairs to his office.

'You can't go,' he said when I had made my request. 'I won't give you permission.'

I was nonplussed until I thought of an answer: 'But the press will want to know why I can't go.'

He hesitated, and finally said, 'All right, you can go, but you're not to *say* anything.'

'Thank you,' I said, smiling.

The family came to the airport to see me off on the first part of the trip—from Adelaide to Sydney—and the Adelaide *Advertiser* photographed me walking through the airport holding hands with the children just before we said goodbye. In Sydney I was to meet other members of the delegation, none of whom I knew, and we were to fly to Tahiti together.

At Sydney's Kingsford Smith Airport Susan met me with her small daughter Mary Alice, who was lurching around in a nappy, sucking a bottle. I overheard Gough Whitlam, who had never met me before, ask an older woman, 'Are you the doctor?' I enjoyed the surprised expression on his face when he realised that the doctor was this thirty-three-year-old woman.

Then Qantas announced that they would not allow us to board the flight because the French government in Tahiti had refused to let us disembark on arrival. Consternation reigned: Whitlam and Jim Cairns, his deputy, moved into a corner and started scheming. A national election was soon to be called and Whitlam would almost certainly lead the Labor Party to victory. It was obvious that he and Cairns would use the Tahitian setback to their own advantage. I felt very annoyed, so I approached them and said, 'This trip must not be seen as a political exercise. The delegation must represent the concerns of all Australians, no matter what their political persuasion.' Susan's little daughter gave Whitlam's leg a kick to emphasise the point, which greatly amused her mother and me.

After a little more discussion and argument, Whitlam and Cairns decided to carry the anti-nuclear protest to the highest level—to the French government in Paris. There would be a delegation of three: Ken Newcomb, President of the Australian Union of Students, Jim Cairns and me. I didn't have a visa, but Jim rushed me to the French Embassy, and with his influence we obtained one within hours. The next thing I knew, I was sitting in a Qantas jet on my way to Paris by way of London, eating prawns, drinking champagne, and listening to Handel's *Water Music* on the stereo system. It was all very strange: my dream had come true. Again, fate seemed to be taking a hand in my life.

In London Jim Cairns and I addressed a large crowd of expatriate Australians and New Zealanders in Hyde Park, all fellow protesters against the French tests. It was amazing to see so many supportive people and to be able to speak in the venerable Hyde Park. But the venue and the size of the audience didn't really faze me. I spoke from the heart about the medical implications of the tests and the arrogant disdain of the French towards all the people of the South Pacific. Then, at the head of a large deputation, we marched to the French Embassy and presented a letter of protest.

The march was widely covered by the Australian and New Zealand press. We hoped that the British government would lend its support to our cause, and tried for a meeting with Jim's old friend, the Labour prime minister, Harold Wilson. But he refused to see us, being too busy with the Common Market debate to worry about the effects of French atomic testing upon the health of Australian people. The fact that Australia was a member of the British Commonwealth seemed to be of little consequence.

Then we boarded a plane for the short hop to Paris. Although I had long dreamed of visiting the city, this was my first trip to France, and it was ironic that it was taking place under these circumstances. As I was totally focussed on my mission, I really saw little of the city's beauty, but one night we were taken to the most magnificent restaurant where the curtains were gold brocade, the waiters were impeccable and the food was something I'd never experienced before.

We applied to see President Georges Pompidou. Fairly predictably, we received no reply, although we did manage to visit François Mitterrand, leader of the socialist opposition. He greeted us warmly in a little dark room, promising that when he was elected to office, he would stop atomic testing and close down nuclear reactors in France. I believed him, not knowing that leaders of the opposition find it easy to be altruistic but their vacant promises are almost never fulfilled when they attain leadership.

We cooled our heels for several days, waiting to see Pompidou. At last we received an invitation to the Elysée Palace, not to see the president but to speak to two men from the Foreign Affairs Department. The palace was flanked by attendants garbed in regal uniforms and gloves, and it was all very grand. I wore a pink shirtmaker dress I had just finished sewing before the trip, and Jim and Ken wore suits.

The conversation that took place was a fascinating exercise

in Gallic logic. The foreign affairs officials claimed that during the years of the Cold War France had constantly tried to negotiate with the superpowers for peace and nuclear disarmament. When these calls went unheeded, the French felt they could be more effective mediators for peace if they developed their own weapons, their own *force de frappe.* This was the first time I had heard that nuclear aggression could be used in the service of peace.

When I confronted them about the medical dangers of radioactive fallout, they asserted, 'Our bombs are perfectly safe.' So Jim asked the obvious question: 'Why don't you test your bombs in the Mediterranean, if they are so safe?'

The blood drained from their faces. '*Mon Dieu,*' they exclaimed, 'too many people live around the Mediterranean!'

And so we heard the truth. I was shaken. These men didn't care if innocent children in Australia and elsewhere died as a result of their atomic tests. Clearly they had never sat beside a grey-faced child dying of leukemia, hairless, with a swollen belly, bleeding to death from every orifice. They had never had to comfort parents stricken with grief who would never recover. This was the first time in my life that I had sat opposite wicked politicians who didn't give a damn if their actions knowingly caused the death of children.

We obviously had no effect upon the mentality of the French, but we returned to Australia feeling that at least the international publicity we had generated had helped the anti-nuclear cause.

At five a.m. one morning in November 1972, I picked up the phone at the hospital still fuzzy from sleep to hear a journalist ask: 'Australia and New Zealand have just spearheaded a successful vote in the United Nations to outlaw nuclear testing. Would you like to comment on this, considering your recent role in the campaign?' I was amazed by such news so early in the morning; the ongoing ramifications of our anti-nuclear protests were hard to believe.

The French immediately countered by announcing a new series of tests to be conducted in 1973, including a one-megaton blast equivalent to one million tonnes of TNT. Would *nothing* stop these arrogant people?

On 2 December 1972, not long after the UN vote, the Australian people finally elected a Labor government after twenty-three years of conservative rule. Bill and I, who were staying with friends at the beach suburb of Mt Eliza near Melbourne, cheered aloud as we watched the towering figure of Gough Whitlam and his almost equally tall wife Margaret appear before an ecstatic crowd and claim victory. We thrilled to what became Gough's signature salutation, taken from the words of John Curtin, Australia's wartime Labor prime minister: 'Men and women of Australia.'

In his speech Gough spoke of idealism and the socialistic and egalitarian principles of the Labor Party. Drinking strawberry daiquiris, Bill and I listened and applauded, like thousands of other 'true believers' all over the country. At last Australia had elected a man with the dignity, wit and intelligence of a true statesman.

Soon after the election Whitlam and the New Zealand government jointly took France to the International Court of Justice at The Hague over their decision to continue nuclear testing. Though the court's decision was equivocal, adverse international publicity forced France to test underground, thus stopping radioactive fallout in the Pacific. This was a partial victory, which personified the dictum of Thomas Jefferson, who said: 'An informed democracy behaves in a responsible fashion'.

CHAPTER 10

I was learning about courage. Treating children who were almost certainly dying of a particularly aggressive disease taught me more about bravery than did my new political career.

I first met Helen Sears after she was admitted to the pulmonary unit of the Royal Adelaide Hospital, an adult facility. She was only ten years younger than me and by the time I got to see her, she was virtually moribund with cystic fibrosis. She was a talented arts student, a lovely, gentle thing, tall with long dark hair, brown eyes and full lips, but very thin, cyanosed (her skin was bluish) and extremely short of breath. It was always so tragic that just when they reached the fullness of youth, these patients had virtually lived out the term of their natural existence.

Because few CF patients lived past adulthood, non-paediatric physicians were not well versed in the intricacies of the disease. Helen's parents heard that I could treat cystic fibrosis and called me in for consultation. There was little I could do for Helen, and she died while still in hospital. Her parents Betty and Harold were devastated, but in their grief, we formed a close and loving friendship that lasted for many years, I think partly because my name was Helen.

Not all stories of CF patients have such tragic endings, however. The most rewarding CF patient I ever treated was a seven-year-old boy named Bradley Taylor, who was deeply cyanosed and so short of breath that he could not walk. He was referred to me in an offhand way by one of the senior consultants, with the implicit but unspoken message that Bradley was dying and there was nothing I could do for him. I took him under my wing and, largely because of our combined willpower, he began to improve. When I visited Adelaide years later, he was twenty-four and only just alive, surviving with twenty-four hour oxygen and becoming navy blue within seconds of his nasal oxygen prongs being removed.

Eventually Bradley was placed on the list for a heart-lung transplant. We said goodbye before the operation in a visitors' room at the Royal Adelaide Hospital and I walked down North Terrace with tears streaming down my face, feeling certain that I would never see him again. However, a perfect match was found for his heart and lungs in Melbourne, and he was rushed to the airport and flown to the Royal Melbourne Hospital in Victoria. When he woke after the operation, his fingernails were pink instead of blue for the first time. The ordeal of the operation seemed insignificant compared with his new lease of life, or perhaps he had endured such suffering that he hardly noticed a little more.

The operation took place in 1990. Bradley's body has not rejected the heart or lungs; he plays golf, and recently he even went skydiving, much to his physician's horror. He is now a part-time public relations officer for the South Australian Cystic Fibrosis Foundation. He and I are extremely close, and every time I visit Adelaide for a speaking engagement, there he is with eyes of love looking at me from the back of the crowd.

Medicine is never without its times of crisis. When I became a paediatric intern, I was rostered on 'take' every three days, which meant that I examined and treated every medical patient admitted to the Children's Hospital for that twenty-four hour period. On some particularly busy days we admitted more than twenty-four, some of whom were desperately ill. All had to be thoroughly examined and have a history taken, each of which lasted for the best part of an hour. I was often frantic.

On a particularly hot day we admitted several dehydrated children, and I treated one little girl with a rapid intravenous drip. Because I intended to return later to assess her progress, I omitted to provide a written order to slow the rate after several hours. In the interim I admitted several other children who were very ill with meningitis, and I failed to return.

At three the next morning, while deeply asleep, I picked up the phone to hear the ward sister say the child was 'fitting'. Wearing only my short yellow flannelette nightgown, I rushed down to the ward and stood at the end of her bed, panicking. She was suffering from cerebral oedema, or swelling of the brain, caused by too much IV fluid; brain damage was a serious possibility. Quickly John Erlich, my registrar, and I gave her large doses of diuretics to flush the fluid through her kidneys, though I was sceptical whether this would work. I was terrified at the thought of facing her mother, knowing how I would feel if this were my child, and I vowed that if this child suffered brain damage, I would give up medicine forever.

However, the next morning she was standing in her cot playing and laughing, perfectly normal. I took weeks to recover from it.

The clinical work was much more challenging that it had been when I was an undergraduate ten years earlier. New research had disproved many of the lessons drilled into us as medical students. New information was now available and I was hungry for it. It became obvious to me that once-definitive scientific dictums change as the research community discovers more, and I learned that it behoves scientists to retain a degree of humility.

For the first time, as my knowledge and clinical acumen increased, I began to feel like a competent doctor. I loved learning and my avid curiousity was rewarded during these years of retraining. I appreciated the feeling in my fingertips as I examined a patient, knowing that my intuition coupled with a thorough knowledge of medicine would reveal even the most obscure diagnosis in most cases. This medical discipline could be compared to the satisfying feeling of solving a difficult esoteric mathematical problem.

It was also a delight working in the same hospital with Bill. He was a brilliant teacher and his radiology rounds were the most popular sessions of the week. He had a subtle, deadpan approach, and he kept us on our intellectual toes. He began the rounds with little comment while we examined several X-rays on the screen, depicting the most rare and interesting case—for instance, a case of congenital hypocalcaemia with associated aortic stenosis. Then he would cross-examine one of us, giving only a few subtle clues, spiced with a modicum of appropriate teasing, until the penny dropped.

The responsibilities of the family were ever present, but often when I arrived home after the arduous days and nights of 'take', I was a physical basket case. The children were around, but in essence, the family continued to function despite me and not because of me. At that time we employed an English housekeeper called Miss Wright, who kept house and family together. She lived in a flat at the back of the garden, and the unlikely combination of our Siamese cat and khaki campbell duck kept her company by sitting side by side on her doormat at night.

After I returned from Paris in August 1972, Bill asked me to refrain from any more political work because he said that it was enough to work eighty hours a week at the hospital as well as keeping some connection to the family, and I agreed.

So the latter part of the year was politically uneventful, but I missed that side of my life.

Thank God, despite my controversial politics, I was duly appointed registrar the next year. Now I moved into high gear for the membership exam, seeing patients at the hospital all day, studying at night, on the weekends and early in the mornings.

I was required to master the latest in paediatric medicine and the vast range of adult medicine as well: haematology, cardiology, gastroenterology, endocrinology, general medicine, neurology and other specialties. This intellectual challenge was not a burden for me, because I loved studying and collating information, but it took me away from the family. Often I sent the kids out of the room when they needed me, because I required absolute quiet in order to concentrate on such things as the feedback loop of the nephron or the intricacies of the inborn errors of metabolism. I feel bad about this now, and I wish I hadn't been so single-minded and had given them time when they needed it. After all, what was more important: my career or my children?

The exam was somewhat turbulent. It consisted of two parts, the written and the viva (oral), several months apart. The first took place in June, and I passed. Only one-third of the candidates passed at their first attempt, a deliberate policy, since it was considered a great privilege to enter this august college.

Then the viva. I was really nervous because I wanted to pass and put this demanding study behind me so that I could concentrate on the family. There were three long cases to examine and diagnose. I sailed through the first two cases, but the third was my downfall. While I examined a little boy seated on a chair, two doctors stood behind me, swaying intimidatingly backwards and forwards in their pinstriped suits and squeaky black shoes, their hands clasped behind their backs. I detected two heart murmurs, which were confusing and difficult to decipher. Forgetting the axiom that 'common things occur commonly', I made an exotic and somewhat unclear diagnosis.

That afternoon I waited with a sinking heart for the results to be posted at the hospital. My name was absent. I was devastated: this was the first time I had ever failed a medical exam. I needed to put these hours of study behind me, and failing a medical exam was a hell of a blow to my self esteem. The truth was that I was still a little green, having only been in clinical paedatrics for a year and a half, not long enough to be greatly experienced. I discovered later that I'd been given a case with an ambiguous diagnosis.

The ambiguity of the case made me very critical of the cardiologist who had presented the child for the exam. I was so cross that I went around telling my friends at the hospital. One evening while working in Casualty, an obsequious little consultant whom I shall call Dr X, a friend of the cardiologist, sought me out and uttered a few veiled threats to the effect that if I continued my criticism I would not be appointed next year. I was stunned.

This man continued to target me. One Saturday morning I brought Penny in to accompany me on ward rounds. When I introduced her to Dr X, he asked her to bend over, and smacked her on the bottom. 'That's because your mother never has time to smack you,' he said, implying that I had no right to work and should have been at home with the children. I was furious. The blatant sexism was beyond belief, but I was trapped because I now knew that if I complained, my job would be jeopardised.

This attitude caused patients to suffer as well as women doctors. One day while I was rostered on Dr X's clinic, we had a patient with a middle ear infection that was unresponsive to antibiotics. The child's temperature peaked every evening and, deeply worried about complications, I suggested that we consult an ear, nose and throat specialist. But Dr X wouldn't hear of it, and then proceeded to wax lyrical about his former days in a famous children's hospital overseas when he had treated middle ear disease, implying that he knew what he was doing. He then went on holiday for a week, and I immediately called the ENT specialist. Within hours the child was on the operating table with the surgeon scooping pus from the lateral sinus in his skull. He recovered.

Dr X returned from leave, and with some trepidation I said, 'I took the liberty of calling an ENT surgeon, and the patient has recovered.' X really ripped into me: how dare I exceed my authority, how dare I go behind his back? The harshness of the attack was so unexpected that I left the ward round and burst into tears in the nurses' office. Like many women at that time, I did not yet have the presence of mind to withstand a direct attack and to fight back, particularly when the aggressor was senior to me.

In November I sat for the viva again, and breezed through. I was now a member of the Royal Australasian College of Physicians, and I received my degree in Melbourne. My friend Rena, who had just passed the membership exam herself, and her husband, Rene, took Bill and me out to a posh restaurant, where we drank so much champagne that by the first course I was almost beyond repair, the relief was so profound.

Now at last I had the authority and the qualification to establish a cystic fibrosis clinic at the Adelaide Children's Hospital as promised by the powers that be on the condition that I pass the membership. But their response to my plan was: 'Oh, we don't believe in luxury clinics,' and permission was refused—the implication being that the clinic would be a luxury for me, a promotion I didn't deserve. The patients didn't seem to be part of their considerations.

Opposition made me all the more determined. A colleague, Graham Vimpani, and I collected actuarial data on the ACH cystic fibrosis patients, which demonstrated that their 50 per cent survival rate was only four years, compared with seventeen years in the combined clinics of North

America. Those same consultants who had considered a CF clinic an unnecessary luxury were silent when I presented this information to them one Friday morning at grand rounds. Permission was finally granted.

The ACH cystic fibrosis clinic was established late in 1974. The only one in Australia, it was modelled on Harry Schwachman's excellent facility in Boston, a combined and collaborative effort with bacteriologists, nutritionists, pharmacologists, physiotherapists, psychologists, social workers, mist tent therapists and lung function laboratories. We established a close working team, reviewing patient care over coffee and sandwiches once a week. Initially I spent at least two hours with each of the sixty or so patients and their parents to elicit a complete history and to conduct a thorough physical examination. I then brought in all the relevant specialists, and the child was fitted into a specific therapeutic regime. I was very excited to finally be providing these patients with the best, most up-to-date care.

I only had six months to consolidate the patients and their treatment before we left for the United States on a year's sabbatical leave for both Bill and me. This situation imparted a tremendous sense of urgency, and I became quite frazzled with responsibility.

As well as setting up the clinic, I continued working sixty hours a week as a registrar. Though I was tired, this was exciting work because I was the acting medical superintendent at night, a unique privilege, and I felt that I could handle any case that came through the door of the casualty department. I was at the peak of my medical knowledge and competence, having just passed the membership. But there was yet another burden to be shouldered.

Shortly after I started the CF clinic with such fervour, I was shocked to discover that the Whitlam government, which we had all considered so visionary, was badly flawed: it intended to export Australian uranium.

I was not well versed in the uses of uranium and nuclear power, so I took myself to the Barr Smith Library at the university, where I borrowed *Poisoned Power* by Arthur Tampin and John Gofman. Gofman, I discovered, was an American physician who had worked for the US Atomic Energy Commission, as had Tamplin. My hair stood on end: never had I read of matters so medically dangerous.

Massive quantities of strontium 90, caesium 137, iodine 131 and two hundred other isotopes are manufactured during the generation of nuclear power from fissioned uranium. The element that really scared me, though, was plutonium. Not only was its half life 24 400 years, but only one-millionth of a gram caused cancer. Five kilograms is required for an atomic bomb. And every large reactor manufactured 230 kilograms of this satanic element every year.

Nobody knew what to do with this radioactive waste. What if it leaked into the environment? What guarantee could any country have that the uranium they exported would be used for peaceful purposes? With three children of my own, and treating patients with cystic fibrosis, I was determined to do what I could to prevent children developing leukemia, other malignancies, or genetic disease from exposure to uranium or its fission products. Another political campaign seemed inevitable. As if my hands were not already full enough . . .

I contacted the press, who thus far had reported everything told them about the French tests, but this time they were uninterested. They implied that uranium could become a legitimate export and that it could improve the country's trade balance. I insisted: 'It's potentially much more dangerous than a little fallout from French tests,' to no avail. Perhaps because the threat of uranium was long term, perhaps because so few people knew of its dreadful potential, my words fell on deaf ears.

However, a chance meeting with an engine driver named

Warren Warwick led me in another direction. A true Labor supporter and an officer in the Engine Drivers Union, Warren shared my concern about the government's irrational decision to mine and export uranium and suggested that I speak to the trade unions on the subject. With his help, I wrote to each of South Australia's seventy-six unions, including the Boilermakers, Plumbers, Pastrycooks, Railway Employees and Metalworkers, and I was invited to speak at many gatherings.

Most of the audiences consisted of men with little formal secondary education, and they were tough. To communicate, my message needed to be direct and dramatic. The Trades and Labour Councils (the representative union bodies in each state) were particularly difficult. The audience was well lubricated the night I addressed the Adelaide Trades and Labour Council, having downed numerous beers in the bar before the main event. I was given ten minutes to speak, with five minutes for questions. 'The audience won't take much notice of you,' I was instructed. 'They always talk over guest speakers.'

I'd worn a pair of black velvet slacks and an ivory-coloured satin blouse—alluring—so that they might at least look at me. But in vain. I could have been wearing a bag over my head for all the difference it made. They continued their loud conversations unabated as I spoke.

At first I panicked, then I had a brilliant idea. I began talking about the medical effects of radiation upon testicles. Suddenly you could have heard a pin drop. Australian workers may not be adamant about many things, but if there is one subject dear to their hearts, I had found it. When I finished, the men shook their heads and said, 'I don't want my kids growing up in a world like that.' The meeting voted to a man to telegram the prime minister of their deep concerns about uranium mining.

I learned something very important that night. Don't overwhelm your audience with data they can't assimilate, because you will lose them. Grab them where they are emotionally vulnerable; once they are with you, the whole occasion is extremely rewarding.

But the pivotal point in the uranium debate came when a railway worker in Queensland was asked to shunt a truck containing yellowcake, or uranium oxide—the name for uranium ore after it has been treated with sulphur during the extraction process—in a railway yard, and he refused on moral grounds. The national railways union went out on a twenty-four-hour strike in support of their colleague, and suddenly uranium hit the headlines, because nobody could get to work by train throughout the nation. This happened several days after I had flown to Sydney to address the federal executive of the Australian Railways Union, a bunch of hard-bitten unionists. When they left the room, I felt I had made little impression—but given the events of the next days, obviously I had.

Shortly after the Sydney trip, I had a rather hair raising experience when I was asked to speak to miners at the Mary Kathleen uranium mine in western Queensland. On arrival in Townsville I was told that passions were running high and some of the miners had actually threatened to tar and feather me. These men certainly did not want a woman doctor coming into their midst to warn them that their occupations and lifestyles constituted significant health risks. They lived in nice houses provided by the mining company, the town had a swimming pool and a good school, and they felt they were well cared for.

We drove hundreds of kilometres from Townsville through the heat of a Queensland day, intermittently overpowered by the stench of dead kangaroos rotting by the roadside. We arrived in the town square just as the assembled crowd were about to catch the six o'clock ABC radio news. The opening theme music ended and the announcer said, 'The Fox Commission has given a green light to uranium mining.' The men cheered. Mining uranium was okay.

My heart sank. This was the greatest possible betrayal. Some months before, the Whitlam government had appointed a three-man team led by Mr Justice Fox to enquire into uranium-mining proposals on Aboriginal-owned land at Jabiru in the Northern Territory. Of concern was the safety of uranium mining, environmental questions, misuse of end products, and the future of Aborigines in the area. Now—and I couldn't understand how the commissioners could have disregarded the significant health effects implicit in the nuclear fuel cycle—the team had approved the establishment of what became the Ranger uranium mine. Two of the commissioners supported the proposal, with one dissenter, Dr Charles Birch, a biologist.

Shortly after the announcement, I was ushered into a beer garden, where a blackboard and microphone had been set up. A group of men and their wives had gathered around tables to hear me; the atmosphere was tense, and the announcement had not made my job any easier.

I took a deep breath and started talking. I explained that the miners were constantly being exposed to radiation while they extracted ore at the mine face, and that inhalation of uranium and radium dust could cause lung cancer, bone cancer and other malignancies. I told them about genes, chromosomes, mutations, the effect of radiation on testicles and their sperm, and the chances of giving birth to deformed children. As I spoke, a hushed silence descended upon the beer garden.

At the end of the talk men waited in queues to speak to me, and one man shoved a viscous green alcoholic drink into my hand in gratitude. They relayed some harrowing stories. One twenty-five-year-old mine worker told me that both his parents had died of cancer and that he was already excreting radium in his urine. I asked him how he knew this and was told that the mining company tested the urine of the men once a week. I tried to reassure him, but he had a grim prognosis.

The following day the management showed me around the open-cut mine, insisting that everything was fine, but I was dissatisfied. None of the men wore a mask, and the hot, dry and dusty conditions that prevailed ensured that everybody was exposed to the inhalation of radioactive dust. It was also obvious that invisible gamma radiation, like X-rays, emanated from the ore face.

We drove away from Mary Kathleen that night through the waves of heat that radiated off the desert floor. I lay on the back seat, looking up at the galaxies of stars and wept for the children born and unborn who would sicken and die from our uranium, for my own powerlessness and frustration at knowing the truth but being overruled by ignorant, powerful men—people who had never borne a child or cared for one as it died.

In the various stratas of society there are scientists who make decisions about uranium and nuclear power but understand nothing of medicine or biology, and businessmen and politicians who, on the whole, are scientifically illiterate. Medical students are not taught the effects of the nuclear fuel cycle, so doctors also tend to be ignorant about these subjects, although they are extraordinarily receptive to the message when they hear it. Like a Cassandra, I often seem to be the only one imparting a message of dire concern, but because I'm a woman, I'm easy to dismiss as 'emotional'. It can be extremely frustrating.

Later I was told that many of the miners left Mary Kathleen after my talk, while others demanded the installation of a clinic. Of course, those who left were immediately replaced by men who were just as ill informed as the others had been before my lecture.

Convincing unionists of the madness in mining and exporting uranium was only part of my plan. A few days after the Mary Kathleen episode I travelled to Canberra to see the treasurer and deputy prime minister, my friend Jim Cairns, to persuade him to oppose the decision of the Labor Party to mine uranium. I knew he must have asquiesced in the policy, and I couldn't understand why. We had gone to Paris together to protest against the French nuclear tests, about which he was so passionate. I could only assume that he had little knowledge about the dangers of uranium itself. Surely when he understood, it would be possible to persuade the rest of the government that Australia's uranium should remain in the ground.

But something had happened to Jim since our Paris trip. A married man with adopted children, he had fallen deeply in love with an exotically beautiful Filipino named Junie Morosi. According to friends in Canberra, he didn't want to leave her side. Because of her, I was told, getting a message through to him would be difficult. The affair was overt and had become a scandal in Canberra. Nevertheless, I decided that even if I had to break into his motel room at three in the morning, I was going to talk to him about uranium mining.

Fortunately, one of his close staff members contacted me as I was wandering the halls of Parliament House to say that Jim was in his office and I should come up immediately. When I walked into the office of the Australian treasurer, it was evident that things were awry. Secretaries sat around filing their nails and chatting aimlessly. 'They're in Jim's office eating lunch,' I was told. Previous to Morosi, everyone had free access to Jim, but Junie had constructed her office as a barrier and nobody could get to him. I walked through her door and noticed a large picture of Jim on one wall. Knocking on the inner door, I entered without waiting for a reply, to find Jim Cairns and Junie Morosi sitting together on the couch eating salad.

Jim was a tall, imposing man with a full head of grey hair that flopped over his forehead. He introduced me to Junie, who glared at me. With her long black hair, sensuous figure and brown skin, she was a very attractive but intimidating woman. Icicles hung in the air because I had had the temerity to barge into her private empire.

I told Jim why I was there and asked whether he knew how dangerous uranium was. 'No,' he said, 'tell me.'

So while Junie stood in the corner, I sat down on the couch and quietly told Jim the medical dangers of uranium mining and the nuclear fuel cycle. Jim was a man of formidable intellect, but before I finished speaking, I knew he was not giving me his full attention. It seemed to me that he was so besotted with Morosi that he could concentrate on little else. I came away from his office feeling sad.

Having failed to interest the treasurer in the problems of uranium, I decided to talk to the prime minister, Gough Whitlam. He was also very intelligent—surely I could persuade him. A day later I was duly ushered into his office. He listened to me talk about the dangers of uranium with only one ear, because he was preoccupied with catching the proceedings of Parliament on the intercom in case his name was mentioned (this was in the days before closed-circuit TV was installed in Parliament House). I left feeling more annoyed than frustrated. The by-products of uranium fission in nuclear power plants were eventually going to kill millions of people, and Whitlam was uninterested. He had no scientific background; perhaps the magnitude of the problem was not apparent to him.

My next appointment was with Rex Connor, minister for minerals and energy, who agreed to see me at his home on a frosty Canberra morning. This portly, balding gentleman of medium build answered the door in a pair of slippers, with his trousers held up by red braces. For several hours I argued the anti-uranium case with him, but he was absolutely unmovable and deaf to scientific logic. Connor's passion was to 'buy back the farm', to make Australia self-sufficient in minerals and energy production; as far as he was concerned, anything to achieve that end was acceptable. He had bought the line of the nuclear industry that atomic power was cleaner, cheaper and safer than coal-generated electricity, and he wouldn't budge.

If the politicians were implacable, there were other avenues. While in Canberra I attended a meeting of the Australian Paediatric Association at the Lakeside Hotel, and during the cocktail hour I circulated with the text for an ad outlining the ways in which uranium was medically dangerous. I persuaded almost every doctor to sign it, which was relatively easy because most had imbibed several drinks before I approached them; if necessary, I used a little flirtation to attain the relevant signature. The ad duly appeared, and medical endorsement of the anti-uranium position gave enormous credibility to the cause. This kind of exercise was repeated when I helped set up Physicians for Social Responsibility in the USA some years later.

I returned to Adelaide to learn that Bob Hawke, then president of the Australian Council of Trade Unions (ACTU), was in town for a meeting at the Waterside Workers' Hall in Port Adelaide. He was an important figure and a rather famous larrikin character, so in his honour I donned my velvet slacks, satin shirt and leather jacket, and off I set. I found Hawke in the rather dilapidated hall at the port, introduced myself, and told him why I was there—to get institutionalised union support for the anti-uranium campaign. I pointed out that I had already spoken to union groups in Mary Kathleen, Adelaide, Darwin and Sydney and that a statement from him about the dangers of uranium mining would really help the cause.

He looked me up and down, apparently liked what he saw, and said, 'Come back in three hours and talk to me.'

I cooled my heels and approached him three hours later, only to find him somewhat inarticulate after the evening's revelries. This time he said, 'I can't talk about this now, I need all night. In fact, I need thirteen days', demonstrating that whatever Bob Hawke was interested in didn't include the problems of uranium and nuclear power. In despair I opened his jacket, placed the relevant anti-uranium literature in his inside pocket, and left.

Several years later, when Hawke became prime minister, his government adopted a pro-uranium stance. I will never forgive him for that, especially after so many Australian unions had led the anti-uranium cause.

A powerful grassroots group called the Movement Against Uranium Mining (MAUM) was inaugurated in my North Adelaide dining room, and we organised protest marches and rallies and placed ads in the newspapers. A related group, Campaign Against Nuclear Energy (CANE), was also initiated in Melbourne.

Many people in society became fascinated by the movement. Sir Mark Oliphant, a highly respected nuclear scientist and then governor of South Australia, asked me several times to lunch at Government House. He had a shock of curly grey hair, a rosy red face and innocent, intelligent blue eyes. We had interesting conversations amid the plush settings of Government House; he was fascinated by the campaign, though he himself tended to favour nuclear power. He had worked on the Manhattan Project with Robert Oppenheimer and Edward Teller, designing the atomic bombs that had been unleashed on Hiroshima and Nagasaki. Some of the scientists on the project felt so unhappy about their actions that they decided to assuage their guilt by harnessing 'atoms for peace'. Being a highly intelligent man, Sir Mark seemed to understand both sides of the argument, but I felt that his involvement with the Manhattan project always preyed upon his conscience.

John Coulter, a doctor employed by the Institute of Medical and Veterinary Science in Adelaide, was a fantastic resource. An excellent researcher, he provided me with data about radiation and cellular dysfunction, as well as moral support. He later became leader of the Australian Democrats.

As the anti-uranium campaign intensified, once again, as with the French tests, I was doing more and more media work. One day I was driving over the railway line in Brompton, a rather depressed inner Adelaide suburb, on my way to the hospital when I switched on the radio and heard a voice that sounded vaguely familiar. I was somewhat taken aback to discover it was my own, and amazed at how professional and articulate I sounded.

CHAPTER 11

My political work has never had a plan. Opportunities seemed to have evolved, and I've grabbed them as they present. It's almost as if I'm not in control of my destiny but I think because I've had such dedication that fate has guided me wisely.

The move to the United States for our sabbatical year 1975–76 was an opening that propelled me into the American political scene, but I was not to know that as we left. It came at an auspicious time in our medical lives. Bill needed a break from his department; he was to pursue further hypertension research with Norm Hollenberg, while I would learn more about CF with Schwachman. I had done as much as I could for the anti-uranium campaign before I left, the cystic fibrosis clinic was off and running, and we left amid high expectations for the great Excited States of Frustration, as one of our friends called it.

We arrived in Boston after a month-long campervan trip through Europe with our three children, which was a character-building experience, to say the least. It's not easy living in close quarters with three early-adolescent children, and the family dynamics were sometimes quite intense. We arrived to a New England summer and rented a house on a hill in Highland Avenue, West Newton, Massachusetts. Penny and Phil went to junior high, while Will attended the local primary school. The elder two settled in well, but Will had a hard time. Being such an individualistic kid, and possessing an Australian accent, he was very different and was teased mercilessly by the boys.

Bill returned to continue his research with Norm Hollenberg on hypertension. He carried out several significant experiments which were written up in important physiology journals. He was very excited by this work.

I returned to the nutrition clinic at Boston Children's Hospital. The CF clinic was my main interest in this department, but I also sought experience in paediatric gastrointestinal disease. Dick Grand, a former colleague who specialised in gastroenterology and hepatology, agreed to train me with his other apprentices. I learned a great deal, but was surprised this time to find the atmosphere of Children's Hospital oppressive rather than stimulating, possibly because I was higher up the career ladder, better trained and more assertive, no longer the wide-eyed young graduate totally impressed by US know-how. I was irritated to find so many ambitious and egocentric young men around the place. They would push me out of the way to peer down the gastroscope or up the colonoscope, or slam doors in each other's faces without so much as a by your leave. I tried to maintain my pleasant Adelaide manners, holding doors open for people who didn't even notice, but after four months I got fed up and started behaving the Harvard way; only then did they seem to treat me with respect. Eventually I became so imbued with this attitude that when I returned home, people found me rude and abrasive until I gradually readjusted to the slower, kinder Adelaide style.

I was also keen to repeat my Australian successes in teaching unions about the medical dangers of nuclear power. Surely, I thought, if I can work with unions in Australia, I could work with the American union movement. All I had to do was speak to the right person or people, and the rest would be easy. I was extraordinarily naive. I decided to go to the top and approach the American Federation of Labor-Congress of Industrial Organisations. I flew to Washington and caught a taxi to the AFL–CIO building, a white marble palace of a place situated near the White House. I asked to see George Meany, the crusty old head of the organisation but obviously my request was audacious. I did manage to talk myself into an appointment with one of the union's top officers, who invited me to lunch at a nearby French restaurant and promised to arrange for me to speak to the Energy Policy Committee.

Some weeks later he called me from a hotel in Boston where he was staying, asking me to bring him some literature about the dangers of nuclear energy. Thinking this would lead to the promised committee meeting, I dutifully drove in and was astonished to find that he had no intention of speaking about nuclear power. Instead, he asked to dance with me and then invited me to his bedroom. I fled.

Still seeking an entree to America's unions, I decided to consider his behaviour as a temporary lapse, so I invited him to dinner with the family one evening. It was pleasant and non-productive, and at the end he scuttled down the front path like a frightened rabbit, and I never heard from him again. So much for the American union movement.

After this fiasco, I explored other avenues to impart my concern to the American people. I contacted Dan Ford at the Union of Concerned Scientists, a group that had already done some magnificent work in alerting people to the dangers of nuclear power. We ate lunch in a small restaurant near Harvard Square, and I told him about my Australian activities. Dan seemed only mildly interested, but within a week I was delighted to be invited to speak at his colleague Ralph Nader's Critical Mass conference on nuclear power in Washington DC early in 1976.

This was the most important seminar at which I had ever spoken, and as the day approached, I grew anxious. I asked a radiologist friend of ours, Roy Strand, to type out my speech; despite what that unionist in Adelaide had said about spontaneity, I didn't want to take any chances. Carefully dressed in a yellow silk shirt, brown and white tweed suit that I had made and brown boots, I faced a large and eminent group of scientists and concerned lay people in a Washington hotel, feeling very nervous. But I was delighted to find that the group was extremely sympathetic to what I had to say, and as I spoke, I gained confidence. It was exhilarating to look out at that huge audience and know that we were in harmony as colleagues, we spoke the same language, we had the same set of values and beliefs.

When I finished speaking, I received warm and sympathetic applause, and almost dazed, I was congratulated by the Swedish physicist Hans Alven. Then suddenly a group of smiling women from California swept me off to lunch. They told me they belonged to an organisation called the Creative Initiative Foundation, which was involved in Proposition 15, a statewide referendum to ban the use of nuclear power in California. The CIF campaign was called Project Survival, and almost before I knew it, I had agreed to spend two weeks speaking in support of their campaign.

I flew to San Francisco, somewhat nervous, having never been to California before, and because of the image this state projects in the media, I imagined gangsters behind each lamppost and the whole state ablaze with advertisements and neon lights. However, I was met at the airport and whisked off to beautiful Portola Valley to meet several members of the CIF clan. The head of the organisation was Emelia Rathbun, married to Harry Rathbun, a former professor of physics at Stanford University. Emelia was a strong-willed and determined woman, and as time went on and our friendship ripened, I came to know that she was sympathetic and very intuitive. At that stage I wasn't told what CIF officially did, but they were clearly efficient when they decided to work on a political campaign.

Next day Jim Birch, a balding, tall, imposing man, bundled me into a car and for the next few days drove me around California. In farmhouses, schools and public halls I told Californians about the nuclear fuel cycle and its extraordinary medical dangers. In Australia I had attracted criticism in certain quarters because I was a young woman who was saying things that some people didn't want to hear. In California, I faced downright hostility. The nuclear industry had conditioned the American people to believe that superiority in nuclear weapons symbolised the USA's strength as a world power, and that nuclear power was safe, clean and cheap. Here I was, armed with facts and figures to show that it was lethal.

While audiences were occasionally restive and suspicious, CIF members were delighted. When the tour finished, they invited Bill to join me in California, which he did. Bill and I were privileged to spend an evening with six courageous CIF members who were about to put their livelihoods on the line. Three of them—Dale Bridenbaugh, Dick Hubbard and Greg Minor—were nuclear engineers who worked for General Electric. They and their wives, Char, Rachel and Pat, had learned how dangerous nuclear technology was. After a great deal of soul searching, the men were about to resign from General Electric—abandoning careers they had pursued all their working lives—and they were now working for the anti-nuclear referendum Proposition 15.

Their resignations caused great consternation within the nuclear industry and attracted much publicity. They flew to Washington as experts to testify before the Joint Committee on Atomic Energy about the inherent dangers of nuclear power and subsequently established their own consulting firm, advising local municipalities and states as well as foreign governments on nuclear problems.

Despite the efforts of so many people, the campaign for Proposition 15 failed. CIF and fellow activists were no match for the national and international oil companies that poured millions of dollars into the campaign to defeat them, companies closely allied to the nuclear industry. As an Australian I was appalled that these companies were allowed to manipulate state elections with impunity. Were there no laws against this?

Some years later CIF members approached me for advice about how best to work on the imminent threat of nuclear war, so I told them to take on and educate Silicon Valley, part of the intrinsic heart of the nuclear war machine. They were located near the valley, and this was their natural constituency. They formed a very effective political group called Beyond War, which did indeed alert and educate many middle- and upper-class citizens of Silicon Valley and beyond.

Meanwhile, my medical activities continued. In October 1975, I flew to Chicago to take part in a 'liver meeting', the biggest medical congress I had ever attended. The sheer scale of the event astounded me—thousands of doctors: how could so many people be specialists in liver disease? I stayed with Sam and Gunvor Refetoff in their old brick pile situated near the University of Chicago. We had met Sam and Gunvor during our sixties stay in Boston. He was an aesthetic, intense, dark-haired Bulgarian who was separated from his parents at about the age of six during the Second World War. He was found years later in Egypt playing a flute to his pet snake. He had survived alone and had even taken himself off to school. He later trained in endocrinology. His wife, Gunvor, was a beautiful blonde Dane who used to work for the Danish airlines. They met in a Canadian hotel: as she walked down the stairs for breakfast, he looked up, their eyes met and they fell instantly in love.

Gunvor was a fervent supporter of my anti-nuclear views, and she decided that I needed some publicity. She called a local TV station, and before I knew it, I was on midday television in Chicago talking about the medical dangers of nuclear power. Dick Grand and my other Boston colleagues, lounging in their hotel rooms during the conference, were somewhat bemused to see me.

Having encountered so much opposition from the medical establishment in Adelaide, I was encouraged and grateful to see that many of my medical colleagues in the States agreed with my views and admired what I was trying to achieve. Among them was Charlie Janeway, chief of paediatrics at the Harvard Children's Hospital Medical Center (CHMC), who pioneered immunisation with human gamma globulin against various childhood diseases. He was so dedicated to the cause of pure medicine that he gave himself the first experimental injection of immunoglobulin and nearly died of anaphylactic shock.

Bill and I first met Charlie and his wife, Betty, in Melbourne airport when we found ourselves caught up in a transport workers' strike, all of us waiting for a plane to the States. Charlie was in his late sixties, thin, with grey hair parted down the middle and intense blue eyes hiding behind a set of mobile, beetling eyebrows. Betty, on the other hand, about the same age, had a pretty round face and was always smiling and looking on the sunny side of life. It was there that they told me about their daughter Lee, who had dressed herself in a hat and white gloves to meet Pat Nixon at a White House garden party. After waiting in a long line, instead of making bland remarks about the weather, she told Pat to use her influence with the president to stop the war in Vietnam.

Betty, Charlie, Bill and I became fast friends. When I wrote my first book, *Nuclear Madness*, unlike other people who cautioned me to be less outspoken, Charlie always urged me to go further. I could not have had a more accomplished or supportive mentor. He was not only my champion, but Bill's as well.

When Charlie retired, he was delighted that the new chief of paediatrics at CHMC was Mary Ellen Avery, a dedicated neonatologist who had done the seminal work on hyaline membrane disease. Mel, as she was called, was an efficient woman of average height, short dark hair and an appealing laugh that put people at ease. During the sabbatical year she called me into her office and invited me to join the Harvard faculty, working in the cystic fibrosis clinic. I was flattered and excited. Bill, who had spent a rewarding year with Norm Hollenberg, had just been appointed to a brand new position—director of paediatric research in radiology at the CHMC.

Both of us were thrilled that prospects for us were opening up in the United States: I was practising the medicine I loved, Bill was about to start a new and challenging job. How could we go back and live in Adelaide when all these wonderful things were happening? There didn't seem to be much of a role for me there; Bill McCoy had told me that there would not be a full-time job for me at the hospital because of my politics, so I could never return to the CF clinic. And if I wasn't going to peak at all, Bill had peaked too early. He was depressed about having attained tenure at the age of twenty-nine, with the prospect of directing paediatric radiology in insular Adelaide for the rest of his working life.

After a lot of discussion and soul searching, we decided to make the jump. We would emigrate to the United States and become permanent residents. There didn't seem to be much against it. Bill and I had never been happier professionally, the kids (except Will) had settled down. I also sensed that there was another role for me in the USA, and it was related to protecting the world's children from the horrors of nuclear power. We didn't feel sad about leaving our friends, and both sets of our parents were dead (Bill's father, George, had died just before we left for our sabbatical year), so we had no long-term responsibilities. It was time to start a new life.

It shortly became clear that we had made the right decision. The kids were thrilled, and Harvard smoothed the path for us. They even provided a lawyer to negotiate our immigrant status (we were known as 'legal aliens', which I thought was a nice term), and they also agreed to pay for the entire move, door to door.

We moved back to Adelaide for six months at the end of the sabbatical year to pack, sell the house, and tidy up loose ends. I also caught up with the Australian anti-uranium movement.

Progress had been made in my absence. Probably nervous about the extent of popular feeling against uranium mining, the Australian government had set up an enquiry into the proposed Ranger uranium mine, and the first people's Nuclear-Free Pacific Conference had been held in Suva, Fiji. The movement welcomed me back, which was great.

Not long after our return Dale and Char Bridenbaugh arrived for a national tour sponsored by Greenpeace. Dale, who is a large, handsome, and cautious man, addressed public and union meetings in Sydney, Newcastle, Wollongong and Perth before coming to Adelaide, where he and his wife stayed with us. These meetings were usually large and supportive; we were elated to discover how many Australians were passionately opposed to uranium mining. I wish they still were. Char spoke to a variety of women's groups. In many ways she reminded me of my mother, short and attractive with a good, sharp mind.

One night I took Dale to the ABC studios in Adelaide to appear on the current affairs program *This Day Tonight.* Opposing him was Leslie Kemmeny, a spokesman for the nuclear industry, who attacked Dale personally during the interview. I sat in the waiting room of the studio watching the show, and I was so furious that I threw an ashtray at the television set. How dare Kemmeny attack one of the bravest and most moral men I had ever met in order to defend the interests of the nuclear industry? Thereafter whenever Dale or I made a major appearance on television or radio, Leslie Kemmeny was there. Somehow the pro-nuclear forces had tapped into our itinerary.

One day Dale, Char and I flew from Adelaide to Darwin to meet with some unionists who opposed uranium mining. In 1954 a uranium mine had been established at a place called Rum Jungle. This had since closed down, but proper health records had not been kept, which greatly alarmed many former workers there. At the same time the proposed Ranger uranium mine was a large and important issue, not only because of its size, but because the new deposits had been discovered on Aboriginal tribal, sacred land.

Dale and I addressed a large outdoor rally with Tom Uren, a staunch environmentalist and a minister in the former Whitlam Labor government, which had lasted only three short years in power. Less than a year before, on 11 November 1975, the governor-general had sacked Gough Whitlam and his government. In the subsequent general election the conservative Liberal Party under Malcolm Fraser had been elected.

After Darwin we flew to Mt Isa in western Queensland for an open-air rally. This was scheduled to take place in a city park at two in the afternoon, but when the time came, the place was eerily deserted. Instead of a throng of miners our audience consisted solely of two reporters, who told us that the mining companies had threatened to sack their employees if they attended the rally. This experience was unnerving.

We were scheduled to leave for Townsville at six that night to address another rally the following day, but at the airport we were told that there was a mechanical fault in the plane, which could not be repaired until noon the next day. I smelled a rat: were we being deliberately delayed? Dale and Char, who had experienced dirty tricks during their anti-nuclear campaigns in the States, were sure we were. But such things didn't happen in Australia, surely?

Nevertheless, our tour was highly successful, reinforcing

the potent grassroots and union anti-uranium movement. The government was forced to continue investigating the medical dangers implicit in uranium mining and the nuclear fuel cycle.

After we returned to live permanently in the United States in 1977, the Liberal government released the first Fox Report, recommending restricted mining but setting out some of 'the hazards and dangers associated with nuclear power'. Thereafter the first national anti-nuclear conference was held in Sydney. This produced a national uranium moratorium campaign involving community bodies, trades unions, and groups of women and Aborigines who organised national demonstrations and educational forums.

Union protests continued over the next few days with wharf strikes in Sydney, Melbourne and Darwin taking place after unionists refused to load ships carrying cargoes of yellowcake. And Victoria, my home state, became a nuclear-free state with the passing, in 1983, of the Nuclear Activities (Prohibitions) Act prohibiting the exploration, mining and processing of uranium.

While all this was happening the Australian federal government was still supporting the mining and export of uranium. In a way my native country had become a paraplegic state: the brain (the conservative federal government) supported uranium mining, but the body politic was paralysed, thanks to an historic resolution passed by the Australian Council of Trade Unions to oppose the mining, transportation and export of uranium.

This ACTU resolution was noble, but ironically, it was repealed when a Labor government was returned to power in 1983. The new prime minister was former ACTU secretary Bob Hawke, the same man who had propositioned me when I tackled him about the uranium issue. He belligerently pushed a pro-uranium mining policy through the 1984 national Labor Party Conference against much opposition. The long-term medical consequences of nuclear waste were not addressed by the prime minister; only the Nuclear Non-Proliferation Treaty was invoked to ensure that Australian uranium exports were not used to produce nuclear weapons. Ironically the policy stated that the party would 'prevent the development of any other mines except for Nabarlek, Ranger and Roxby Downs'—the three mines that just happened to contain about 85 per cent of Australia's total reserves of uranium. It made a few ritual noises about workers' health and safety, safeguards, and so on, but no mention of human radioactive contamination via the food chain from radioactive waste. Obviously, 'nonproliferation' was a clever move to side-track the health and safety issue.

The Labor government's determination to stay in the world uranium market was obvious. Australia's uranium was feeding into a common world pool via enrichment in the USA and the USSR that could provide fuel for nuclear weapons; it was pointless to pretend that batches of Australian uranium would not contribute to the proliferation of nuclear arms. Members of the ALP Left were resentful and unhappy about the pro-uranium policy, but their faction was too weak to have any influence. Not when their prime minister was so strongly courting the big-business interests that favoured the mining of uranium.

The family returned to Boston in January 1977, tanned and fresh from a summer in Australia, to be greeted by ice and snow. Before we left the United States we had bought a massive English tudor house in West Newton that looked like a Grimms' fairy tale house, complete with a crooked chimney. It was so big that we discovered it cost a fortune to heat. The weather was frigid and the movers could hardly stumble up to the front door with our furniture without slipping on ice or piles of snow that lined the footpath.

The children were despatched to their various schools, Bill

began his new job with high hopes, and I decided to defer work for six months while I decorated our house. I had never had a big house to work on before, and I loved buying curtain material and carpets, covering lampshades, sewing curtains making blinds, and painting walls bright and zany colours.

Soon after we settled in, our neighbours Bill and Beverly Carmen lent us their home for a meeting about the medical dangers of nuclear power. Peggy Taylor, editor of *New Age* magazine, attended the meeting and after my talk she asked me for an interview. Not long after its publication, I received a phone call from the publisher of a small company, Autumn Press.

'Would you write a book on nuclear power?' he asked.

I had never imagined myself writing a book, and besides, as I told him, I was too busy, but he was very persuasive. 'You don't have to put the words down,' he said. 'You could try talking into a tape recorder; we could transcribe it.' It seemed like a feasible proposition, so I reluctantly agreed.

It didn't take long for me to discover the trials of authorship. I had several problems, apart from my ignorance of the art of writing. First, there was an enormous amount of material about nuclear power, most of it scientific, and it was vital that the non-specialist reader understood it. Translating my speaking skills and knowledge of dramatic presentation into print was very difficult.

The publisher wanted a 'white paper' on nuclear power. 'We'll get you a co-author,' he said, 'somebody who can arrange your material and help make it readable.' He found Nancy Herrington, a former journalist, a tall, pretty woman with a mop of curly brown hair and an authoritative manner. I spent weeks drafting the book in a little walk-in wardrobe near our bedroom, and twice a week Nancy came over and we went through the material together. We sat on the powder blue carpet of our bedroom, drinking hot chocolate and discussing the rudiments of nuclear power. Somehow Nancy fashioned chapters out of my ramblings and the whole thing began to resemble a manuscript. Nancy introduced me to her friend, Mary Benjamin, who decided to make a documentary film about me. More about this later.

There were gaps in my own knowledge of nuclear issues, particularly nuclear war, which I'd never really investigated before. The physician Donnell Boardman had already introduced me to two classic papers on that subject published in 1962 by the *New England Journal of Medicine*, but I needed to know more.

At this point—and fortunately—I met Randall Forsberg, former secretary of the Swedish Institute for Peace Research in Stockholm and now enrolled at MIT to study the complexities of the nuclear arms race. I drove to her home one cold afternoon in Stetson Street—named after the man who invented the hat, to my amusement—in Brookline. Randy, a pretty, dark-haired and highly articulate woman, had the statistics of nuclear weapons and war at her fingertips, and in the couple of hours we spent together she told me some mind-boggling facts: that a total nuclear war could be over within an hour and that intercontinental ballistic missiles (ICBMs) deployed by the USA or the USSR could reach their targets within thirty minutes. Why hadn't I known this?

I came away very shaken. Nuclear power was certainly destructive, but nuclear war had the potential to eliminate most life on earth. Nevil Shute's *On the Beach* indicated that such an event was possible, but now I had the information to know precisely how feasible this really was. Until my meeting with Randy I had not understood the complex and satanic brilliance of the technology invented solely to destroy the earth.

When the book was finished, I was sitting on my yellow kitchen stool one night when the phone rang. It was the publisher, who asked 'What are we going to call the book?' Without giving it a second thought, I replied, '*Nuclear Madness*'. Since then many other '*Madnesses*' have appeared.

CHAPTER 12

Giving a speech is like composing a symphony on your feet. It begins with a prelude or overture, then moves into the allegro, which ripples along at a fast and buoyant pace. Then it descends into the adagio, which is slow and thoughtful, occasionally mournful, and flows into a cadenza of unpremeditated musings, lifting the audience with new melodic insights. The last movement is usually profound, rising in a crescendo to the end so the audience is left with a feeling of exhilaration and hope for the beauty and love of life.

I usually approach the podium with my mind more or less a blank. Though I read voraciously, it seems that my structured thoughts are never really given full expression until I am on the platform, and I am often shocked when I articulate connections and ideas that I had not formally recognised.

The audience plays a vital role in my speeches. If they applaud when I come out on stage, I am swept along by their energy and enthusiasm. When an audience is with me, the evening is fun, particularly when they have a sense of humour. If they sit leaden when I crack the first joke, I know the night will be difficult. I need to be quiet and respectful with them and to resonate with their mood, but the talk becomes slow and heavy.

During the first fifteen minutes of a speech I assess the audience and discover their area of special interest. This is sometimes easy, occasionally difficult. But each audience is imbued with its own unique character, like individual patients in a consulting room, and responds only to certain approaches. Once I read in the *New York Times* that people's attention span had declined because of the 'sound bite' mentality; they can only listen to a talking head for about fifteen minutes. But this has never been my experience. I can usually engage an audience for one and a half to two hours at a stretch, depending on their energy and excitement, and mine.

The most interesting part of any speech is usually question time. It's fascinating to discover people's reaction, and the interchange is fun and often more provocative than the speech itself. I know that I have affected people deeply when there is almost an electric buzz of conversation in the hall and the foyer at the end, and people hang around talking and don't want to leave. I usually experience a sense of comfort and satisfaction at the end of the night, and return to my hotel feeling deeply fulfilled. Mind you, I have sometimes been so extraordinarily exhausted on the road that even after a hot soaking bath, meditation and a comforting book, my mind races and I still can't get to sleep.

I give a speech intending to change people's lives that day or that evening. Interestingly, usually the most controversial statement I make is the one that tends to stay with people for years and changes their attitudes, however annoyed they might be with me initially. I consider it an insult to give a boring speech when people have made the effort to venture from their comfortable homes to hear me. It is also a pointless exercise if they go home saying, 'That was a nice speech', and forget about it the next day. I consider myself successful if half the audience loves what I say and the other half hates it. At least I have moved people to consider and reconsider their previous attitudes and beliefs.

The initial presentation and image are very important and are responsible for at least 90 per cent of the impact upon an audience. If you look attractive, people consider you trustworthy and they tend to believe your logic, however radical. I used to say, 'If you wear pearls, you can say anything.' It stood to reason, then, that my Jaeger suits and pearls made the grim message about the medical dangers of nuclear power and nuclear war more accessible to middle America.

By 1977 life was moving into hectic gear as people around the country began to hear of me and ask me to visit their areas to spread the word about the dreaded nuclear power genie. I tried to accept every invitation because I felt the matter was one of urgent preventive medicine and public health. I met fascinating people in my travels and it was an exciting existence. But this activity was still occurring against a background of family and medicine. Bill was okay with it all, but, understandably, he occasionally became resentful if I was away too much.

On 29 April 1977 I flew to Denver to take part in a huge march at Rocky Flats, a plant that manufactured plutonium triggers for the US nuclear weapons arsenal. The grounds of the factory were heavily contaminated with plutonium, as were the adjacent suburbs and water catchment areas. Even Denver became contaminated when several extremely serious accidents occurred there.

Rocky Flats is a quiet, brooding sentinel of evil, which sits on a plain at the base of the Rocky Mountains. The march had been effectively organised by Pam Solo, a nun who lived in Denver, and her friend Mike Jendresick. Pam is about 162 centimetres, has dark, short, straight hair, wears thick spectacles and is very serious. Tens of thousands of people arrived from many parts of the United States. They walked slowly to the factory's boundaries and then sat while they listened to some very powerful speeches. Meanwhile, the national TV networks were drumming the air with their helicopters, and that night they played us on the news programs.

This was the first large demonstration at Rocky Flats. The American people were beginning to awake. Pam Solo was delighted. She had worked for months to bring the event to fruition, and I admired her enormously. She was living an exemplary life, doing what Jesus would have done, speaking the truth about good and evil. Although other people were involved, Pam was the initiator.

The next day I flew to Barnwell, South Carolina, the site of a huge nuclear weapons complex located on the Savannah River. The river and its marshy precincts are heavily contaminated with radioactive pollution, and it is a terrible mess. We marched to the fence at Barnwell and some of us gave speeches. But my most vivid impression was of a dirt-poor community of tobacco and food farmers living in a sinister radioactive shadow, unaware that their food, air and water had been contaminated with radioactive isotopes.

On a bitterly cold day in May, Pen and I joined a ragged march down the main street of Seabrook, New Hampshire to the municipal rubbish dump, where a nuclear reactor was to be sited. The anti-nuclear group known as the Clamshell Alliance asked me to speak. This march was a sober affair and its participants quite determined. I stood on a central mound of the dump and talked to the crowd through a hand-held megaphone. 'Plutonium lasts for half a million years,' I told them, 'and every reactor manufactures five hundred pounds [225 kilograms] of it per year. If one pound [450 grams] of this could be adequately distributed, all human beings on earth would eventually die of lung cancer; ten pounds [4.5 kilograms] is enough fuel for a nuclear weapon.' The people listened silently and erupted in applause at the end of my speech.

The intensity of the rally proved to be a precursor of the years to come, for Seabrook became the scene of the greatest protest marches since the Vietnam War, and police and protesters struggled bitterly for years. But the utility company went ahead anyway and built the nuclear power plant over the next ten years. Because it is within walking distance of an extremely crowded beach and close to the border with Massachusetts, Michael Dukakis, governor of Massachusetts, refused to endorse evacuation plans, so the completed reactor could not be fuelled. But when New Hampshire governor John Sununu became chief of staff to President George Bush, he overruled Dukakis and, without an evacuation plan, instituted the fuelling and start up of Seabrook. It was tragic that the will of the common person was violated by a few powerful men, thereby imposing a toxic cauldron in their midst.

At this time I began to receive invitations to speak at conferences outside the United States. In May the Irish Council of Trade Unions asked me to a conference in Dublin to talk about the medical hazards of nuclear power; the Eire government had plans to build nuclear reactors in Ireland. It was here I met Petra Kelly, the future leader of West Germany's Green Party, which helped to change the face of Germany in the 1980s. In her late twenties or early thirties, Petra was small, blonde and pretty, with finely chiselled features. We became friendly during that week in Ireland because we were on panels together and we visited traditional Irish pubs and night clubs. We were very similar in our approach to the subject: passionate, well informed and insistent. She said that we were sisters.

Petra's mother was German, her stepfather an American

military officer, and she had spent much of her adolescent life in the United States at college before returning to live in Germany. But her real mentor and love was her German maternal grandmother, whom she adored. Her younger sister had died of a retinoblastoma, cancer of the eye, at the age of twelve, and Petra had been so affected that she dedicated her life to the prevention of cancer, specifically in the area of nuclear power and nuclear war.

She spoke almost faster than I did, in didactic, carefully crafted sentences. She was brilliant and utterly persistent when pursuing her political ideals. After Ireland we saw each other at rallies in London, West Germany and elsewhere in Europe, and Australia, and we became very close. She always had an older man in tow, both in Ireland and later. Eventually she fell in love with General Gert Bastian, a former officer in Hitler's army, who became devoutly anti-nuclear. She adored him in a totally devoted way.

It was an interesting phenomenon that in the 1980s Petra was really the passionate instigator of the anti-nuclear campaign in Germany, and I played a similar role in the United States. And we were both, in a way, outsiders in the countries in which we were to have the greatest influence.

Years later as I was watching the nightly news, I heard that Petra had been found murdered in her apartment in Germany and Gert was also found dead, with a gunshot wound to the head. Their bodies were not discovered for two weeks. Some thought that they had been killed because of their role in the nuclear power debate after the collapse of the Cold War. But the general consensus is that Gert killed them both; he was becoming old and frail, and Petra frequently said that she couldn't live without him.

❖

I celebrated my fortieth birthday on 7 August 1978 with real joy. Bill gave me a white negligee, a gold bicycle and a bunch of red roses, and I fantasised about riding down Commonwealth Avenue on my bicycle in a white negligee, clutching my red roses to my chest. My family was in great shape, and my major work was yet to come.

On a hot day later that month a thin, dark-haired young man sought me out in my small office in the Enders Research Building at Harvard. He introduced himself as Ira Helfand, an intern who worked at the Mt Auburn Hospital in Cambridge, Massachusetts. He said he had been involved in an anti-nuclear referendum on the ballot in Cambridge. If it passed, all medical and military uses of nuclear isotopes would be outlawed, severely affecting academia and related military nuclear work at Harvard, MIT and other industries located in Cambridge. The nuclear industry was fighting the referendum for its life. California's Proposition 15 all over again.

Ira and I commiserated about the medical effects of nuclear power for some time, then I suddenly turned to him and said, 'We need doctors to become involved because this is a medical issue.' It was obvious that doctors have such societal credibility that they could use their authority to educate people and change opinions on this subject. Within a week Ira and I had called together a small group of physicians to meet in my study. Besides Ira and Bill, they included Eric Chivean, an intense psychiatrist dedicated to the environment who had previously attended one of my public meetings, Richard Feinbloom, a tall, pleasant family practitioner, Rick Ingrasi, an 'alternative' psychiatrist, and two medical students, Katherine Kahn and Andy Kramer. We were from a variety of specialties, but had one thing in common: we were all passionately concerned about the medical implications of nuclear power.

We decided to form an official doctors' organisation to promote the dangers of nuclear power. We would recruit fellow members of our profession and work in unison to spread the message. The next order on the agenda was to choose a name. Richard Feinbloom told us that there used to be a doctors' group called Physicians for Social Responsibility, of which he was the secretary. It was started in 1961 by Jack Geiger, Victor Seidel, Bernard Lown and others, who wrote the two definitive articles on nuclear war for the *New England Journal of Medicine.*' Richard said the group folded in 1973, but he thought the name was still registered in the state of Massachusetts. We decided it would be easier to use this name if possible, rather than go through the bureaucratic hassle of registering another one. But this decision proved to be a grave mistake.

From its beginning PSR was exciting and time-consuming. Initially the embryonic organisation met every week in what we called the 'broom cupboard', a small office at Richard's health care practice on Massachusetts Avenue, Cambridge. I was elected president.

We decided to use grand rounds as the best way to teach and to recruit other doctors to our cause. When I was invited to speak at local hospitals, my audience of doctors may have expected to hear about the latest treatments for kidney disease, but instead they heard about the medical effects of nuclear power and the nuclear fuel cycle. Doctors are notoriously conservative and many were initially dubious about attending a lecture on such a controversial topic as nuclear energy, but when the talk finished, many of them, recognising the true medical nature of the problem, grabbed PSR membership forms and filled them out on the spot.

On one notable occasion in 1979, I was invited to be commencement speaker at the Tufts Medical School graduation. To my surprise Georgia Dullea, a reporter from the *New York Times,* asked if she could cover the talk. The ceremony was held outside in the Boston spring amidst rolling green lawns and trees covered with veils of new leaves. I gave the usual speech outlining the medical implications of nuclear power, then for some reason I advocated the socialisation of medicine. I came from such a system in Australia and I naturally assumed the medical faculty would support me. At the end of the speech I received a standing ovation from the graduates and parents, and I felt comfortable that all had gone well.

We were walking away across the lawn, when Georgia turned to me and asked, 'Why didn't the faculty stand up and applaud you?' I hadn't noticed because they were seated behind me on the dais. This was the first time that I encountered the entrenched attitude that any form of socialism, even socialised medicine, is not congruent with American values and is akin to communism.

The *New York Times* article was quite flattering. More importantly, however, it gave me and our fledgling PSR the official recognition that an anti-nuclear revolution was in the making.

But even in the early days of PSR, all was not smooth sailing. We arranged a national meeting in Boston's Faneuil Hall, and had a very difficult time with some forthright medical students who adamantly insisted that the membership include nurses and other health care workers. While I understood their sentiments and sympathised to some extent, I was firm that PSR had to remain an organisation composed exclusively of doctors, dentists and medical students. In the public mind these were the medical authority figures; if they spoke against the horror of the nuclear industry, they would be heard.

While I was pursuing a career as a lecturer in hospitals and medical schools, I continued my full-time job in the CF clinic. I had about forty patients in my care. It was challenging work treating children who were in various stages of death and dying. I was particularly fond of the babies and younger children. We played crazy games together; I would roll my eyes up into my head when they entered the room, and they would be fascinated. From that point they seemed to trust me completely. They felt almost like my own babies as they snuggled into my lap while I examined them. Lumbar punctures and injections were a breeze because of our relationship. But if they became acutely ill at home and a strange doctor was called in who hurt them, it sometimes took months or years to regain their trust.

I found my adolescent patients challenging and paradoxical: they had the bloom, fresh beauty and rebelliousness of youth, and they were also dying. They were therefore very hard to handle, doing the opposite of what I advised, using me as a catalyst for their anger, being extremely manipulative. I either made close friends with them, or, if they were really impossible, passed them on to Dr Kon Tai Khaw, another doctor in the clinic. Khaw was Chinese, of stocky build, with a broad smiling face. He was terrific with these patients, authoritarian so that they respected him, yet friendly and somewhat playful.

There was one patient, called Suzanne, whom I remember with great affection. She was tall and thin, with long, straight black hair, and we developed a close relationship. I taught her to meditate to calm her fears, because we both knew that she was quite ill. She was married to a lovely fellow, but an air of impending doom always surrounded them—tragic.

In their rebellion the girls sometimes became pregnant to prove they were normal. This was dangerous because as the baby swelled in their bellies, it pushed the diaphragm into the thorax. This loss of chest volume severely inhibited lung function, making the disease worse for them. Sometimes they became so ill that they died soon after the delivery. The baby usually did not have CF, but it was always a carrier of the gene.

After every clinic, three a week, the nurse practitioners, social workers and doctors held a conference at which we reviewed the progress of every patient. These meetings were often very stimulating and great fun. After Harry Schwachman retired, Harvey Colten became the new chief of the CF clinic. Harvey, although attached to his research into the rudiments of the inflammatory process, was also an excellent clinician. I respected him greatly and in some ways he reminded me of my father, with his red hair, freckled skin and unpredictable, fiery temper.

At times we clashed about my anti-nuclear work, although our differences didn't affect our working relationship. One day I was leaving work early to travel to Nashville to take part in a protest against the Tennessee Valley Authority (TVA), which was planning to build several new nuclear reactors. I was pleased that I was about to challenge TVA publicly, but my attitude was like a red rag to a bull. Harvey roared at me that the TVA had provided thousands of jobs for the unemployed during Roosevelt's New Deal and for years had been the social conscience of the South. I insisted that it was irrelevant what TVA had done in the past; its nuclear power program was now blotting its copybook.

I was actually quite affected by Harvey's reaction and lack of approval and wept on the plane on the way down to Nashville. It was here that I met the tall, impressive Jeanine Honicker, a passionate anti-nuclear activist. She is slim, middle aged, with wavy grey hair and a twinkly smile, and she doesn't suffer fools gladly. In her broad Nashville accent she coined the phrase: 'The solution to pollution by dilution when it comes to radiation is fallacious.' Her adolescent daughter had developed leukemia and had been given no hope of recovery. At three one morning, Jeanine had woken from a deep sleep knowing with absolute certainty that a bone marrow transplant would save her child. Against great opposition she and her husband Rolph persuaded the doctors to perform the operation, and her daughter survived, which proves the medical dictum—listen to the mother, she's always right. That kind of gritty determination came to the fore again in Jeanine's anti-nuclear work. By means of persistent lobbying, she and her friends actually managed to block the construction of one of the TVA reactors.

Not long afterwards I participated in a rather extraordinary event: an anti-nuclear demonstration at the American Association for the Advancement of Science in Washington, DC, to be opened by the firmly pro-nuclear senator Mike McCormack from Washington state. I was promised five minutes to speak from the platform before McCormack opened the conference, so quickly and passionately I listed the dangers of nuclear power. Most of the scientists in the audience were shocked, both by the information I imparted and because they were unused to their planned and sedate opening being usurped by any sort of demonstration.

I remember noticing a grey-haired, conservative-looking woman sitting in the front row during my short speech. She followed me out, pestering me with questions. It transpired that she was the famous syndicated columnist Mary McGrory, who promptly wrote an article about the meeting. Somewhat embarrassed, I arrived at the clinic the next day to be greeted with Harvey's ribbing: 'The next thing we know, you'll be invited to the White House.' He was prophetic.

It was fascinating to discover that the 'conservative' meetings at which I spoke were very sympathetic to my cause. On 3 January 1979 I was the keynote speaker at a huge conference of Catholic bishops and their flock in Detroit which was a seminal event. The people arrived in droves, having driven through a big snowstorm to listen to my anti-nuclear warnings; the conference initiated great soul searching.

Though traditionally the Catholic Church had been conservative and anti-communist, I found it to be a flexible institution. This meeting was typical of many; I was surprised and gratified to find that some members of the hierarchy were in fact revolutionary thinkers. After hearing me and other anti-nuclear speakers talk about the medical effects of nuclear power and nuclear war, they accepted Einstein's dictum: 'The splitting of the atom changed everything save man's mode of thinking, thus we drift toward unparalleled catastrophe.' Over the ensuing years influential members of the Catholic Church in the United States played a pivotal role in halting the nuclear arms race.

At about this time I came face to face with one of my

mentors. For years I had admired the fascinating life and work of Margaret Mead, especially her strength as a leader in her field of anthropology. I was to speak at a women's conference in Houston, and as I approached the podium I saw Margaret Mead seated in the front row. I must have given a good speech because I received a standing ovation; even Margaret Mead was standing up, clapping. I felt as if all my birthdays had come at once.

Mead was the next speaker. Stiffly, she climbed onto the stage, wearing a long brown cloak and leaning on a tall wooden staff. I has said that women are the civilisers and that society cannot flourish without us. Mead endorsed my words, adding, 'When we were troglodytes, the men hunted for food while we stayed in the caves and nurtured our children. We also nurtured the men and guided their lives.' This was one of her last speeches. Not long afterwards she died of pancreatic carcinoma. I felt so privileged to have heard her.

As my visibility was increasing, so PSR was expanding, its membership inspired by a goal greater than themselves. I managed to pick up doctors everywhere. I remember one talk I gave in a high-rise Chicago apartment to a small but rapt general audience. After I finished, a thin man with a large mop of black curly hair and black beard introduced himself as Richard Gardiner, a radiologist, and told me that he wished to work for PSR. A few weeks later he turned up at the office in Boston wearing jeans and sneakers. I told him to get his hair cut and to buy a suit and proper black shoes. At which point Richard disappeared into the bathroom, then emerged with his hair sleeked down over his head and asked, 'Is this all right?' I told him no, he should get it cut. He did, and proved to be one of the most effective members of PSR, in charge of Chicago and the Midwest, as well as one of my most loyal supporters on the board.

In December 1978 PSR placed an advertisement in the *New England Journal of Medicine* enumerating the medical dangers of nuclear power and carrying an endorsement from twenty-five eminent American physicians. We called for nuclear disarmament, phased withdrawal of existing nuclear reactors, a moratorium on new reactors, and a comprehensive program to conserve energy and develop energy resources, and we included a membership form. Serendipitously, it was published on 29 March 1979, the day after Three Mile Island melted down, and we suddenly received five hundred new members.

CHAPTER 13

On the morning of 28 March 1979 I was in Sydney perched on the throne in my sister's downstairs bathroom when she burst through the door and announced: 'A nuclear plant has had an accident in America.' Thus I heard about Three Mile Island, the nuclear facility not far from Harrisburg, Pennsylvania, which was experiencing a meltdown. Two huge nuclear reactors had been built slap in the middle of the richest dairying area in the United States, and not far away was a Hershey Chocolate factory, which used the local milk. The situation looked horrific.

I had to know how serious it was, not least because of the children. If the accident was big and the wind blew towards Boston, where they were staying with some dear friends in our house, they would be at risk. I was on the phone immediately, arranging for the children to fly to San Francisco to stay with friends. It was not clear for several days whether or not they would be safe.

For years I had been talking my head off about the dangers of nuclear power. Now this had happened: an accident that must have scared the living daylights out of the American public, particularly those living in the Harrisburg area. Who knew what the consequences would be? Surely this would be the seminal event that would instigate the end of nuclear power in the United States and possibly the world.

When I returned to the States, however, I was surprised to discover that information about the accident was hard to come by. The Nuclear Regulatory Commission, the Three Mile Island utility itself and the White House apparently had no real idea of the problem's magnitude. Specific radiation monitors measuring radiation release went off scale early in the accident and remained so for forty-eight hours, so official accounts of radiation release were nothing more that guesstimates.

But I couldn't believe how people in positions of responsibility were ignoring the magnitude of the nuclear threat. President Jimmy Carter actually took his wife Rosalyn into the damaged reactor, at just the time when the accumulated hydrogen bubble could have exploded. Their yellow macintoshes and boots looked very nice on television, but what about the potential danger they faced from radiation? As I said in a speech, 'If I had a wife, I wouldn't have taken her in there.'

Several days after my return, I was asked by the people of Harrisburg to speak to them about the medical dangers of their situation. They knew very little about how reactors worked, and why they were potentially so dangerous. Nobody had taken the time to explain what had actually happened, nor what the consequences could be. I faced a frightened audience of thousands in the gym of the local school; the place was packed. Using a blackboard and a piece of chalk, I drew and explained the possible medical implications of the accident. The *Today Show* filmed the whole event and broadcast it nationally the following morning.

I also spoke to the local doctors, who knew surprisingly little about how isotopes concentrate in the food chain and therefore in human bodies, and their specific predilection for various bodily organs. I couldn't believe they were so ignorant; anybody with a basic medical education and general knowledge, I thought, *must* know what the by-products of nuclear fission can do to people, although it is also true that the medical implications of nuclear power are not taught to medical students—not a wise omission, for in the event of a serious radioactive release we would be responsible for the injured patients.

When, then, do the faculties in medical schools ignore this ubiquitous threat?

When I asked this question, I encountered a phenomenon I have since come to understand very well. *Psychic numbing*, a phrase coined by the psychiatrist Robert Lifton, is used to describe a state of denial which is, I think, similar to the first stage of grief described by Elisabeth Kübler-Ross in her landmark book *On Death and Dying*. It affects individuals and groups of people who are unwilling to come to terms with the magnitude of the nuclear threat; they block it out of their consciousness. The medical profession—and doctors are not the only ones—has still not accepted the responsibility and reality of a world laced with nuclear reactors.

Because the Three Mile Island catastrophe had created so much panic, and because there was so little public information, I knew my book *Nuclear Madness* was more important than ever. It should have been distributed as widely as possible and read by everybody who wanted it; there was a huge demand out there. But my publisher was oddly reluctant to reprint to meet the demand. I wanted him to ship truckloads down to Harrisburg, but he refused—after having reassured me for months that the book could be a best-seller. So I consulted a lawyer, who incidentally informed me that I had signed a ridiculous contract, giving Autumn Press total control over the book and any others I might write in the future. I was caught in a serious double bind.

Eventually I had to take the publisher to court; the case, which proved to be a shocking burden, cost $60 000. After many months we reached a settlement and I got the contract back and owned my future again.

Mary Benjamin was proceeding with the documentary about my crazy life as an anti-nuclear activist, but I told her that she would never adequately capture my spirit unless she filmed me on my home turf. It so happened that I was due to return to Australia in March 1979 for a book tour related to *Nuclear Madness*, and I persuaded her to come. She had absolutely no money, but she booked the whole tour for the film crew onto her credit card with no guarantee that it would ever be paid off, and they flew off in a Qantas jumbo jet, bound for the great Australian experience.

I left before the others for Hawaii, where I was to appear as a witness for a militant organisation called Catholic Action, which was bringing a case against the US navy because of the medical hazards of radiation emitted from stored nuclear weapons. I had been invited by Jim Albertini, a dedicated Christian who had done a great deal of work in alerting the public to the dangers of the navy's nuclear operations on Hawaii.

I'd never been to Hawaii before, and as I stepped off the plane it embraced me with its soft, warm tropical air perfumed with the scent of frangipani and ginger flowers. Noisy birds sang in the trees throughout the night above my bedroom on the university campus—an instant love affair. The next morning Jim took me to his dark little office and somewhat tentatively showed me a paper written by an investigative journalist, Howard Moreland, describing the construction of an atomic bomb. But this was not the main intent of the document. For the first time many of the US corporations involved in the manufacture of nuclear weapons were identified. Until then they had carried out their nefarious activities in secret, free from public scrutiny. The American courts had refused Moreland permission to publish this material in the *Progressive* magazine because they said the information was dangerous. Could I try to have it published in Australia? 'Certainly,' I agreed blithely, without a second thought.

Bill caught up with me in Canberra after I'd been there for several days, and he accompanied me on the trip. He subsequently became almost as passionately interested in the anti-nuclear movement as I; a stalwart founding member of PSR, he has shown himself an excellent speaker at public meetings. Our relationship always flourished whenever Bill and I worked together for a common cause, and I depended on his calm good sense and support.

Our first port of call was Melbourne, where I gave a press conference. The reporters covering it were cynical, rather bored and unengaged until I waved Moreland's paper in front of their noses. I explained what it was and told them, 'This can't be published in the United States, so here's your opportunity.' They perked up immediately and led me out to the front lawn of the motel, where they took photographs of me holding the paper.

As it happened, the paper was not published in Australia, but that was not the end of the story. The journalist who interviewed me in Melbourne notified his editor, who told Sir Philip Baxter, the head of the Australian Atomic Energy Commission, who then informed the FBI. I was wise enough to burn the paper before I left Australia, but as I flew one way across the Pacific, the FBI was flying to Australia to investigate this appalling breach of security.

I found the political climate in Australia to be somewhat difficult. It was a case of two steps forward, three steps back; sometimes I felt that segments of this country, which had been so firmly against the French tests, hadn't absorbed the anti-nuclear message in any significant way. I discovered this when I had to deal with the press (and Mary's crew captured some memorable examples on film). During an interview in the ABC radio studio in Canberra, an aggressive, redheaded middle-aged man asked me, 'Where do you get your funding?'

'What funding?' I asked.

'The money that enables you to travel around the world with this message,' he replied, implying that some world organisation—perhaps the Communist Party—paid for me to travel and speak. I patiently explained that my publisher and the Australian groups that sponsored my visit covered my expenses, but he was not to be convinced.

Another never-to-be-forgotten scene took place in Adelaide, again on ABC radio. The interviewer juxtaposed me with a 'nuclear expert' via a telephone line. At one point this Englishman confidently and patronisingly remarked, 'The problem of nuclear waste has been solved.' I was just about to reply, disputing almost everything he had said, when the interviewer interrupted and said, 'We're out of time, I'm sorry, Dr Caldicott, we don't have time for a reply.'

I was so upset that I was almost weeping with frustration. I told the interviewer, a woman who happened to be pregnant, that the nuclear industry had dominated the debate since I'd left, that she hadn't given me time to reply, and that he was lying. She said in measured tones, 'I think I treated you fairly.' I picked up my patent leather handbag and swung out of the studio with Boyd Estus, the cameraman, chasing me down the hallway, lens focussed.

I must say it's a strange feeling to be continually under surveillance by a film crew. I was permanently wired for sound, and if they lost me, they would turn up the volume. I could well have been in the lavatory. No privacy. And every time I turned around, I had a camera pointing up my nose. This situation continued throughout the three-week tour of Australia.

Bill and I were invited to address key members of the Labor Party in Sydney at a meeting chaired by Lionel Bowen, who became deputy prime minister when Labor swept back into office in 1983. In the late 1970s the conservative Fraser government was trying to have two bob each way, attempting to placate the anti-nuclear lobby with alleged 'safeguards' against the manufacture of nuclear weapons by countries buying our uranium, while encouraging the nuclear industry to expand. Big business was happy. What alarmed me was the response of the unions: owing partly to the influence of ACTU president, Bob Hawke, anti-nuclear sentiment was much weaker than it had been. While I'd been away, the uranium industry had quietly gained the upper hand.

The 1977 Fox Report commissioned by the Whitlam government had given the conditional go-ahead to uranium mining. Bill and I went to the area where the potential Ranger uranium mine would open near Jabiru, about 200 kilometres south-east of Darwin, on the eastern edge of the Kakadu National Park. It is a beautiful area, its cliffs covered by ancient Aboriginal rock paintings, and is situated adjacent to Magela Creek, a wide waterway filled with pink and blue fragrant waterlilies, teeming with fish and crocodiles. It was a stunning, untouched wilderness, like so much of Kakadu.

After mining began, it soon became obvious that the restrictions imposed upon Ranger were not nearly stringent enough. For instance, one condition recommended that tailings (the radioactive waste sludge) be covered by two metres of water at all times to minimise the risk of radioactive radon gas release. But the Kakadu–Ranger area is subject to high and unpredictable monsoonal rainfall, and tailings seepage had proven difficult to contain. In September 1983 workers went on strike because the drinking water system was connected to the tailings effluent system and because they were concerned about high radioactive dust levels and about the company's disregard for their health.

Incidents of this nature gave a clear indication that businesspeople and large companies don't really care about the environment or their employees. They provide environmental impact statements only because they must comply with the law, but their primary motive is to remove the uranium and make money.

I saw how this affects Aborigines when I visited Crocker Island, north of Darwin, with the film crew on hand. Aborigines are a quiet people, and they filed slowly into their hall—an old tin shed—to hear what I had to say. The Navajo Indians from Grants, New Mexico had given me some colour transparencies documenting the death and disease suffered by their people who had mined uranium, and they wished to share this tragedy with native Australians. I showed the slides, with Navajo commentary, and asked for questions. There was silence for several minutes until a tribal elder named Dick spoke. Putting his hand on his chest, he said, 'I don't know, it's real wreck it.' Later he said, 'It hurts my heart here to see those people.'

Later when I was leaving the hall, I was stopped by a full blood Aboriginal woman in a bright yellow dress, carrying a child on her hip. She said to me, 'Some of my relatives want money from this mining. But I don't want money. I want my land, my father's land, my forefathers' land. It's my land.' She was strikingly direct, and I had never heard a simpler and better statement of Aboriginal belief.

While I was in Australia, Eric Chivean and my other colleagues conducted interviews for a new position of executive director for PSR. The organisation certainly needed one to handle our exploding membership in the wake of the *New England Journal* ad. But they chose someone who did not work out. This was serious, but his departure meant that we were bound together to save our fledgling group, which we found stimulating and enjoyable. We argued vigorously with each other, but there was no rancour. We laughed and loved and supported each other as we watched our peers flocking to join us, and I felt that we had the potential to prevent a nuclear war. I used to say that if we had ten thousand doctors, we could save the world 'with faith, hope and trust, and a little sprinkling of pixie dust'. Our excitement was so intense that our feet hardly touched the ground.

At that stage the board consisted of Bill, Rick Ingrasi, Henry Abraham, Katherine Kahn, Tom Winters, Ira Helfand, Eric Chivean, Richard Feinbloom and me. I was the leader, but not autocratically so; while the others deferred to me, they also challenged me. We were like a quarrelling, excited, creative, affectionate family. And as time went on, we stuck together through thick and thin, never frightened to take anyone on—presidents, generals, politicians.

Because we had taken over the PSR name, we felt it was right and proper to invite the original members to be sponsors. They agreed to allow us to use their names on our stationery. We called them the 'old guard'.

One of the old guard was Bernard Lown, a cardiologist at the Harvard School of Health. In July 1979 he invited me to his home. He was of medium height, with dark, balding hair, intense brown eyes and an indefinable accent that was Central European in origin. I was gratified by his interest but slightly puzzled; we hardly knew each other. His home was a grand place in West Newton, and I remember feeling somewhat cautious as I looked at the photographs on the walls of Lown with Fidel Castro, Isaac Stern and other greats.

Lown's approach disconcerted me. 'You're too radical,' he said, 'you shouldn't be talking about nuclear power; nuclear war is the really important issue to tackle.' He spoke to me as if he knew best; I was just a little girl who didn't know what she was doing. I did not appreciate this. The truth was that my colleagues and I had created a thriving new medical organisation that was growing bigger almost every day. I felt apprehensive when I left Lown's house; it seemed to me that he was wary of our achievements and wanted to reassert his former power over PSR. This did not augur well for future relationships.

PSR continued to attract passionate and stalwart helpers. One was Peter Joseph, a doctor from San Francisco who was as committed as I to the anti-nuclear issue. He became the main San Francisco contact. And shortly after the Three Mile Island disaster a young woman, Carol Belding, rang. She told me she had been sitting in a rocking chair with her newborn baby when she heard about the accident, and she was so appalled that she knew she had to do something. She called the Clamshell Alliance, which worked against the Seabrook reactor, and other anti-nuclear groups, but nobody wanted her, so she contacted us and offered her help. We gratefully accepted, and almost immediately Carol became the 'engine' of the group. She was extremely beautiful with china blue eyes and a face like a Dresden doll, and a dry sense of humour. She collated and answered the hundreds of letters that poured into our broom cupboard every week, and was soon indispensable. Shortly afterwards Abe Claude arrived. Tall, good-looking (a little like Abe Lincoln), an excellent tennis player and a stable and forceful man, he helped hold PSR together through some trying times. Carol and Abe were a wonderful team.

Setting up and organising PSR accounted for less than half of my anti-nuclear work. I continued to preach the message wherever and whenever I could. And fortunately I found an enormous amount of support in all sectors of society, not just among the medical profession. The warmth and enthusiasm amongst the people I met more than compensated for the schedules I set myself, which were often gruelling to the point of exhaustion.

Four weeks after our return from Australia, still followed by the Mary Benjamin film crew, I flew to Rocky Flats for another demonstration. Pam Solo had set up a second huge protest rally at the factory, and this time she had speakers who represented nuclear victims. One of these was Dorothy Robertson, a shy but determined woman whose husband had died of cancer several years before, after being exposed to fallout from an underground nuclear test site that had accidentally vented. The horror of his story was that he had been forgotten in the turmoil; he was a watchman and, not knowing what had happened, he had stayed at his post for nine hours, becoming covered with fallout.

Dorothy had never spoken in public before and she was shaking with nerves. The day was bitterly cold, there was a huge crowd, and she was almost unable to face them. I urged her to speak from the heart about her husband, taking her through what she wanted to say, urging her to tell the audience about the dreadful things that had happened to the man she had loved. She climbed onto the platform, and from the moment she began to talk, her words carried conviction and quiet power. 'I will know to my dying day that the government killed by husband.' The crowd was absolutely silent as she spoke.

The next stop was Grants, New Mexico, where I wanted to thank the Navajo people for the slides they had given me to show to the Aboriginal people in Australia. We travelled past huge piles of uranium tailings at a milling plant, silently leaching their carcinogenic radon gas into the air. The people who lived in the area, including the Navajo, were all subject to the risk of developing lung cancer down the time track.

I had to climb onto the back of a truck to speak. Many in the audience were quiet. Beautiful Native American women were seated on the ground dressed in colourful ankle-length skirts, silver and turquoise bracelets, necklaces and earrings. Their men, equally sombre-faced, stood behind and around them. I looked at these people whose very lives were threatened by Gulf Oil, which had dug the world's deepest uranium mine at the foot of Mt Taylor, sacred to the Navajo people, and as I began to speak about the mine, I was suddenly overwhelmed. I couldn't express my grief; we were killing these beautiful, innocent people, we were raping their land, ignoring their spirituality in favour of building bombs to blow up the earth for money. I no longer had any words, and began to weep. After a few minutes I pulled myself together and continued to speak, thanking them for the slides.

I have never cried like that before or since while on the platform. I was still jetlagged from my trip to Australia; I hadn't stopped since I hit the United States and I was dealing with potent emotional material. Clearly my own emotional threshhold had been lowered by tiredness and the dreadful situations I had been speaking about, trying to comfort and reassure people in their fear.

Still not stopping for a breather, on 6 May I took part in a huge rally in Washington, DC, organised by the Mobilization for Survival to protest against the potentially catastrophic events at Three Mile Island. This was set up for the greatest possible media coverage: I was invited to help carry a black coffin symbolising irradiated dead babies with Benjamin Spock and others as pallbearers. We marched down Pennsylvania Avenue from the White House to the Congress, surrounded by singing children. We walked in the spring sunshine, and the contrast between the bright day, the children's joy in living and the spectre of the nuclear death America had almost experienced was almost too much to bear.

Tens of thousands gathered at the steps of the Capital to hear a star-studded lineup of speakers. Prominent among them was Jane Fonda, fresh from her starring role in *The China Syndrome*, the film that had eerily foreshadowed the events at Harrisburg. She wore skin-tight trousers and a strapless black suntop and was followed anxiously by her then husband, Tom Hayden. Her speech was well written and full of feeling: 'Some people,' she said, 'think the movie is fiction, not reality. But in this case, reality copied fiction.' When I met her later, I found her to be a passionate, knowledgeable and sincere supporter of the anti-nuclear cause.

Ralph Nader, the guru of consumer protection, gave a speech in his measured and loud tones, and Benjamin Spock spoke with graceful and passionate commitment. My contribution was to draw the crowd's attention to the dreadful realities of a massive meltdown. Thousands of people could have died horribly if things at Three Mile Island had been slightly different. The line between an unfortunate accident and horrible devastation was gossamer thin.

Some weeks after this march, I was working in my clinic one afternoon when I received a phone call. 'Federal Bureau of Investigation here,' announced a serious male voice. 'Is that Dr Helen Caldicott?'

When I assured the voice that it was, it said: 'We would like to come and see you.'

'Sure,' I said, rather wondering about the 'we', but feeling no sense of intimidation at all. I had been expecting the call and knew it concerned the paper I had taken to Australia listing the names of US companies involved in nuclear weapons production. I was rather looking forward to my encounter with the feds.

I rang my lawyer and friend Juli Sosnik, who wasn't nearly as confident as I was. 'I'm going to see the FBI'—'No you're not, not without me,' he replied.

We sat waiting for them in the hospital coffee shop, which overlooked the front door of the hospital. It was amazing how many suspicious-looking characters it is possible to see if you happen to be looking for them. I kept asking Juli, 'Is that one?' whenever anybody even vaguely different walked in.

He shook his head no repeatedly, then to my surprise he said, 'There's one.'

I looked. The man seemed perfectly ordinary. 'How do you know?' I asked.

'Striped shirt, raincoat, grey pants,' he said briskly. 'A senior guy, by the look of him. And there's the other one.'

'Other one?'

'Mm-hm. He's a big cheese, too. Clothing's more upmarket.' The second FBI agent looked like an ordinary businessman in a suit covered by the ubiquitous Humphrey Bogart raincoat, collar turned up.

'Come on,' said Juli. We got up, sauntered over to the two men and introduced ourselves. I enjoyed their how-did-you-know-it-was-us reaction. Juli and I escorted them to a small room in the radiology department, where, without a pause, they plied me with questions about the paper.

Big Juli took over. 'We refuse to answer any questions,' he told them flatly, citing the Fifth Amendment. They were miffed and frustrated by this approach, but had no choice except to withdraw. From then on, I had no trouble with the FBI. It later transpired that the information that was necessary to design a nuclear weapon was freely available on the shelves of the public library at the Lawrence Livermore Labs. So the case was dropped, and the *Progressive* magazine duly published Moreland's article.

Part 3
The Global Stage

CHAPTER 14

The year 1979 was a turning point in my life. I experienced the feelings of heat and torture associated with the Hiroshima–Nagasaki bombs, I breached the Iron Curtain at the height of the Cold War, and I made an illegal trip to Cuba, America's nemesis in the Caribbean.

Invited to be the keynote speaker at the commemorative anniversary conference in Hiroshima on 6 August, I stepped off the plane into the relentless humidity of a Japanese summer and was whisked away to the Hiroshima Peace Park. A large crowd had gathered to remember the bomb that vaporised and lethally burnt 200 000 people, injuring many more. (The incidence of cancer among the irradiated survivors is still rising.) The park is beautiful, adorned with statues of children, but rising above it is the Hiroshima dome, the skeletal steel remains of a building not melted by the nuclear heat. At exactly 8.15 a.m., the time the bomb was dropped, tens of thousands of white doves were released to soar silently into the air on outstretched wings—symbols of peace, in mute contrast to the fires of hell unleashed thirty-four years earlier.

The museum at Hiroshima will always be a dreadful, stark reminder of humanity's folly: melted clocks stopped at 8.15 a.m., huge pottery vases collapsed into a blob, silhouettes of people burned into the landscape at the moment they were vaporised. If anyone needed to see the horror of nuclear war, here it was. I came out of that museum with tears in my eyes.

I spoke later that day in a huge unlined shed of galvanised iron. It was stifling, waves of heat radiating over the tens of thousands of Japanese—almost entirely men dressed in grey suits—seated inside. I nearly fainted as the temperature rose; one kindly gentleman handed me a fan. For the first time in my life I worked with an interpreter, which cramped my speaking style somewhat. I would say one short sentence, she would speak for five minutes. It really threw me; what on earth was she saying? The success of my speeches depends on establishing a rapport with an audience, watching their reaction as my words sink in. But I had absolutely no idea what the interpreter was saying and, as the audience sat silently, impassively with closed eyes throughout the speech, it was impossible to gauge their reaction.

Later I was driven through neat, bright green rice fields to Nagasaki. Thousands fled there after the bomb dropped on Hiroshima, believing that, because it was the only Christian centre in Japan, the Americans would never bomb it. How wrong they were. Three days later 150 000 people lost their lives when the second nuclear bomb exploded. My most vivid memory of Nagasaki was a statue of Mary blackened on one side, leaning over the entrance of a devastated church.

I was surprised to find that though there was a vigorous anti-nuclear movement in Japan, its members were virtually ignored by the government and the general population. Japan has built many nuclear reactors, and the authorities are still turning their backs on the mounting problem of nuclear waste, trying to ignore its existence. While I was familiar with this sort of denial, I found it puzzling—even bizarre—that this nation, which had suffered so greatly from the effects of nuclear radiation, should be wilfully blind to its dreadful consequences. The other awful legacy of the American bombs is that the *hibakusha,* as the radiation victims are called, are ostracised by their own society.

I became very homesick in Japan. When I returned home three weeks later, I felt sober, and grateful for the existence and support of my family. The children had decorated the dining room with balloons and streamers and made a cake in honour of my birthday, which had been on the 7th of August. I took the rest of the month off and had a wonderful time with Bill, the kids and our friends, lazing around, swimming, eating tandoori chicken, marinated mussels and pasta, and drinking gallons of red wine. Then for several weeks I returned to work at the clinic, squeezing in talks to medical students at various universities.

In 1979—the year before Ronald Reagan's election—tensions between the superpowers escalated. It was against this background that I was invited to participate in a delegation formed by the American Friends Services Committee to visit the Soviet Union. The delegation also included Everett Mendleson, professor of the history of science at Harvard; Arthur Macy Cox, a former CIA employee and now an arms controller with a conscience; a dedicated peace worker named Marta Daniels; and William Sloane Coffin, the minister of Riverside Church, in New York. We were guests of the Soviet Peace Committee, an institution that had existed in the Soviet Union since the end of the Second World War.

On the way to Moscow I stopped off in Frankfurt, West Germany to address an international conference about women and the nuclear issue. It was held in a large bare room in a school. My audience was made up of strong, liberated women, dressed in loose-fitting, colourful clothes with their hair hanging long and relaxed around their heads. I didn't understand a thing that was going on (I had only studied German in school for one year). I struck up conversation with several middle-aged women who did speak English, and was shocked to hear some of them openly admitting that they were admirers of Hitler—one woman even said that she was still in love with him. It was clear to me from this and other visits that many Germans had not felt guilt, even after the might and power of the Allies had devastated their land and cities.

On 18 September I flew to Moscow. I had been looking forward to my trip to Russia, but the surge of intense excitement I felt as I crossed the Iron Curtain in the plane was totally unexpected. Later I travelled by train from Moscow to Leningrad, waking in the morning to look out onto trails of blue smoke wending their way among the golden autumn leaves from tiny peasant houses. The scene was so familiar as to be quite an eerie experience. I had a strong sense that I had been there before.

Our delegation's first impressions of the Soviet Union were disappointing. We were taken to an ugly modern hotel where we were billeted, each floor of which was controlled by a tough old *babushka* who intimidatingly kept the keys to all our rooms and who spoke no English. The plumbing was erratic, the long halls dark and gloomy, and the food boring—black bread, potatoes, peas like chewing gum, and glasses of tasteless yoghurt for breakfast. At least the beds were clean and reasonably comfortable.

The Soviet Peace Committee had drawn up a rigid but comprehensive schedule for us. We began by meeting committees of lower-echelon bureaucrats who fed us the propaganda line: the Soviet Union had always wanted peace but their desires had been thwarted by the war-mongering United States. We were also told that hundreds of peace committees existed right across the land, funded voluntarily by the Soviet people since the Second World War. Finally, they asserted that their radioactive waste was strictly controlled. I was particularly sceptical about this last statement.

To underline the point about the USSR's nuclear safety, we were taken to the town of Novovoronisk, where there were four operating reactors and one under construction. This was a grey, depressing place, built in typical Soviet style—rows of unadorned concrete apartment blocks in which most of the population lived. I became alarmed about Novovoronisk the moment we started our tour of the town, when I was told that it was heated by steam generated from the reactors. This secondary coolant was radioactive. I took up this point and other questions later during a meeting with some of the officials of the nuclear establishment. The officer in charge of health, who was dressed, like the others, in a dark suit and tie, blandly denied (through our interpreter) that the reactors emitted radiation into the air and the water.

'But they must; all reactors do,' I said.

'No, certainly not.' He was bland but firm, and he added under questioning that the workers were never accidentally exposed to radiation. I was flabbergasted. I was also terribly concerned to learn that the reactors had no emergency core cooling systems, no containment vessel; worse, I could see that the concrete structure housing the reactors was cracking. I persisted with the health spokesman, challenging him about worker and public exposure to radiation. When he was more or less accused of lying, he became so furious that he stormed out of the room. His feelings were soothed that night only by the mutual imbibing of a great deal of vodka.

I wasn't worried about questioning these bureaucrats; we all did. Interestingly, the more we challenged, the faster we were moved up the official bureaucratic ladder. I think they quickly realised that we knew what we were talking about and respected us. All our meetings were formal, conducted in old, aristocratic mansions and palaces then owned by the Communist Party. We sat around long polished wooden tables and were supplied with soft drinks and mineral water from green glass bottles; they always served us excellent thick black coffee and delicious biscuits. The Russians smoked like trains and sipped their coffee through sugar cubes in their mouth.

Everett Mendleson was extremely well informed and well versed in the recent history and important players in the Soviet Union; Arthur Macy Cox was intimately aquainted with the arcane intricacies of new weapons systems of both superpowers and the status quo of the arms control negotiations; and Bill Coffin, the comedian of the group, kept us supplied with witty aphorisms that filled one half of my notebook.

Mr Morosov, the deputy director of the International Atomic Energy Agency, gave us a lecture about the storage of high- and low-level nuclear waste, the proliferation of nuclear weapons, and the efforts of the International Atomic Energy Agency. He agreed that the IAEA needed more sensitive monitoring, and that both the money allotted to the agency and the number of inspectors needed to be upgraded. He also worried that some countries had not signed the Nuclear Non-Proliferation Treaty and were not members of the IAEA. He was passionate about stopping nuclear proliferation.

I found myself warming to him; it was reassuring to find that such a senior bureaucrat held these views. Knowing that the USSR enriched uranium from other countries and that both Finland and Japan built reactors with the assistance of the Soviets, I asked how the Soviet Union was dealing with nuclear waste. Unfortunately, Mr Morosov was less than frank about this, so I was left with a feeling of disquiet.

However, I was impressed by a group of scientists from the Institute of Physical Chemistry who knew a geat deal about oil and world energy supplies. Their discussions of energy problems in the emerging Third World showed that they understood that these countries needed renewable sources of energy, such as solar and wind power. In 1979 this was visionary thinking by government leaders: I had never heard an American official speak in these terms. The scientists told us that uranium 238 was being bombarded with neutrons—the process that makes instant plutonium—at the Brookhaven National Laboratories in the United States. I was amazed that they were aware of this. The scientists even quoted Albert Einstein, who, when asked what weapons would be used in World War III, replied that he wasn't sure, but those in World War IV would be spears and stone axes.

I became aware that many officials in the Soviet Union were knowledgeable and progressive about nuclear disarmament. A scientific delegate from the Soviet Peace Committee told us about tentative proposals to remove the Soviet Union from a military footing, re-employing military personnel in civilian capacities and redirecting the money allocated to massive weapons programs to such civilian programs as poverty control. I couldn't believe I was hearing this from the heart of a superpower.

It was in the Soviet Union that I made some horrific discoveries that affected my subsequent work.

At the time of our visit Moscow was negotiating the Strategic Arms Limitation Talks (SALT II) treaty with the United States. I was sitting with Arthur Macy Cox on a bench in a little leafy park in Leningrad when he told me that despite ongoing negotiations with the USSR, the United States planned to place in Europe two kinds of missiles armed with hydrogen bombs that would totally negate the arms control process. The first was the Pershing II, to be deployed in West Germany, which would take a mere three minutes to travel from launch site to target. The Soviet leadership would have no warning of their impending demise, because their satellites would be unable to detect the missile launch and relay the data back to Moscow in three minutes, nor would officials have time to press the button to launch their own missiles. So in order to save their missiles and pre-empt the Americans, they would have to computerise the launch of their missiles with no human input: the so-called launch on warning.

The second kind of missile was the cruise missiles, six metres long, armed with computers in their nose cones that contained a map of their transiting terrain. Extremely accurate, these could enter the chimney of a targeted factory thousands of kilometres from their launch site. And because they move close to the ground during flight, they are undetectable by satellite. Before they are launched, they cannot be detected by satellites because of their small size—they could be hidden under haystacks, in buildings and the like. It was frightening to learn that arms control totally depended upon satellite camera verification. I heard about these satanic devices with horror and dread. Their existence signalled the end of arms control, an arms race totally out of control, and nuclear war run by computers.

This was much worse than I had envisaged. I now knew that my efforts to alert people to the dangers of nuclear war must be redoubled. People had to be told about these evil things, people *had* to listen. It was my mission, my duty, to make sure they *did* listen. I felt somewhat desperate.

We eventually reached the highest levels of government when we met with Ambassador Usachev, who was in the process of negotiating the SALT II Treaty, at the Foreign Office in Moscow. He underlined my fears by telling us that the belligerence and stupidity of the United States were very discouraging. 'I would ask you to concentrate on alerting public opinion to the dangers of your country's new aggressive policy,' he said. He added that after seven years of negotiation, the US Senate still refused to support SALT II.

Usachev and his government wanted nothing less than a nuclear weapons freeze—an end to the production of *all* nuclear weapons once the SALT II Treaty had been signed, to be called SALT III. Quoting Andrei Gromyko, Soviet ambassador to the United Nations, Ambassador Usachev said, 'The arms race has surpassed a reasonable point. Additional weapons do not give real strength, they only create more difficulties and possible military conflict.' He added that trust between the superpowers was most important and that since 1942 the USSR had introduced no fewer than 140 disarmament initiatives, only a few of which had been supported by the United States.

He was deeply disturbed by the American initiative to give nuclear arms to China. 'You are trying to make China strong,' he said, 'and tomorrow you will be sorry.' He spoke of the 'China card' being wielded by Zbigniew Brzezinski, foreign policy adviser to President Jimmy Carter, to threaten the USSR. He pointed out that China has never supported any disarmament proposals at the United Nations and that in 1959 Mao Tse-tung had maintained: 'Nuclear war is not so dangerous, and some people would survive.' This, he said, was still official Chinese policy. 'The China card', he added, 'could involve the United States and the USSR in nuclear war.' This was the most sobering meeting of all the discussions we had in Moscow. I came away deeply shocked that my adopted country, the USA, could be so blind to the folly of its planning.

At the end of our stay, after about ten days, we went to the American Embassy in Moscow. Here we met two brash young techno intellectuals who proceeded to lecture us enthusiastically about nuclear strategies and counterforce politics. These young men were obsessed with numbers, with strategies, with moving figures and missiles, with first strike and winnable nuclear war. They were chilling: to them nuclear war was a bloodless contest played out between antagonists on computer screens, a matter of strikes and misses, the biggest computer game in the world. They displayed no emotion except excitement about their plans. They were young and clearly immature. They lacked, I felt, any comprehension that people were at stake here, that the planet was threatened with annihilation.

Later we met a delegation of doctors whom I was eager to persuade to start a Soviet-style PSR. My aim and vision was eventually to create a worldwide interlinked movement of doctors to teach the public and the politicians about the medical dangers of nuclear war and nuclear power. It was happening in the United States: it also needed to happen in the Soviet Union. I was so anxious to get my point across—

this was our only opportunity to meet with Russian doctors and I was the only doctor in the group—that one of our delegates, Marta Daniels, later admonished me for 'dominating' the meeting. The others agreed with her, or at least they stayed silent, and by their silence assented. They clearly hadn't understood my agenda, which I tried to explain, but to no avail. I knew they wanted consensus in the group. But my sense of urgency was so great, and as this was the only meeting with doctors, I felt I must be as persuasive as possible. I ended up in the Berioska, the tourist shop, feeling like an outcast, reminiscent of my early schooldays.

Throughout our stay in the Soviet Union we were constantly told of the dreadful suffering experienced during the Second World War; 20 million had died. We visited Leningrad cemetery and saw row upon row of mass graves containing the victims of the Nazi siege in 1942. Children were placing bread on the graves of their aunts, uncles and grandparents as a symbol of Russia's suffering. The graves lined the path on both sides for about half a kilometre; at the end of the avenue stood a large statue of Mother Russia holding an olive branch.

I walked arm in arm down this path with Arthur Macy Cox while the strains of Bach's Double Violin Concerto, that affirmation of civilised humanity, softly washed over us from a loudspeaker concealed nearby. We were silent for a long time. Then I turned to him and said; 'Arthur, if we have a nuclear war and if anybody survives and comes to visit this cemetery, they will say: "They didn't learn." '

After I returned to Harvard, I realised I could no longer continue the practice of caring for individual patients when all the world's children were at risk. The nuclear arms race was almost out of control—launch on warning and the end of verification! I watched people in the Harvard labs pouring and repouring solutions into test tubes with such dedication to science and such conviction and I thought to myself, 'What are you doing that for, when we won't be around for much longer unless we all *do* something?'

But how could I leave the career I had wanted and loved so much? So much of my being was bound up in being a physician. I was at Harvard and I could, I believe, have achieved anything I desired in medicine. And yet I knew I had to do more. My personal ambition as a doctor was much less important than working towards saving the world from unimaginable catastrophe. I talked with Bill, and he was sympathetic to my plight.

I agonised for months. Several times I had my hand on the door knob of Harvey Colten's office, intending to go in and resign, before I pulled it away and fled. At the back of my mind remained the niggling question: if I wasn't a doctor, what was I? What would I be if I left medicine? Finally, late in 1980, I plucked up courage and entered Harvey's office.

'I have to leave,' I said.

'I know,' he replied quietly.

We didn't speak for very long, because he understood my conflict and convictions. I left him and walked out into Longwood Avenue feeling stunned, bereft, knowing that whatever lay ahead of me, a significant part of my life had ended.

However, my extra conviction, the energy that sprang from my urgent sense that something must be done, had an overwhelmingly positive effect. Not long after my return I spoke about nuclear power and nuclear war to a packed auditorium at Boston University. I felt powerful: I knew I was carrying the audience with me every step of the way. When I finished they stood up and cheered, tears pouring down their cheeks. I looked over the sea of faces and I *knew* what was possible. Carol Belding said later that if I had asked that audience to follow me over a cliff, they would have done it.

In November PSR was asked to give a presentation to the Rockefeller Family Fund. On behalf of PSR, Bill and I had already made a fund-raising presentation to the Stern Fund of New Orleans, a foundation that dispenses substantial sums of money to non-profit organisations such as ours. They gave us $10 000; I had never encountered such generosity, and we were extremely grateful. The concept of raising funds was new to me.

Bill and I knew we were a good fund-raising team, but the Rockefeller Family Fund was really big. Halfway through my talk, however, one of the members of the fund interrupted and challenged me belligerently on the philosophy of nuclear power, after which he left the room. But the other family members stayed and listened sympathetically, and the Family Fund duly forwarded a cheque for $36 000 to help cover the cost of hiring an executive director and a direct mail consultant. We went on to build a list of donors whom we could tap twice a year. Our campaign proved to be very successful, raising over a quarter of a million dollars in a six month period.

PSR held its first official board meeting in November 1979, a milestone for us: we were really becoming official. I chaired it, as I had done other meetings. Some of the members of the original PSR came, including Bernard Lown. Because of their presence, the atmosphere was rather tense, which was unusual for us. A bitter wrangle developed between Howard Kornfeldt, a member of the new PSR and co-president from the bay area chapter, and Bernard Lown. Howard felt we should change the name of PSR to one which more clearly stated our anti-nuclear objectives. Bernard Lown fought him with an energy that was very destructive. Not for some time did I understand why he was so insistent upon keeping the original name of PSR. Lown won.

I spent much of 1979 travelling. On 15 December Bill and I set off for Cuba, accompanied by Norma Becker and a friend of hers named Paul. Norma had arranged the trip specifically for the four of us. I never really asked her why, but I presume that she wanted us to see Cuba so that we could demystify it for the American people. As it was illegal for anyone from the US to enter Cuba we had to travel via Jamaica to obtain our visa. Cuba was beautiful: pristine beaches, translucent turquoise sea, clean countryside, no rampant consumerism and a feeling of pride among the people. I was surprised: the standard United States line was that the people of Cuba were brainwashed and repressed.

We stayed in a once-grand hotel in Havana for about ten days. The US embargo and the poor economy determined that most buildings were in a state of disrepair. We were shown around by government guides and representatives, which was interesting, but on our days off we were free to roam the streets at will. Paul spoke Spanish and we were able to engage in many conversations. On the whole the young people were discontent, because they heard American radio stations and they wanted jeans, transistors and all the other accoutrements of Western life. The older people, on the other hand, seemed happy with their relatively new situation. One old lady, when asked what she thought of Castro, puffed up with pride and said, 'My son's a doctor.'

Before the revolution, when the country was run by Juan Batista and the US mafia, most of the population were illiterate, hookworm and tuberculosis were endemic, and infant and maternal mortality were high. However, after Castro took control, literacy increased, TB was eliminated, and pregnant rural women entered hospital at least a month before delivery to ensure adequate maternal and infant health, with excellent results. There was a universal free health care system: so good that Julius Richmond, the surgeon general under President Carter, considered using it as a model for nationalising medicine in the United States. (Julius was a brilliant man, the head of psychiatry at the Harvard Children's Hospital and a friend of ours. He tended to amble along, and I once asked him, 'How do you achieve so much when you walk so slowly?' His eyes twinkled mischievously as he replied, 'That's the secret.')

The United States had of course embargoed all trade with Cuba since 1959, when Castro and the Communists prevailed, but many European countries as well as the USSR traded with Cuba and gave the country their support. (We asked the Cubans: 'If everybody in the world had a uniform standard of living, would yours have to go up or down?' Their answer was: 'Down.') Castro, we were told, was so loved by most of his people that he could arrive at a university at any hour of the day or night and be greeted by an audience of thousands, eager to hear him orate—sometimes for five hours at a stretch—about the revolution, Cuba and international affairs.

It was a shock to be told that the Cubans were determined to build a Soviet-style nuclear reactor not many kilometres from Miami. We argued well into the wee hours with one particularly obstinate nuclear engineer who seemed to be in charge of the enterprise, but nothing we could say would dissuade him.

Just before Christmas, while we were still in Cuba, I developed severe pain in my upper left arm, which intensified until it was more agonising than childbirth. When I returned to Boston, I was put onto heavy analgesics and had a cortisone injection, which eventually helped. The kids were amused with me when we went to church on Christmas Eve—'Mum's wasted,' they said. Little did I know that this remark implied that they had absorbed some of the drug-related jargon of their peers.

Bill and I were so disgusted with the dripping consumer affluence of American shops after the sparsity of Cuban life that we decided on a Cuban Christmas for the family that year and followed the custom of hanging blessings to each other on the tree—no presents. It was the most loving Christmas we ever had. This is what Bill wrote to me:

My paternal great grandfather, Gracius Jacob Broinowski.

Jane Smith, my great grandmother, who married Gracius when he came to Australia from Poland.

Jim Coffey, my mother's father, in about 1942.

My maternal grandmother,
Ethel Clarke Coffey.

Dad's mother, Grace Creed Evans, whom we called Dais. Here she is as a young mother, holding my father in her lap. On her left is my Uncle Bob.

Dad in his twenties. He was a talented and passionate tennis player.

Mum holding me.
I am three months old.

In my playpen at about nine months.

On a holiday with Mum and Dad.

A family portrait taken in the early 1940s. Richard is three, Susan is five months, and I am five.

Aged about ten. I was dressed to the nines by Mum but I hated the outfit.

A Fintona girl.

A medical school dinner. I was particularly proud of the *Vogue* designer pattern dress that I'd made myself.

Mum and Dad's silver wedding anniversary on 30 November 1960. Dais is sitting directly behind me. Dad died two months later.

Dad in his office several months before he died.

Medical school graduation. I was a doctor, aged twenty-three.

Marriage to Bill, 1963.

Bill's parents, George and Dot. Mum was on my left.

I loved being a mother. Here I am with Nookles at six months.

A pensive Penny.

Philip is three, Penny two, and Nookles, seven months.

The beginning of my public life in August 1972. Saying goodbye to the children as I left for Tahiti to protest the French nuclear tests.

A Hollywood glamour shot arranged by Pat Kingsley.

Bill and I at a WAND conference.

Lobbying Tip O'Neil with Tom Halsted.

Randy Forsberg, the inventor of the Nuclear Weapons Freeze.

Bill and I at a congressional reception with George McGovern.

Congressman Ed Markey, who sponsored the 'sense of the Congress' resolution on the Nuclear Freeze. Here he is at the WAND ball the year Meryl Streep received the Helen Caldicott Peace award.

Linus Pauling, a two-time Nobel Laureate.

Me in action, describing the explosion of a twenty-megaton bomb.

Alfred Eisenstadt photographed me for *Life* magazine in 1982.

At a WAND ball in the mid-1980s with Sayre Sheldon, President of WAND, and T. Berry Brazelton, who received the Peace award that year.

With two untiring supporters of mine and the movement, Sally Field and Lily Tomlin, who jointly received the Peace prize at the WAND ball in 1984.

A rite of passage. Becoming a grandmother has given me one of the greatest joys of my life. With Penny's daughter, Rachel, aged three months.

Dearest Hen,

Helen, it is too much to ask for more from our relationship. I wish for your arm to be free of pain and for you to continue to exercise the influence you already have on world events and for PSR to become a major force. I want you to continue to find more peace in your own life and to see more clearly the love your parents had for you. I share your hopes for peace in the world, a downturn in the arms race, and real love between people. I will continue to give you all my love. Bill.

CHAPTER 15

The large hall in Harrisburg was packed with people and the atmosphere was tense as they watched a nationally televised debate chaired by Jim Lehrer of MacNeil-Lehrer fame. This evening commemorated the first anniversary of the Three Mile Island meltdown on 28 March 1979. The panel included Dr Norman Rasmussen, a wily old pro-nuclear engineer from MIT; Ed Markey, a beautiful, enthusiastic young congressman from Massachusetts; and me. During the debate, Rasmussen turned to Markey and said, 'Congressman, you're not an expert on these issues,' to which Eddie retorted, 'The people don't trust the experts anymore.' The people applauded wildly.

I reminded the audience that the Hershey Chocolate factory was only twenty-one kilometres as the crow flies from the reactor and that the company used milk from the surrounding area for their chocolate. At the end of the debate a woman from the city council angrily approached me and demanded, 'Did you say that on purpose?' to which I replied, 'I certainly did.'

At one stage I was invited to receive an environmental award presented by Lola and Robert Redford! Ever since I saw *The Sting* and *Butch Cassidy and the Sundance Kid* I had been smitten by Redford. So I took Bill with me as a form of insurance policy. We rang the bell of the Redfords' Fifth Avenue apartment, and the door was swung open by this golden-haired man more beautiful in the flesh than on celluloid. 'Hi, I'm Bob,' he said as I collected myself to say, 'How do you do?' I can't remember the conversation during drinks, but I do remember that it was a fabulous apartment overlooking Central Park.

Lola's commitment to environmental and anti-nuclear causes was obvious. At one point I asked her, 'How do you get such public attention for these environmental awards?'

She smiled and answered, 'Marry Bob Redford.'

It was in June 1980 that I had quite an extraordinary experience with one of my then heroines. I flew out to La Cross, Wisconsin, to address the American Holistic Medical Association and was delighted to learn that my fellow speaker was Elisabeth Kübler-Ross. I had enormous respect for her theories, which described how people reacted when confronted not only by death but by the thought of a nuclear holocaust. I was delighted at the thought of meeting her and looked forward to talking with her.

My speech about the horrors of nuclear war made quite a sobering impression on the audience. Then Kübler-Ross rose to speak. She is a small sparrow of a woman, with thin, brown hair and bright, intelligent eyes.

'Don't worry about nuclear war,' she told the audience. 'It will never happen.' She continued in this vein throughout her talk. I was staggered. How dare she? Not only did her speech effectively mitigate the impact I had made, reinforcing the audience's denial, but more importantly, it went against her own dictums. How could she say these things when her whole message told people that they must face reality? Well, after I recovered from that experience, I continued to recruit PSR members by travelling around the country developing new chapters.

I had been told that in Seattle lived a bright, enthusiastic woman doctor who would be a really good contact for PSR. I gave Judy Lipton a call and told her that I was coming to Seattle and asked her to arrange grand rounds in the major hospitals and a series of public speeches for me.

I loved rainy, leafy Seattle, whose climate reminded me of my native Melbourne: overcast and dripping with rain or sparkling in the sun, beautiful in the summer because of its rhododendrons, lilacs and deciduous trees. But as we approached the airport, I was acutely aware that we were flying over kilometres of Boeing aircraft factory, which received much of its income from federal government funds to produce cruise missiles and other nuclear weapons and delivery systems. I later discovered that the sparkling waters of Puget Sound harboured the Trident submarine fleet; each ship carried 240 hydrogen bombs, enough to destroy every city in the northern hemisphere. The 23rd Psalm played in my head: *Though I walk through the valley of the shadow of death I shall fear no evil, for Thou art with me, thy rod and thy staff they comforteth me . . .*

Judy, who was small, shorter than my mother, with dark hair, brown eyes and beautifully shaped, delicate lips, and her husband, David Barash, a bearded, intense man, greeted me enthusiastically. When I arrived at their house, I was introduced to their huge black, furry, rather smelly dog called Genevieve. I don't like dogs at the best of times. And it happened that I was to sleep downstairs below ground level, where the window was left open to air the room and Genevieve somehow managed to pour pounds of gravel from her smelly resting place above the window into my bed. The doglike odour never disappeared.

Judy is a powerhouse of energy, and she and I became close friends. The visit went very well, and on the morning of my return to Boston she nestled in my arms and sobbed on my shoulder, saying she couldn't contemplate her baby being consumed by the fires of a nuclear holocaust. I gently told her that she had to grow up now and help save the world for her children, as I was doing.

And she did. In double-quick time Judy and her newly constituted PSR chapter held a symposium on the medical consequences of nuclear war in Seattle, co-sponsored by the University of Washington Medical School. It took place in April 1981 and was so successful that people were scalping tickets at the door. But Judy didn't stop there. A year later she arranged a one-week event called Target Seattle, in which she and her team bombarded the population with the medical implications of a nuclear bomb exploding over the Seattle area. Bank managers, business leaders, schools, corporations, churches, all the media and 600 000 Seattle residents participated in this educational effort, and no fewer than sixteen public forums took place throughout Seattle.

Judy, who has a morbid sense of humour, also helped initiate a 'Run for Survival', which also received tremendous publicity. Sprinters who took part had thirty minutes (the time required for a nuclear missile to travel from Russia to America) to flee from ground zero to a safe point away from the blast. Of course, they never made it. This illustrated the fact that everybody would be trapped by a nuclear attack, that there is no escape.

Towards the end of the first Target Seattle I arrived at the airport to be greeted by an exhausted Judy. She laughed and said, 'Helen, you told me to save the world, and now I give you Seattle on a silver plate.' She then drove me to the King Dome stadium for a rally, where another speaker was Archibald Cox. The dome was not full, but held between 25 000 and 30 000 people. After my speech, volunteers passed around plastic buckets, and we raised no less than $40 000, just like that. Target Seattle became an annual event in a city whose economy depended largely on the military industrial giant the Boeing corporation, and it was emulated by other states, including Connecticut—also a militarised state.

Fascinating events were occurring in the early days at PSR, though not without their difficulties, I must say. Late in 1979 Eric Chivean, who had helped me found the new PSR, decided that we should hold a two-day symposium on nuclear weapons and the medical consequences of nuclear war, sponsored by Harvard and Tufts medical schools. Without keeping the rest of us informed, he consulted closely with George Kistiakowsky, who had participated in the design of the implosion mechanism for the first atomic bombs and later became science adviser to President Eisenhower. George, a tall, sandy-haired, balding man with a stoop, was a professor of chemistry at Harvard University; he also headed a group called the Council for a Livable World, whose aims closely paralleled those of PSR.

It was a good thing that they planned this symposium together because George had wonderful connections with many of the original Manhattan Project scientists, and the event would be lent great authority if they were involved. So I thoroughly endorsed the move. At the same time, however, I had mixed feelings. I was the president of PSR, and I was consulted only peripherally; further, Chivean and Kistiakowsky did not invite me to be on the panel of speakers. This felt awkward. I think that George was uncomfortable with my avid stand against nuclear power because he was one of the scientists who assuaged his guilt by thoroughly supporting the development of 'atoms for peace'.

But we forged on, and PSR was beginning to make its presence felt. Shortly before the symposium we published a letter in the *New York Times* headed 'Four Dangerous Myths about Nuclear Power' signed by members of the board.

On a grey, cold Boston winter's day, 20 February, an overflow crowd of seven hundred packed a Harvard lecture theatre. Howard Hiatt, the tall patrician dean of the Harvard School of Public Health, included this sentence in his opening remarks: 'Where treatment of a given disease is ineffective or costs are insupportable, attention must be given to prevention. Both conditions apply to a nuclear war.'

George Kistiakowsky described how a nuclear bomb is made. Jack Geiger—a member of the PSR old guard, appearing on the scene for the first time—quoted data from the two classic *New England Journal of Medicine* articles published by the old PSR in 1962 which described the effects of a bomb dropped on Boston. Other eminent people in politics, the military and medicine gave eloquent and effective presentations.

The press were amazed and fascinated. During a packed press conference on the first day, reporters seemed unable to understand why *doctors* were so concerned about nuclear war: wasn't that a subject best left to the politicians and the military? We were telling them it wasn't, leading them through the medical data for the two days of the symposium. As a result, the *Boston Globe* published an article describing the concentric circles of specific destruction that would be induced by a hydrogen bomb exploding over Boston. There were many other subsequent articles. I was excited to see that our message was finally being addressed.

Taking a leaf out of my Australian experience after being so inspired by the success of the symposium on the first day, I drafted the text for a full-page ad, which the faculty and Eric Chivean helped to edit, to be placed in the *New York Times.* It took the form of an open letter to President Jimmy Carter and Soviet president Leonid Brezhnev warning them of the medical consequences of nuclear war, signed by seven hundred prominent physicians and other citizens. That ad, headed 'Danger, Nuclear War', was published on 2 March 1980, was reproduced in newspapers across the USA, and became a classic.

We sent a copy to President Brezhnev, but decided to present the letter to Jimmy Carter in person. Four days after the ad appeared, Alex Leaf, chief of medicine at the Massachusetts General Hospital, Howard Hiatt, Eric Chivean, John

Hopkins psychiatrist Jerome Frank, who wrote a seminal work on nuclear war called 'Sanity and Survival', and I travelled to Washington for that purpose. The president would not see us, but we met Lloyd Cutler, counsel to the president. He stonewalled us, not even bothering to give us a proper reply, his response cool to the point of boredom. We left feeling frustrated and dissatisfied.

Several weeks later, however, PSR received an urgent phone call from the Soviet Embassy in Washington: Ambassador Anatoly Dobrynin, the longest-serving member and dean of the ambassadorial corps in Washington, wished to see us immediately. On 22 March Chivean and Jim Muller, a cardiologist who spoke fluent Russian, accompanied me to the Soviety Embassy. American paranoia about Russia was particularly acute at this time, and the CIA had a base opposite the embassy to monitor all incoming and outgoing communications. We were fairly certain that our movements in and out of the Soviet establishment would be tracked.

We felt nervous, not knowing why the meeting was so urgent, as we were ushered into an elegant drawing room and served delicious Russian pastries and thick black coffee. In strode Anatoly Dobrynin, a large, friendly man with balding pate and a commanding presence. To my amazement, he handed me a letter from President Brezhnev, written two days before, on 20 March. It read as follows:

> Esteemed Ladies and Gentlemen,
>
> I have studied your statement 'Danger, Nuclear War' and I fully share your concern as scientists for the fate of mankind in connection with the danger of nuclear war. Since the time when the atomic energy was first used for military purposes the Soviet Union consistently stands for banning these and all other types of weapons of mass destruction and annihilation.
>
> The US scientists can substantially contribute to the explanation of disastrous consequences for mankind of a nuclear conflict between the USA and USSR, which would inevitably

assume a global scale. Such explanation will further strengthen the will and activity of those who come out for stopping the arms race, for maintaining normal relations between all the countries, including, of course, the USA and USSR.

You may rest assured that your humane and noble activities aimed at preventing nuclear war will meet with understanding and support in the Soviet Union. With best wishes,

L Brezhnev

This letter and our open letter was published by the Soviet news agency Tass, as was a reply by Soviet medical experts.

Dobrynin spent ninety minutes with us in a wide-ranging, amiable discussion. I told him that he was a charming, wonderful man who was nothing like the Russian bear most Americans thought of and that he should appear on American TV to let people see what he was really like. Dobrynin said that he had tried that with Tom Brokaw, but the news people had edited the interview down to just a few seconds, and he now felt it would be a high-risk venture.

I was also delighted by Brezhnev's astonishing document. It was clear from the highest quarters that the Russians were much more concerned about the impending threat of nuclear war than was the US administration. I was unsure about how to use the letter politically, but Dobrynin counselled us wisely. He tactfully suggested that we should be guarded during this time of high Cold War paranoia in the United States when we faced the media with the letter, not flaunting it, lest people think we were pro-Soviet, which would do the anti-nuclear cause no good. Dobrynin also said there would be Soviet support at the highest levels for an American, Japanese, Soviet physicians' meeting to discuss nuclear war, an idea originally proposed by Jim Muller. We weren't pro-Soviet, just a group of doctors determined to educate all we could about the medical effects of nuclear war.

I took his point, and I felt more determined than ever that Carter should respond to our letter. I rang the White House again and told one of his aides, 'If we don't receive the president's reply soon, we will publish the original 'Danger, Nuclear War' ad again, with the reply from Brezhnev and an empty space for Carter's.' This worked: we had an answer from Carter very soon, though it was short on detail. We published both responses in a full-page ad in the *Washington Post* on 30 April 1980.

Carter then sent a personal telegram to Dr Mary Coleman, president of the PSR chapter of the District of Columbia. It read: 'Your statement on the danger of nuclear war is a grim reminder of the almost incalculable price the world would pay in the event of a nuclear conflagration. By describing so forcefully the terrible human costs of nuclear catastrophe, you have made a valuable contribution to its prevention.'

On the day that we had the abortive meeting with Lloyd Cutler, we were eating lunch together in a French restaurant in Washington when I received a call from an anonymous donor wishing to contribute money for future symposia. This was wonderful news. I then suggested an idea that had arisen at the Harvard Symposium—that we should develop a 'travelling road show', taking the symposia nationwide. This meant that the Symposia faculty would contribute its time and expertise for nothing, and it readily agreed. So on the plane trip that night back to Boston, Eric Chivean and I put together a financial proposal on the back of an envelope. We estimated that we would need $120 000. I submitted this figure to the anonymous donor, with a brief outline of our proposal; we weren't given the full amount, but we did receive $75 000, which to us seemed an amazing amount in itself. We were off and running; we began planning symposia for New York, San Francisco, Seattle, Chicago and Los Angeles.

PSR thus began a journey that was to have enormous ramifications within the United States and indeed in many other countries. As our sponsorship and membership increased, we were able to move from our broom cupboard to a small office in Beacon Street, Watertown, and then to a larger office in

Watertown Square. Carol Belding, our stalwart office supervisor, helped to recruit the speakers for the symposia and also set up a speakers' bureau, because we were now receiving numerous requests for public meetings. At the same time, she ran the rest of the office, and before long I realised that we needed someone extra whose job would be exclusively to organise the symposia. Halls had to be booked, faculty contacted, medical school sponsorship set up, local chapters of PSR mobilised and supported. After interviewing several people, I chose Mary Lord, an economic development specialist. She was very methodical and efficient, just what we needed.

I had great fun planning the format of each event, inviting the medical speakers and requesting medical school sponsorship. George Kistiakowsky's Council for a Livable World were co-sponsors, providing the relevant scientists as speakers. I decided that the dean of the local medical school should open proceedings in each city, and that every session should be chaired by a prominent community or medical person. This was deliberate policy: I wanted these people to become emotionally involved as they listened to the dreadful, unrelenting data on nuclear war.

For our second event, in New York on 27 april, we persuaded Cyrus Vance, who had recently resigned as President Carter's secretary of state, to moderate a session. We also found Jonathan Schell, a brilliant journalist from the *New Yorker* magazine. He subsequently wrote *The Fate of the Earth*, a classic book outlining the extraordinarily bizarre thinking behind nuclear war preparations and the prospects for the planet after such an event. Beautifully written and persuasive, the book became a best-seller, powerfully influencing public opinion.

Our San Francisco symposium, arranged by physicians Peter Joseph and Howard Kornfeldt, was one of our best. It was sold out. The local medical schools—Stanford and the University of California—sponsored the event, and continuing medical education credits were available for the attending medicos. The symposium was held in a grand location, the San Francisco War Memorial Opera House, where the charter of the United Nations had been signed.

Joseph Boyle, president of the Californian Medical Association, moderated one of the panels: subsequently the CMA became a major sponsor of resolutions against nuclear war within the American Medical Association. On the first day the subject was the medical consequences of nuclear war, how bombs are made, and what possibilities make such a war likely.

Most Americans still thought that everything their government did was fine and that the Russians were the evil ones. Typical of those listening was my dear friend Bea Herrick, who said that until she heard the data presented that day, she had had absolutely no idea what the United States or Soviet government was planning. She became physically ill as a result of her experience, so disturbed that she could not attend on the second day.

At the end of the second day, as I summed up the data, I was deliberately emotive. I faced the audience and said quietly, 'What is the point of making sure your children eat good nutritious food and clean their teeth every night when they probably don't have a future?' At the cocktail party afterwards, people told me: 'You made me cry.' That was precisely what I had intended. An emotional release after two days of unrelentingly awful information.

Filmmaker Ian Thierman recorded the whole symposium, turning it into a very powerful thirty-minute film, *The Last Epidemic*. It became a classic, and we showed it to hundreds of thousands of people in city clubs, Republican and Democratic clubs, churches, public meetings, schools, academic societies, editorial boards and TV stations. It usually brought people to tears. We also produced a complementary book in league with the *Bulletin of the Atomic Scientists*, which reinforced the symposium data, and we sold it all over the country.

I never had any trouble recruiting speakers. In the two years or so that followed, we heard powerful speeches from George Kistiakowsky; Jonas Salk, a small, spritely, highly intelligent man; Jerome Weisner, the president of MIT, and formerly President Kennedy's science adviser; burns specialist Glen Geelhoed; and Admiral Noel Gaylor, an elegant, authoritarian figure who had become ardently anti-nuclear. Dr Lewis Thomas, the famous medical philosopher, spoke to us about the social and psychological aspects of the nuclear arms race; economist Lloyd Dumas discussed nuclear war and the economy; and Marshal Shulman, an authority on the Soviet Union, spoke about negotiating with this superpower.

It was wonderful to hear knowledgeable people speaking the truth at last. I was so emotionally involved that in my enthusiasm I once clapped so hard the diamonds flew out of my engagement ring. The message was getting through to ordinary citizens, people who had previously heard nothing about the arms race except arcane military jargon. Now it was being presented to them in accessible ways via the media, who remained fascinated and supportive. Now we were getting the facts across, leading an information revolution. And once people understood the facts, how could they avoid them? How could they not act on what they knew, doing whatever they could to counter this appalling threat to the future of life itself?

Before long, other professional organisations began to emulate the PSR model, and we assisted them with advice, sometimes even helping them financially. Educators for Social Responsibility rented an office down the hall from us; we helped them through some of the growing pains we had experienced. Not long afterwards Psychologists for Social Responsibility was founded, followed by the Lawyers Alliance for Nuclear Arms Control and similar associations of architects, computer professionals, businesspeople, high-tech professionals and performing artists. All these groups approached the nuclear question from their own angles.

Morticians even formed their own anti-nuclear society, after inviting me to address their annual convention, declaring that they objected to embalming radioactive bodies. (They apparently failed to understand that by then they themselves would also be radioactive and dead.)

I was now speaking before a wide range of groups with different approaches and interests, and I had learned enough about public speaking to tailor my talk to the audience. I spoke to physicians as a fellow professional, coolly bombarding them with medical data, because doctors are generally not able to handle much emotion. For women's groups I would stress motherhood and the intrinisic nurturing qualities of women, speaking about babies and the future. Religious groups were easy. Scriptural texts using quotations from Jesus were eminently applicable to the prevention of nuclear war. I consistently emphasised that anyone can be as powerful in his or her on right as the most influential person who ever lived.

It was fascinating to observe the psychological reactions elicited by what I had to say. I left many stunned people in my wake, which was my intention. They tended to move through the classical stages of grief, initially reacting with shock and disbelief; sometimes they would use a small factual error to discredit everything I had said (it's not 553 cruise missiles, it's 528). Then people often became depressed, a state that could last for a period of weeks to months, until they entered a stage of anger and found a new perspective and sense of direction, knowing with certainty the course of action they would take. There are indeed many hundreds of inspirational stories of people who after months of grief suddenly knew their course of action and set out to save the world.

I never knew what sort of audience I would come upon next. One day I found myself in the Harvard yard, having arrived sweaty and late, leading a long procession of people garbed in academic dress towards the Sandars Theater. I was somewhat confused by the make-up of the crowd, who included bent up, very old men and young, gangling youths. I was to give the Phi Beta Kappa address, a society that doesn't exist in Australia and with which until then I was unfamiliar.

I stood on the stage and, as I usually did, dropped a metaphorical nuclear weapon on the audience. As I described the scenario—vapourised bodies, melting eyeballs—I could see the Boston dowagers in their wide-brimmed, flower-covered hats gradually sinking lower in their seats, and I realised I was being too grim. Quickly regrouping, I began to talk about preserving the beauty of the dogwoods and lilacs. The atmosphere changed and I could see relief on the faces in front of me. At the end they rose and gave me a standing ovation.

On 15 March 1980, PSR organised an important meeting at the Harvard Science Center, addressed by Alice Stewart, an English epidemiologist who had done pioneering work on the relationship of childhood leukemia and prenatal X-rays, and a brilliant statistician, George Kneale. Although the meeting was highly successful, we had a few rumblings of disquiet from some old guard PSR members, who felt that we should concentrate above all on the effects of nuclear war, and that emphasising low-level radiation—which wasn't terribly important or dangerous in their view—was counterproductive. They had bought the nuclear industry's fallacious line that this so called low-level radiation was safe. But the point is that small amounts of radioactive iodine in the thyroid gland can expose the surrounding cells to high doses of radiation while the rest of the body incurs no dose.

Of course, it was obvious why the industry would spread this sort of propaganda: to reassure the public about the quantities of radioactive isotopes being emitted from nuclear power plants and the weapons industry, which were contaminating food chains and the general population. Some PSR members were clearly becoming dupes of the nuclear industry, whether they knew it or not.

On 30 March I attended the new England Environment Conference at Tufts University, where I spoke for an hour about the medical implications of nuclear power and nuclear war. Renate von Tsarner, an elegant, very alert Swiss woman with lively hazel eyes, told me was deeply moved by my words. After some discussion, we decided to form the Women's Party for Survival, which later became Women's Action for Nuclear Disarmament (WAND). I thought women would be easier to mobilise than doctors, but I was mistaken; they were shy.

As national opposition continued to build towards the frightening nuclear arms race, more and more citizens became involved, and the increasing dissent was beginning to assume the status of a popular revolution. Yet its ultimate aim—persuading the Pentagon and the Kremlin to dismantle existing nuclear weapons—was remote. We knew neither side would back down and show itself 'vulnerable' to the other, and too much money and patriotic emotion was invested in the arms race to make this practicable anyway.

Early in 1980 Randall Forsberg came up with a brilliant approach to the problem. She suggested that instead of calling for a bilateral dismantling of nuclear weapons, both sides should just stop building them. They should maintain their existing stockpiles at present levels and cease deployment. In short, there should be a nuclear freeze.

Anti-nuclear groups, including PSR, seized on this as the answer. It was eminently practical, fair, uncomplicated and, above all, feasible, not biased either towards the United States or the Soviet Union. Over time four state legislative bodies passed resolutions to support the freeze, and in 1982 the House of Representatives and the Senate passed similar resolutions, though they were not legally binding. Many members of PSR and other anti-nuclear organisations assumed leadership roles in local freeze movements throughout the country. Things were changing at last!

CHAPTER 16

Families – Biological

One morning as I was preparing breakfast, at about seven o'clock, I answered the phone and heard an unfamiliar voice say, 'We've got your son here and he's had an accident.'

'Where is he?'

'Just around the corner,' the voice said, giving me the street name and number. Bill and I hotfooted it to the relevant house, to find Will's twelve-year-old face swathed in a nappy. When we undid it, he was covered in blood, one front tooth missing, one broken and another cracked. Oh my God, I'd waited years for these beautiful new teeth to emerge, and now they were shattered.

He had been out early on his paper route when the front wheel of his bike had disengaged and he'd landed face first onto the roadway. Bill searched the street and found the tooth, and we rushed him to the dental school. In the end, after years of corrective dentistry and much courage from Will, he lost both front teeth and was destined never to look quite the same.

The family were as important to me as ever, and I poured myself into their care despite the fact that I was away so much and responsibilities were piling on responsibilities. Will was ever on my mind. Still unable to adapt to the American way of life, he made somewhat inappropriate friends. I was worried about sending him to a rough junior high school in the district, so after numerous enquiries we decided to enrol him in a private upper-crust secondary school with the grand name of Nobles and Greenough. For this he had to dress in grey slacks, tweed jacket, shirt and tie. He rushed out each morning still looking somewhat dishevelled and spent his day learning Latin, algebra, Spanish, English literature, and so on. He never really fitted in here either, but at least his education was comprehensive.

Philip and Penny seemed to be settled in at Newton North High School, said to be one of the best schools in Massachusetts. Both Phil and Pen were on the track team and were fantastic runners, and Will was a big-time wrestler at Nobles.

In my absences our huge house on Commonwealth Avenue became very dusty. I clearly needed a housekeeper, but Bill was insistent that we clean the house together as a family. Of course, such a scheme was impossible. I would return from a trip absolutely exhausted, with no energy to supervise a cleaning session, so the house got more dusty and untidy. Eventually I took the law into my own hands and hired someone to do the job.

As Bill gradually grew more and more involved in the antinuclear movement, he became a very effective speaker. We were a great pair on the stage—he looking dapper and tailored in his beautiful pinstriped Jaeger suits, giving excellent chapter and verse statistics, followed by me in my Jaeger gear and pearls speaking of the philosophy and psychology that propelled the nuclear arms race. These actitivies were exciting. There is something very special about working with your partner for a higher cause.

However, Bill was also in a double bind. It must be difficult for spouses when the mate is in great demand and is rarely home, particularly for men. On the other hand, I know he appreciated the work I was doing, and I kept thinking that if I were a man, my wife would almost certainly be supportive. Looking back, I suppose what I needed was a wife. So there was an element of tension and some resentment superimposed upon the family and my work, let alone Bill's research. I know the children were fretful about my absences, particularly Penny. She really needed her mother during her adolescent years, and often I was not to be had. Furthermore, I would sometimes make a date to spend the day shopping with her in the Chestnut Hill mall, but if something important arose like a TV interview, I would often put her off.

Now, of course, I can see that nothing could have been more important than my beautiful, vulnerable adolescent daughter. I had my priorities wrong. I used to think that I must save the world for them. It was a legitimate mission, but one I pursued to their detriment. The trouble is that I am very black and white, no grey—when I set off on a course of specific action, I find it almost impossible to deviate from this journey. I've developed, I think, some moderation as I've grown older, but if I hadn't been so driven, my impact would never have been as great. To my regret, it is too late for my children, who today still carry some resentment from those days, while they also understand that because of the efforts of the anti-nuclear movement the world is now a safer place for them and their own children. Mine was a dilemma, I believe, that could have had no completely satisfactory solution.

Each summer Bill and I would pack the kids and cats (Mishka and Sasha) into the car and head off to our little four-storeyed doll's house in Annisquam, a tiny old New England village on the edge of Ipswich Bay, whose charming white houses were surrounded by gardens full of phlox, delphiniums, roses, lilacs and wisteria. The small village store served pancakes, maple syrup and bacon on the weekends, and I loved strolling down late on Sunday morning with Bill and sitting at the counter reading the *Boston Globe* while we ate a delicious breakfast. At lunch they served sweet boiled New England lobster, which the family ate as the drawn butter ran down our chins. The children and their friends swam and windsurfed in the cove, dragging themselves out of the water to drape their beautiful young bodies over our soft green lawns. At night we would wander through the winding lanes of Annisquam inhaling the evening perfume of honeysuckle while the tide rose silently in Lobster Cove, and we all went to bed salty, sunburnt and deliciously tired.

So we muddled through—a relatively functional family, all things considered.

Families – Extended

As I reached out to more and more people, others entered my life as a form of extended family. Richard Gardiner became a soulmate who took me into his family and loved me as if I belonged there. His wife, Judy, was a lecturer in English literature at a Chicago university, and we used to sit around their kitchen table in Chicago with their two gorgeous adolescent daughters, Corita and Vivica, reciting Shakespeare. Because of their influence I always ended my speeches with the love sonnet 'Shall I compare thee to a summer's day? Thou art more lovely and more temperate . . .'

Then there was the lovely and vulnerable Judy Lipton, who organised the city of Seattle. Judy is a psychiatrist of extremely high intelligence who always looks at things from a slightly wry perspective. When I'm in Seattle we always visit the Dilettante, founded by the chef to the last czar, where we eat wickedly delicious chocolate morsels washed down by frosted hot chocolate as we talk about our latest family fiasco or about the intricacies of our adopted family, PSR. Judy and Richard were loyal unto the last at PSR.

Claire Ryle was another member of my extended family. I met her when I embarked on a lecture tour of Europe, which she and her friend Jim Garrison had conceived. I stepped off the plane at Heathrow, utterly exhausted, to be greeted by this angel-faced young woman with a skin like skimmed milk. She blushed at the slightest hint of embarrassment and was one of the kindest, most gentle persons I had ever met. She was about my height, five foot five (165 centimetres), and was so poor that for the three week European trip she wore the same dull green woollen jumper and brown tweed skirt every day. Her father, whom I met when I gave a lecture at Cambridge University, was Sir Martin Ryle, who during the Second World War had discovered radar. He was so overcome with guilt about the way radar had been used to plan for nuclear war that he once whispered to me in a quiet moment, 'I wish I'd been a farmer.' I became very close to Claire during those three weeks, and she became one of my confidants in the difficult years ahead.

The Saxons, a couple in Los Angeles I consider members of my own family, founded the PSR chapter there. Richard, a droll and loving orthopaedic surgeon, and Pauline, his dynamic, intelligent, fascinating wife, became my dearest friends. Their house reminds me of a Norman Rockwell house that I used to covet when I read the *Saturday Evening Post* as a child, not really believing that people could live in such style. Whenever I arrive at their house, I drop my bags, walk into their kitchen, put on the kettle, and make myself a cup of tea, feeling totally at home. We sit around their small kitchen table until one or two in the morning chewing the fat about the latest dreadful political situation, or what we are going to do to save the global environment from nuclear devastation.

And finally there was Pat Kingsley, who came into my life after hearing me speak at the LA symposium. Pat happened to be one of the major publicity agents for Hollywood film stars, and she offered her services free to me. At that stage I was so naive I didn't even grasp the magnitude of the offer, but because of Pat the issue of nuclear war became a major story in every women's and news magazine in America—*Vogue, Ladies Home Journal, Redbook, Life, Time, Newsweek* and the like—and I found myself featured on such TV talk shows as *Donahue, Merv Griffin* and *60 Minutes.* Pat, a Southerner who speaks with that laconic drawl, is tall and blonde, with a strikingly attractive face. She can be as tough as nails and as gentle and caring as a loving mother. It was this latter role that she played for me. She was there through thick and thin; I called her every day from every part of the country, and her support and love were absolute. Without Pat during those years of enormous responsibility and trauma I could not have accomplished what I did, and I would not have made it in one, though slightly dishevelled, piece. To her I owe an enormous debt of gratitude, as I believe does the world.

Families – Adopted

And then there was my surrogate family, to which as an initial instigator and president of PSR, it felt as if I had given birth, and had nurtured, fed and protected as it grew from infancy to childhood through to adolescence. Doctors and staff came on board as they were drawn to the work, and each gained a place to exercise his or her talents and creativity. I believed in delegating responsibility, and the office flourished, as did the executive committee.

There comes a time in the life of every family unit, however, when degrees of dysfunctional behaviour begin to manifest themselves. Adolescents need to challenge their parents, to assert their independence and individuality, and the stronger the parents, no matter how much they love, the stronger the rebellion. Although clearly a strong, capable and, from time to time, overbearing parent against whom the members could test their mettle, looking back I can see that in one important way I was not as effective a leader as I might have been. I naively expected that everyone at PSR would respect and support each other in our enormous mission. I wasn't wily enough to foresee that organisations are composed of human beings who can be jealous, insecure and envious. That was my downfall.

On the other hand, I knew that I could inspire large crowds of people and had created two powerful political groups. Further, I was a potent fund-raiser. Yet in many ways I was still a little girl batting around in an adult world.

As I crisscrossed the country, I had the sense that all was not well within my PSR base at home. Surely and steadily my leadership came under challenge from several members of the executive committee and board. When I returned to the meetings, I could feel a degree of deviousness and deceit that was palpable but difficult to prove. It was to lead to one of the turning points in my life.

CHAPTER 17

In October 1980 Claire Ryle, my angel-faced friend, and I wearily dragged my suitcases across Europe on a mission to extend the PSR message to other countries. We jokingly called ourselves the anti-nuclear bag ladies as we struggled from train to train.

Our first stop was Amsterdam, which we visited at the invitation of Laurens Hogebrink, who worked with the Interchurch Peace Council in Holland. Laurens and his energetic wife, Win, lived in a tiny house right on a street in the city. There was hardly enough room to swing a cat, but they looked after me beautifully. I was severely jet-lagged, exhaustion heaped upon tiredness. They gave me a hot bath and some delicious Dutch hot chocolate and put me to bed.

The next day I was inundated with reporters from the major newspapers of Amsterdam and The Hague, hungry for stories about the nuclear threat to their country. I sat or almost lay on cushions on the sitting-room floor and conducted interview after interview. Because of the saturation media coverage, our tour had positive political ramifications in Holland. Laurens and a wonderful, persistent middle-aged physician, Dr Emile Wennen, arranged a large meeting of doctors, which led to the establishment of a doctors' anti-nuclear war organisation in the Netherlands called the Medical Campaign Against War.

Our next stop was Brussels, not nearly as comfortable or, indeed, hospitable. Our contact failed to meet us at the airport, so we were left to drag our way to his house by train. On arrival he greeted us with less than joy and showed us up to an attic. Claire and I struggled up a set of narrow stairs with my suitcases, only to discover that we would have to sleep together in a single bed. The weather was rainy, grey and very cold; I was depressed and longed to go home. Several meetings with some prominent members of the European Parliament had been arranged, but they were poorly attended. The media response was desultory compared with Amsterdam, but we did meet several distinguished doctors who helped initiate a thriving Belgian medical campaign for the prevention of nuclear war led by a very effective physician, Dr Jeff De Loof.

On to Hamburg and Berlin, a trip organised by two strong women doctors: gynaecologist Regine Armbruster-Heyer in Hamburg and Barbara Hörving in Berlin. Our presence generated great excitement, especially among women's groups and doctors, who then established their own PSR-type campaigns. We were greeted here by a very enthusiastic press.

The last leg of our trip took in the British Isles. Upon our arrival in London we were ushered into a packed press conference set up by Jim Garrison, Claire's energetic partner, who initially conceived the trip. Anthony Tucker of the *Guardian* wrote a full-page article, complete with photographs, and medical journalists wrote excellent pieces in the *Times* and other papers, by far our best response.

The next day I attended a meeting at University College Hospital, held expressly to form the London chapter of the

Medical Campaign Against Nuclear Weapons (MCANW, the title chosen instead of PSR). I spoke to an audience of about sixty doctors, and afterwards John Humphrey, a brilliant and highly regarded immunologist, was elected chairman. There followed a heated discussion about whether the organisation should be concerned with both nuclear power and nuclear weapons. This lasted until John slammed his fist on the table and said that he would resign if MCANW dealt with nuclear power. So that was that.

Claire and then I travelled to Bristol and Edinburgh, where we oversaw the formation of two other chapters of the British MCANW. I remember being so cold on the visit to Scotland that I crouched naked over a single-bar radiator in my room to try to elevate my body temperature. For the life of me I couldn't understand how elderly women who walked the streets in thin raincoats and lisle stockings could possibly survive in this spartan climate. I had obviously become soft skinned living in the United States, with its comfortable central heating.

As well as speaking to a group of doctors and attending the inaugural meeting of the Scottish MCANW, in Edinburgh I addressed a huge public meeting in the Edinburgh Playhouse. I also spoke at a primary school one evening to an enthusiastic mothers' group. They made a tape of this talk, which was shown all over Scotland and led to the formation of a very effective and large anti-nuclear women's organisation in Scotland.

The Medical Campaign Against Nuclear Weapons grew and flourished, and eventually became the strongest anti-nuclear organisation in Europe, sponsoring significant articles on nuclear war in the British medical journals. Claire Ryle was appointed full-time coordinator of the various branches, presiding over their growth and achievements with some very dedicated doctors. A direct offshoot of the English campaign was a thriving Italian medical group against nuclear war organised by Dr Alberto Malliani of Milan and Dr Ettore

Biocca in Rome, both of whom worked closely with Dr Paul Wallace of England and with Claire.

So the movement initiated by Claire and me spread throughout the European continent. It was thrilling! We were helping to undermine the plans of the Pentagon, which was determined to deploy cruise missiles at Greenham Common in England, in Holland and in West Germany. When I returned to the USA after this tour, I felt encouraged by the progress that we were starting to make globally. Many more people were becoming anxious about the prospect of nuclear war; influential community members and professionals were at last coming out in support of prevention. Educational campaigns were beginning to flourish in the USA and in Europe.

In Germany, I had told audiences that I thought Ronald Reagan could well become president in the forthcoming elections. They laughed at me incredulously; how could the American people possibly take this corny B-grade actor seriously? But I was well aware of the prevailing mood in the United States, how easy it was to foster extremely conservative and nationalistic values. I knew the power of the New Right, carefully crafted and propagated with the aid of millions of dollars. On election day, 4 November 1980, I gave a speech to a small student audience at Hamilton College in New York State. When I finished, I went to the common room, where most of the students were playing video games and drinking beer. The TV set above the bar was broadcasting the election results, but nobody was watching or listening. I couldn't take my eyes off it; as time went on, I was mesmerised as I watched the forces of conservatism moving like a hurricane across the country. State after state fell to Reagan; by the end he had taken almost every one, and the students drank on.

It was as inexorable, as unstoppable, as an avalanche. And while I watched, the appalling facts about nuclear war preparation haunted me. The USA possessed about 30 000 nuclear weapons, the Soviet Union about 25 000. And Reagan had pledged to increase America's nuclear capacity. Furthermore, the great majority of Americans supported the arms race. Popular awareness of the nuclear industry was growing and the number of anti-nuclear groups was increasing (including, of course, PSR), but there was a long, long way yet to go. My mission became more urgent than ever to me.

On a hot Boston day in 1980, soon after my trip to Europe, I was a guest at a luncheon at Bernard and Louise Lown's house in Newton. Lown had invited several physicians, including his junior colleague Jim Muller, a cardiologist who spoke Russian and who was deeply concerned about the nuclear arms race, and Eric Chivean. There was also a public relations man from New York. I felt uneasy about his presence, but the reason for the lunch soon became clear. Lown said he wanted to establish an umbrella organisation that would incorporate all the national medical groups, including PSR, as well as a newly developing group of Soviet doctors. It was Jim's original suggestion that the Russians be invited. Ambassador Dobrynin had also earlier suggested this course of action. Lown said that he had already made contact with Brezhnev's cardiologist, Evgeni Chazov, a medical friend, who had expressed interest in the proposal.

At one juncture Lown said he thought that the movement would take some years to establish; whereupon I became agitated and responded, 'We don't have time,' expressing a sense of urgency that cruise and Pershing missiles were about to be deployed in Europe, which would signal the end of arms control and initiate 'launch on warning'—computerised nuclear war.

Something didn't feel right. Obviously, though, it was a good idea to develop an international medical network. I was pleased when people took the initiative, because I couldn't possibly oversee the international movement alone, and I strongly believed in the delegation of responsibility. Thank God someone had stepped in. We agreed to name the group International Physicians for the Prevention of Nuclear War

(IPPNW), which, like PSR, would be based in Boston.

About a week later I received a call at work from Jim Muller inviting me to lunch at the Harvard Club. I was delighted. After we were seated, I told him I thought that, building on the established success of PSR, IPPNW could be an important international movement. But before I got very far, Jim interrupted.

'Helen, I have to tell you something,' he said. 'Bernard Lown doesn't consider that you're appropriate to be involved in the IPPNW organisation.'

I was absolutely dumbfounded. 'Why not?' I asked, as calmly as possible.

He couldn't or wouldn't give me a straight answer or a good reason. The rest of the lunch was tense and miserable.

Lown's office was conveniently across the road from the Harvard Club, in the School of Public Health. I should have confronted him then, informing him that his behaviour was unacceptable. Either he adhere to the democratic principles PSR had always observed or he step down. It was inappropriate for him to take on the mantle of international organiser of the medical community that Claire, I and others had conceived and developed. But by that time I was physically and emotionally exhausted from all the travelling and enormous responsibility. Now I can see, too, that I was somewhat immature, not yet the person I was to become, and I felt uneasy about confronting a distinguished Harvard faculty member who was my senior.

After that episode things moved fast. Several months later in early December 1980 in Geneva, Bernard Lown, Jim Muller and Eric Chivean met with three physicians from the Soviet Academy of Medicine—Evgeni Chazov, Leonid Ilyin and Mikhail Kuzin—and formally founded the International Physicians for the Prevention of Nuclear War. They did not consult with the executive committee of PSR, other members of the PSR board or, of course, me.

In the months ahead I continued to travel, lecture and

recruit for PSR, while feeling somewhat insecure. I couldn't be absolutely sure which members of my board supported Bernard Lown; a rift was developing. In June 1981 we held a symposium in Chicago, which, like all the others, was co-sponsored by local medical schools as well as the Council for a Livable World. Working with the council also presented difficulties. They were a respectable and experienced group of scientists and economists who wanted things to be done a certain way, but I had definite ideas about the symposia format. Before long I heard that George Kistiakowsky had gone behind my back and was complaining about me to some old guard members of my board and Lown.

I was ropeable and rang George. 'You're cross with me,' he said, and I had no difficulty in agreeing. So he invited me to his Harvard chemistry lab to discuss the situation. I told him that in future if he disagreed with me, he was to tell me directly because we were both presidents of our respective organisations. He accepted this, but I ended up sitting at his feet listening to a monologue about his glory days as science adviser to President Eisenhower. Once again I felt that I was being put in my place. I could have left, of course; today I would.

These personal dynamics, I suppose, were inevitable amongst people with big egos, particularly when a strong woman was involved, but despite these few anxieties, the symposia continued to be extremely successful. The fourth was held in Albuquerque, New Mexico, America's nuclear heartland, in September of 1981. The Manhattan Project was instigated in the hills near Santa Fe and Albuquerque in the early 1940s when the federal government secretly acquired a boys school and over several years converted it into a huge and dangerous facility called Los Alamos Labs. Since then New Mexico has been so abused by extensive nuclear facilities and radioactive contamination that the federal government designated it a 'national sacrifice area', meaning that some states had to be polluted for the national good. It was the site of nuclear testing, extensive uranium mining, a proposed national nuclear waste repository depot and huge military facilities. The single largest employer was the military, and the MX missile was slated for deployment here.

The irony is that New Mexico is breathtakingly beautiful, with vast blue skies filled with fluffy clouds, red desert sands, cactus and desert flowers. I fell in love with it immediately: its grandeur and space reminded me of Australia. I understood why an artist such as Georgia O'Keefe would choose to spend the last years of her life there. But I also felt a deep sadness. Here was yet another wonderful part of the natural world defiled by the nuclear monster.

Holding a symposium in this state was not without problems. The nuclear industry and its offshoots were very sensitive to our presence. The press, reflecting its constituents, was less than wholehearted in its support for us, and the State Board of Medical Examiners was reluctant to issue credits for the event, despite the fact that all our previous symposia had been approved by medical schools. I later discovered that the University of Albuquerque derives a large portion of its research funding from the military–industrial complex. But credits were granted at the last minute, and the symposium became the largest medical meeting in the history of New Mexico, attracting excellent media coverage.

I saw this ambivalence about the dangers of nuclear weapons at work again some days later when I spoke to the staff and scientists of Sandia Labs, where nuclear bombs and missiles were constructed (I'd been refused permission to talk to the Los Alamos staff). Several thousand curious and occasionally hostile men filed into a large steel shed. These were men who were well informed about nuclear physics and engineering, so I gave a carefully reasoned speech full of documented data about the medical consequences of nuclear war.

The onslaught began as soon as I finished. A man rose slowly from his seat and said, 'The *Boston Globe* quoted you as saying that people who work for the nuclear industry are either dumb, stupid or highly compromised. Is that true?' I could tell that a lot of men in the room were thinking, '*Now we've got her.*' I took the wind out of his sails by responding: 'I did say that, and I'm sorry.' I actually still agreed with those sentiments, but careful diplomacy was the order of the day in such a delicate situation. It worked: he sat down, deflated. The audience lined up to ask questions at the end. I was intrigued to notice that practically every man said: 'That was fascinating, he needed to hear that,' pointing over his shoulder to a man behind or next to him. No one said: '*I* needed to hear that'!

Our symposia were provocative in this conservative Reagan climate and we continued to receive extensive local and national media coverage, including wire service stories and radio and TV reports. And other ramifications became apparent. On the day following the very successful, standing room only, Los Angeles symposium, the American Public Health Association, many of whose members had been present, passed a resolution opposing the development and deployment of nuclear weapons and calling for a freeze and multilateral arms limitation talks.

The meetings also stimulated a spontaneous movement of local physicians around the country to form new chapters, and many started working for the anti-nuclear cause individually. They wrote for newspapers and became local TV and radio stars. By the end of 1980 we counted 10 000 members, with 75 chapters and 40 in formation.

PSR members were enthusiastic to learn the techniques of public speaking and media presentations. Because they were also uncertain how to go about recruiting their colleagues and introducing grand rounds, I often visited the new and established chapters to advise and consult, and gradually the local leaders assumed responsibility for speaker training. The board divided the country into regions to cope better with our exploding membership, and a representative from each region was elected to the national board. Sometimes I felt like a mother hen caring for her chicks: there were times when I couldn't believe that from its beginnings in a broom cupboard, we now had a national organisation divided into geographic areas. It seemed truly amazing.

Jonathan Fine, chairman of the executive committee, put together an interesting series of study groups. Every Sunday we met at his Cambridge house for brunch, to be briefed by some of the country's most important thinkers in the nuclear area, including Nobel laureate Salvatore Luria; Jerome Weisner, president of MIT, who worked on the Manhattan Project; and Bernard Feld, editor of the *Bulletin of the Atomic Scientists.* I was fascinated to learn what the 'arms control' community actually thought about nuclear war, and as a result, my own talks at grand rounds and elsewhere gained a new depth of analysis.

Anyone who supported the universal principles of love, compassion and responsibility for life on earth—the principles Jesus Christ espoused—could not possibly be in favour of nuclear war. I quoted freely from the New Testament when I spoke to conservative groups such as the Southern Baptists, and I could hold them in the palm of my hand, even though they were ardently anti-communist—there was no argument.

I always felt that God was on my side when I spoke from a pulpit. It was not difficult to convince a congregation that the mere preparation for, let alone the thought of, nuclear war was evil and that the life process was something to be revered as God's creation. I entered preacher mode from the sanctity of the pulpit, particularly in a cathedral. But I was often disturbed by the attitudes of some of the representatives of organised religion. The issue was pressingly obvious—the Reagan administration was telling us that we had to prepare for nuclear war—yet when I encouraged certain priests and ministers to preach about this topic, they would typically reply, 'Oh I couldn't do that, contributions would drop off, and I couldn't pay for repairs to the church.' I used to look at them and ask, 'What would Jesus do?', thinking of Jesus and the money lenders. They would be speechless.

As my own spiritual journey has progressed, I have become increasingly cynical about organised religion, which is more about power and control than about love and compassion. I think that each person's spiritual path is totally individualistic and has absolutely nothing to do with anyone else. While I appreciate the sense of community derived within churches, I never found any sense of God or a higher power within religious groups. Nevertheless, they are full of wonderful people who do extraordinary things for their fellow human beings.

On one occasion 30 000 Methodist women sat transfixed as I described the awfulness of nuclear holocaust; they were so profoundly affected that they rushed home to their ministers and demanded to know what the church was doing about the threat of nuclear war. The ministers were somewhat nonplussed, but because the women insisted, they agreed to examine the facts. The Methodist Church eventually produced a powerful pastoral letter condemning America's nuclear war preparations.

They were not the only church group to be so affected. After much consideration the Catholic bishops of America issued a pastoral letter that also opposed nuclear war, recognising that both the Soviet Union and the United States were taking similar positions. This was a landmark move: the Catholic Church had always been strongly anti-communist and supported US militarism against the Soviet Union.

With some trepidation I also confronted the Church of Christ of Latter-Day Saints, better known as the Mormons; this patriarchal and conservative church had been enthusiastic supporters of the Cold War, and I had little hope of bringing about a change in attitude. I travelled to Salt Lake City, where I met with Spencer Kimball, the church president, an old, frail, bent man in his nineties with enormous power. I spoke to him at length about the medical consequences of nuclear war and he acknowledged that vaporising the major cities and towns of the United States was not necessarily a patriotic act. I was delighted that after my visit the Mormon Church issued a statement opposing the decision to base the MX missile in their home state of Utah—a big move on their part.

Over several years I was the keynote speaker at the annual conventions of the Mennonites, the Church of Christ and the Southern Baptists, and at a huge breakfast meeting of Presbyterians. These church groups became very influential upon societal opinion and helped to lead the growing American opposition to nuclear arms.

The formation of IPPNW had an unfortunate effect, one that could have been predicted. PSR and the new group began to compete for funding within the United States. PSR was running a highly successful direct mail campaign that eventually brought in half a million dollars a year. But IPPNW began sending mailings to our donors—after agreeing not to—and presented money-raising proposals to foundations that had previously been helping us. Naturally the funding community became confused, and animosity infiltrated the PSR board, who felt they were being bullied by IPPNW. But some members of the board were reluctant to say anything because they were close friends and colleagues of Bernard Lown, and a couple were involved in both organisations.

There was no doubt that those in IPPNW considered themselves to be high fliers. At the group's first conference in West Virginia in March 1981, Bernard Lown invited a delegation of Soviet doctors, several from the British Medical Campaign Against Nuclear War, and some senior physicians from American medical schools. In all, eleven countries were represented. During the speeches Lown took credit for the anti-nuclear work that physicians had done to that date. It was somewhat unnerving. Lown dominated the proceedings, with Chazov and the Soviet delegation sitting on his right.

Unfortunately, the Russians came with a provocative statement that they wanted the conference to endorse and release to the press, blaming the United States for its role in the nuclear arms race. Reagan had just been elected president, and the Cold War was hot; such a statement would have totally discredited PSR in that conservative nationalistic climate. As IPPNW was the umbrella organisation, anything they did would directly involve PSR. The press were hanging around like vultures ready to label us Soviet accomplices at the slightest provocation. That would have destroyed us.

As president of PSR, representing 10 000 US physicians, I insisted that the statement not be released to the press. This really upset Lown and the Soviet delegation, and we ended up debating the issue through the night, with the Russians stalking out of the room when they believed themselves misunderstood. It felt as if we were at the SALT talks. I stood firm, and only Jonas Salk supported my position and stayed by my side until the issue was resolved. Jonas didn't look his age—a slight but imposing figure with kind eyes, he always seemed to be in the centre of the action. I gave Bill a call several times for moral support, and he urged, 'Keep at it.' In the end Jonas and I prevailed. I don't think Lown ever forgave me.

In all, it was a very uncomfortable meeting. It felt like a hostile takeover bid, the sort of thing that happens on Wall Street every day.

Despite the formation of IPPNW, I continued to play an active role on the European scene both publicly and within the medical profession. I returned to Europe late in 1981. Belgium had really taken off: a medical meeting in Ghent was packed with doctors from all over the country.

My trips to Sweden, Norway and Finland initiated extremely active physician movements that became potent factors in halting the nuclear arms race. In Sweden and Finland, in particular, the medical campaigns became two of the most important in Europe. I was a little apprehensive about Finland because it was close to the Soviet camp, but I picked up little tension among the people. The Finnish medical organisation in fact became a particularly effective force. So keen was this group that they translated my book *Nuclear Madness* into Finnish, and it was widely distributed there.

In the year since my last visit to Europe the nuclear issue had really entered the political agenda, partly because of ongoing education by doctors and strong effective anti-nuclear campaigns, but also because Reagan was scaring the hell out of the Europeans by saying that it was possible to fight a nuclear war in Europe without the global button being pressed. There was a huge anti-nuclear rally in Bonn, where Petra Kelly and I were co-speakers. I was fascinated and somewhat amused to see how attitudes towards the United States had changed. German youth in particular showed absolutely no respect for Reagan, who was lampooned everywhere. I saw models of him on horseback with missiles in his hands; there were cartoons, T-shirts and caricatures. After the cloying patriotism of the USA, where the president was idolised, right or wrong, this was refreshing.

In Britain, where I started new chapters of MCANW in Glasgow, Cambridge and Birmingham, the mood was more serious. I spoke at a monster rally in London arranged by the Campaign for Nuclear Disarmament to protest against the stationing of cruise missiles in England. The crowd was sober and attentive, except for a small group of black-clad anarchists who stationed themselves next to the stage within close range of the microphone. Their role quickly became clear: as soon as somebody started to speak about the impending dangers of nuclear war—and there were some magnificent orators, including Tony Benn, the famous English historian Edward Thompson and Michael Foot—they drowned them out with anarchic chanting.

When it came my turn to speak, I was determined to shut them up. I took the microphone, drew a deep breath and painted the most graphic picture I could of the medical effects of a nuclear bomb landing on London, describing the concentric circles of destruction—vapourisation, melted eyeballs, severe burns, amputated limbs and the like.

The anarchists were shocked into silence.

During 1981 I had several instructive meetings with journalists from some of the major American dailies who requested briefings about the medical consequences of nuclear war. Arms control expert Bill Kinkaid and I first tackled the staff of the *Boston Globe.* The journalists gathered in a large auditorium to hear our speeches and the response was very positive. Shortly afterwards the *Globe* editor, Tom Winship, who was also president of the national Newspaper Editors' Association, arranged for me to give editorial briefings to the *New York Times,* the *Washington Post* and the *Miami Herald.*

This was a wonderful opportunity to warn jounalists about the consequences of nuclear war. However, I felt I had little influence over the rather self-important *New York Times* journalists, who were not about to drop their guard for a young woman doctor who came to lecture them.

The *Washington Post* meeting was one I anticipated with some pleasure. Having recently read Woodward and Bernstein's *All the President's Men* as well as seeing the film, here I was, visiting the familiar halls of the hallowed *Post* and being greeted by its editor, Ben Bradlee. I found him friendly and sharp, but possessing a short attention span because he picked up facts quickly and was easily bored. We moved into a large room full of journalists, who started ripping me apart about the Soviet Union, accusing me of being naive and not understanding Soviet intentions—almost before I had uttered a word. I told them to be quiet and watch the PSR film *The Last Epidemic* before they said anything more.

When the lights went on at the end, some members of the audience were in tears, their cynicism completely gone. Ben Bradlee leant back in his chair. 'I guess I'm numb,' he murmured, to which I replied, 'Yes, you've entered the first stage of grief', and I explained the Kübler-Ross grief process. Later the Pentagon correspondent Walter Pincus followed me round with a quizzical half smile on his face.

'What's the matter, Walter?' I asked.

He said, 'I've never thought about nuclear war like that before.'

'Why?'

'I've never thought about what it does to human bodies.'

I was shocked: how could anybody write about the subject of nuclear war without thinking about its logical outcome?

Ben Bradlee beckoned to a woman reporter, who whisked me off to do a long interview, and then on to the photographic department for some pictures. It was a very good piece, hard-hitting and provocative. But it was published in the *Post*'s 'Style' section accompanied by a flattering photograph that made me look like Jackie Kennedy. That episode taught me that no matter how much I moved an audience, no matter how many facts I had at hand about nuclear war, I was not considered hard news—because I'm a woman. Here I was, a leader of the anti-nuclear movement, a fact acknowledged by the article but apparently not worthy of front-page comment. If I'd been Henry Kissinger, I would certainly have been featured on the front page of the *Post.* Not once was Randy Forsberg or I ever given the time of day in the 'hard news' sections on arms control or disarmament during the extraordinary years of the freeze movement.

Mary Benjamin's film, entitled *Eight Minutes to Midnight,* was nominated for an Academy Award in 1982. Everybody was thrilled, though I had slightly mixed feelings: I thought my Australian voice sounded really strange on film, and I didn't like the way I appeared obsessive and hypermanic—I was like a chook running around without its head. I seemed to calm down, though, towards the end of the film, when I talked directly to the camera about the sanctity of life and the beauty within a single cell. I said, rubbing my forehead, 'I can't contemplate the fact that it all could be destroyed.'

That wasn't the end of my film involvement. In May 1981 I was to give a speech in the upstate New York town of Plattsburg, which was located adjacent to a strategic air command base. When I arrived at the hall, I was greeted by an enthusiastic crew from the National Film Board of Canada: microphones, floodlights, the lot, ready to record the event. Terri Nash from the NFBC had heard me speak in Montreal, decided to tape me next time I was near Canada, and tracked me down in Plattsburg. I was so tired that I didn't know how I would have the energy to speak, let alone perform for the cameras, but I said what I had to then staggered off to bed in a motel located immediately below the flight path of B52s loaded with nuclear weapons.

Some months later, after a speech at the Riverside Church in New York, Dorothy Rosenberg from the National Film Board made me sit down and look at the rough cut of the film, now entitled *If You Love This Planet.* I still hated seeing myself on film, but the producers had managed to get hold of some very effective Pentagon footage of Hiroshima, which had never been shown before. *If You Love This Planet* won the Academy Award for best documentary of 1983.

Normally winners of documentary Academy Awards aren't given a great deal of attention—everybody's more interested in the awards for Best Picture, Best Director, Best Actor and Actress—but not this time. The US Justice Department labelled *If You Love This Planet* (plus two Canadian films on acid rain) as 'foreign propaganda'. Until then the press had been totally uninterested in a speech I was about to make at the National Press Club in Washington, but suddenly they snapped awake. Before I knew it, Senator Edward Kennedy was on the phone, asking whether he could introduce me. I said sure, and later he reprinted my speech in the *Congressional Record.* He introduced it with these words: 'Dr Caldicott is one of the most eloquent voices on earth for the prevention of nuclear war.'

The distribution of *Planet,* along with the two Canadian films on acid rain, has been severely limited in the United States, even though it won an Academy Award and was seen by the majority of Canadians. Viewers of the film had to register with the Justice Department each time it was screened; this policy had a definite inhibitory effect.

Planet was used as a test case before a congressional committee that was trying to eliminate an antiquated law preventing certain people, books and films from being aired in the United States, despite the First Amendment. When a spokesman from the Justice Department finished his testimony before the committee, defending the decision not to play the film, one of the congressmen looked at him and said, 'Using that kind of logic, you would justify the concentration camps.' The case went as far as the Supreme Court, but with Reagan appointees holding the balance of power, *If You Love This Planet* has remained a limited item for years. It has never been shown on national TV in the States.

Part 4

Glory Years

CHAPTER 18

Pat Kingsley brought actress Sally Field to one of my first talks in Hollywood, held in a lavish mansion. They sat together on a low, round divan in the middle of the room as I spoke. Sally was small and very pretty and was lit up by what I had to say. She was a mother of two young boys, and from that time on she was amazingly supportive and helped to catapult the subject of nuclear war into the mainstream media.

Pat also represented Candice Bergen, Goldie Hawn, Lily Tomlin, Margot Kidder and Debra Winger, women who were very concerned about the imminent prospect of nuclear war. They were enrolled in the cause and were enlisted to appear with me on television shows. To my delight, Sally and Lily appeared with me on *Donahue*. The scene in the make-up rooms and corridors before the show began was extraordinary. Lily, with reams of notes and papers in her hands, was striding up and down doing a crash course on the strategies and tactics of nuclear war, while Sally, rigged up with hair curlers, sat quite composed while being made beautiful in the makeup chair.

I was nervous, but for the first half hour of the show Lily and Sally were on alone. Lily, in particular, performed brilliantly. By the time I appeared, she had covered all the relevant details and there was little to do but reinforce her opening statements. It worked. Several days later the Women's Action for Nuclear Disarmament office in Watertown, Massachusetts received 6000 letters from all over the country. Our membership increased dramatically.

My very first national TV appearance was on the *Merv Griffin Show* in Los Angeles. I wasn't sure about Merv because he was a close friend of President Reagan's. Pat was like a cat on a hot tin roof as she paced up and down in the green room during the interview. I had no idea what I was getting into when Merv interviewed the first guest, Eva Gabor. Heavily made up, her hair a bright blonde bouffante, she was dressed in an off-the-shoulder pink taffeta evening dress with a flounce that covered her ample breasts, and was wearing diamond drops the size of pears. She was there to tell everybody what it was like to be Eva Gabor in Hollywood.

Soon afterwards I walked on to the sounds of clapping from the live audience and the blare of a band, looking very much like a doctor in my sensible Australian tweed suit. No greater contrast to Eva Gabor could have been imagined. And when the conversation turned from Hollywood to the nuclear holocaust, the audience became confused. As I struggled to convince them that nuclear war would be 'bad for their health', Eva cut in: 'But the Russians roll over children, with tanks. They are evil, they can't be trusted.' This got a big hand from the audience, who obviously agreed. How was I going to deliver a clear message that there had to be cooperation between Russia and America? I picked up a glass of water with a shaky hand to calm my nerves and accidentally poured it straight down the front of my blouse. Luckily we then went to a commercial break and the lights dimmed, giving me a few moments to collect myself and work out a new strategy.

As the lights went on again, I turned to Merv, a man of stocky build with a head of grey hair, and said, 'Do you know that our children are frightened and think they have no future because of the threat of nuclear war?' This worked; I spoke movingly about children, as a mother and paediatrician, and I could feel the audience shifting to my side. As the show ended they applauded. I got in just under the wire and felt enormously relieved. So did Pat. I suspect that if I hadn't made the grade that day, she would have thought twice about working with me.

Pat continued to schedule more television shows, including *Good Morning, America*, the *Today Show* and *60 Minutes*. I was aggravated by the talk show format. It's almost impossible to talk about the ramifications of nuclear war to an audience of 60 million when you've only got three minutes and you're sandwiched between an actress talking about her latest facelift and an author hawking his new novel. No wonder people lose perspective on priorities in a confusing world where every issue, no matter how mundane or important, is treated with a similar affect and gravity. But every second of air time is worth millions of dollars, so I quickly grew accustomed to ignoring the interviewer if the question was not relevant. Instead I turned and talked directly to the camera and said my piece.

In February Pat arranged for me to meet Candice Bergen at the Russian Tea Room in New York; she was to introduce me later to her friends at *Nightline*. She arrived with her husband, the French movie director Louis Malle, and director Mike Nichols, who joined us during the meal. They seemed fascinated by the conversation, which duly turned to the subject of nuclear war. Candice is a classic beauty, an elegant, graceful woman who emanates a sense of calm and peace, not at all like the frenetic, sassy Murphy Brown she plays on television. I greatly enjoyed the meal, though I was initially somewhat nervous. She and I chatted about families and marriage as we walked back to her apartment for coffee. Then we headed to the ABC offices, where we met Brian Lord, the producer of *Nightline*, who grilled me about nuclear war and its ramifications. We got on well and he seemed to respect what I had to say. He invited me some weeks later to appear on *Nightline* just after the announcement of cruise missile deployment in Europe. The show turned out to be a disaster, but more about that later.

Pat scheduled two more *Donahue*s, one with Sally Field again and a priest, whom I remember because he had a severe case of dandruff flaking all over his collar, and another with Margot Kidder and Jane Alexander. Jane is an elegant and dignified actress who starred in the anti-nuclear movie *Testament.* She joined WAND as soon as she heard about it because she had been plagued by nuclear nightmares for years and was incredibly relieved that she could now do something constructive. She quickly became a leader, always in the front line of decision making and responsibility within the organisation. She and her husband, Ed, became our dear friends.

Margot Kidder, a forthright, beautiful Canadian, also became a good friend. We agreed politically on all issues and she was a close confidante and working partner. I first met her at a press conference, where I turned to her and in my typical up-front fashion asked, 'Who are you?' Margot, who had played Lois Lane in the movie *Superman*, smiled and said, 'Superwoman'. I'd never seen a Superman film, although I'd devoured the comics as a child, so her answer did not ring a bell. When she told me her agent was Pat Kingsley, I felt that Pat would kill me not knowing who Margot was.

At that time Margot was closely involved with Pierre Trudeau, then prime minister of Canada. Because of this relationship she was able to arrange a lunch for us at the prime ministerial residence early in 1983. I stayed in a Toronto hotel the night before, and she rushed into my room the next morning, straight from an early shoot. She had a quick bath, powdered herself and put on a gorgeous soft, white creation, and off we went to see Trudeau. She turned to me as we left the room and said with a wicked grin, 'This is what you call whoring for peace.'

Trudeau, who was accompanied by his foreign policy adviser, was most gracious. He was extremely charming, shorter than I had expected, balding at the front, with an interesting, puckish face and greenish eyes. After an elegant meal, we started discussing nuclear issues. I was quite surprised to find that he was not particularly knowledgeable about the subject of nuclear weapons and was shocked to discover that he didn't even understand the flight characteristics of the cruise missile then being tested over western Canada; his adviser was not much better informed.

I grew frustrated with them both, insisting that the majority of Canadians did not support the test flights. Trudeau's reply was: 'If I believed in majority opinion, everybody would have guns.' I took this point. Later in the conversation, when his adviser was being quite patronising, I interrupted and said, 'I am going to tell you something that may irritate you, but you are both behaving like typical men!' The adviser's face set like stone, but Trudeau burst out laughing. I finally got to the seat of his soul by asking him how he visualised the future of his three little sons. He stopped talking and became very thoughtful.

Some months later Trudeau asked me to brief the Canadian cabinet on nuclear war. Bill accompanied me on this trip. When we entered the room, I was surprised to find that two other people had been invited: James Schlesinger, former US secretary of defence, a noted hawk, and Eugene Rostow, also an American Cold War warrior. The meeting, chaired by Deputy Prime Minister MacEachen, was held at a resort in the Laurentian Mountains on a beautiful summer's day. Schlesinger, a large, sandy-haired, balding man with an authoritarian and intimidating manner, spoke first. He was very dictatorial, subliminally threatening his Canadian colleagues, by indicating that they should toe the party (the US) line. He also implied that US policy in Central America was fine, that if people had to be killed in the name of anti-communism, so be it, and that Canada had no right to interfere with or even comment on American foreign policy. The Canadian cabinet—about twelve men—was clearly intimidated by this man, and throughout the ordeal I kept thinking, 'I'll get you.'

Then it was my turn. I described the medical ramifications of a nuclear attack on Toronto and the ecological results of a global nuclear war, deliberately speaking as unemotionally as possible. I gave them facts. 'Enormous overpressures will create winds of up to five hundred miles [800 kilometres] an hour,' I said, 'causing hundreds of thousands of injuries. A normal hurricane wind has a velocity of approximately one hundred and twenty miles [200 kilometres] an hour. These winds will literally pick people up off the pavement and suck them out of reinforced concrete buildings, together with the furniture, converting them into missiles travelling at one hundred miles [160 kilometres] per hour. When they hit the nearest wall or solid object, they will be killed instantly from fractured skulls, brain trauma, fractured long bones and injuries to internal organs.

'Glass is also vulnerable to overpressures. Windows will be popcorned—extruded outward or inward—by these forces before they shatter into millions of shards of flying glass. Travelling at a hundred miles an hour, these shards could penetrate human flesh, producing shocking lacerations and haemorrhage.'

There was much more; by the time I had finished, most of the men in the room were looking rather pale. Then I turned to Schlesinger, looked him straight in the eye and said, 'Every human life is as precious as yours, and you don't kill people in the name of foreign policy.'

He said nothing, but I learned that after the meeting he was standing beside a lake at the resort, absent-mindedly throwing stones into the water, when a cabinet minister came upon him. Schlesinger turned and said, 'She's got a point.'

The press were everywhere. All I told them was that the cabinet had listened carefully and seemed moved by what I had said. Sometime later Pierre Trudeau brought six countries together in a peace group called the Five-Continent Six-Nation Peace Initiative, to work for a cessation of the nuclear arms race. Another step on the never-ending road towards nuclear disarmament.

In March I spoke in San Francisco's Grace Cathedral at an event arranged by our newly formed Women's Party for Survival. Pat organised for *60 Minutes* to film it. This was an important evening; the cathedral was packed. My talk on this occasion included a description of the ludicrous Crisis Relocation Plan devised by the Pentagon and the Federal Emergency Management Agency. In the event of a nuclear war everybody was supposed to evacuate his or her relevant city to designated small towns in the country. To avoid panic, cars with odd-numbered plates would leave on the first day, then those with even-numbered plates would follow the next day. People should remember to take bankbooks, credit cards, change of address cards, tampons, and so on, but leave behind pets and drugs. If the car stalled on the freeway, instructions were to move it to the side, pull out a trusty shovel, dig a hole, park the car over the hole, and shelter under the car until the nuclear war was over.

During the thirty minutes of an all-out nuclear attack people were to dig themselves holes three feet (90 centimetres) wide and six feet (180 centimetres) long and cover them with two doors and three feet of dirt. At what stage they entered the hole was not exactly clear. T. K. Jones, deputy under-secretary for defense for strategic theater nuclear forces, actually said: 'It's the dirt that does it,' and 'With enough shovels we'll make it.' (Robert Sheer from the *Los Angeles Times* subsequently wrote an anti-nuclear book titled *With Enough Shovels.*)

Large parts of my speech were broadcast on *60 Minutes*: what an excellent forum after years of struggling around the country addressing small audience after small audience. Next day the ticket clerks at the Los Angeles Airport greeted me with: 'We saw you on TV last night. It's very serious, isn't it?'

I had some fascinating experiences over the years dealing with the media. On one occasion I was interviewed in a Chicago TV studio together with a retired brigadier-general by a woman journalist who was very conservative. Throughout the segment, the military man spoke in logical and reasonable terms about the prospects for nuclear war, describing how retaliation against the Soviet Union could be necessary. I tried to make the counter-argument that such an event would probably end all life on earth, or at least kill hundreds of millions of people. As the lights went out in the studio at the end of the interview, he turned to me and said aggressively, 'You should go to Russia.' I thought rapidly for several seconds and decided to let him have it. 'I fucking want my kids to grow up.'

He turned scarlet with fury. This man could talk coldly and clinically about nuclear war, but when a woman said 'fuck' to him, he was undone. He seemed about to attack me on the floor of the studio, when the producer rushed out of the control room and separated us. I could just see the headlines: 'General Attacks Peace Activist on Floor of TV Studio'.

The most off-putting interviewer I have ever had, I think, was the noted CBS correspondent Eric Sevareid, then near the end of his career. He would ask a question, and as I answered, his eyes would glaze over. Then he would glance at his script and ask the next question. It was acutely uncomfortable.

Occasionally media celebrities, I found, could also be disconcerting. Soon after I started working with Pat, she arranged for me to meet Barbara Walters at her large New York apartment. Walters' secretary answered the door, and I waited some minutes in the opulently furnished living room before Barbara appeared.

She was very offhand, and clearly wasn't drawn to me. At one point she asked, 'Why are you doing this work?'

I had noticed a large portrait of a small girl on the wall. 'Is that your daughter?' I asked.

When she nodded, I said, 'I'm doing this work so she can live.'

Walter Cronkite, on the other hand, was charming. When I met him and his wife, Betsy, at dinner one night, Walter amazed me by saying that if he had his way, he would remove all US nuclear weapons from Europe. 'What would the Russians do then, roll over people with their tanks?' he asked.

I said, 'The American people love you, Walter. Why don't you tell them that?'

He laughed and replied, 'I'm only loved because they *don't* know what I think.'

Mary Benjamin showed *Eight Minutes to Midnight* to her new acquaintance Meryl Streep, who was so inspired that she decided to host a showing at a theatre on Broadway. This was a very exciting prospect, so Bill and I decided to take the kids. I dressed in a simple white satin blouse and my burgundy velvet skirt, and off we set. As we approached the theatre, I saw my name written in lights beside the title of the film on the marquee. Me? Up there? On *Broadway*? I felt almost as if I were in a dream.

When the children were seated in the front row, Bill and I went backstage, where we found an agitated Meryl. She is small and pretty, but she wouldn't stand out in a crowded street; it's the quality of her acting before the cameras that brings her to life and makes her glow. She kept running to the bathroom to brush her hair.

'What's the matter, Meryl?' I asked. 'Your hair looks great.'

'I'm nervous,' she told me.

'How can you be nervous when you act in films all the time?'

'I only work from prepared scripts. I've never spoken extemporaneously.' I was amazed that someone so accomplished could be so nervous.

We waited in the wings, and when the film finished, just before Meryl and I were due to go on stage, I turned to her and said, 'Do you have any children?'

'A baby boy,' she answered.

We looked into each other's eyes and wept a little. Then we clasped hands spontaneously and walked out on stage together. The crowd rose and clapped for about five minutes.

Meryl gave a moving speech, saying how much the film had affected her. 'Helen Caldicott has been my inspiration to speak out,' she said. It was a wonderful evening, made even better when *Eight Minutes to Midnight* received its Oscar nomination.

Pat was incredibly generous with her time. Just days after she had committed to work with me, she flew to the East Coast and stayed with my family for several days to get to know me. Subsequently, she often flew to New York to accompany me during media interviews. She was very stringent with the journalists; when she saw me flagging, she would say, 'That's it,' and they would leave. No mucking about.

Full-page articles and photographs of me and the family appeared almost every week in major magazines: *People*, *McCall's*, *Time*, *Life*, *Yankee*, *Vogue*, *Penthouse*, *Family Circle*, *Ladies Home Journal* and others. Many of them were along the lines of 'Attractive Australian-born Dr Helen Caldicott, a wife and mother, wants to save the world'. I hoped they would encourage people to think about the horror of the nuclear arms race and join together to prevent it. Sometimes I couldn't bear the almost wilful ignorance I observed in people. Didn't they realise what danger they were in? Perhaps I was obsessed, and they were in a state of normality, but it was all so obvious to me. I would look in disbelief at mothers casually filling their supermarket trolleys with cartons of Coke and other goodies for their children, people walking around

Chestnut Hill mall, buying ever more expensive clothes and things for their houses. What, I wondered, maintained their absurd denial while Ronald Reagan was endorsing plans for first-strike, winnable nuclear war?

At one stage, just after I had returned to the States from a trip to Australia, Pat organised a fund-raising party for PSR in Los Angeles at the home of a friend of hers that was attended by many of her film mates and clients. We raised $30 000 that day, so I returned home with a nice present for PSR.

By now I was becoming adept at fund-raising. I learned how to enter the room and meet the various guests, while simultaneously calculating how best to approach each one for the greatest gain to PSR: being seductive, aggressive or grief-stricken as the occasion demanded. It required some play-acting on my part—whatever it took, I did.

Life in the fast lane was relentless. Often the producer of *Good Morning America* or the *Today Show* would ring and ask me to appear on the program in New York at a moment's notice because some nuclear issue had hit the news. At the same time, I frequently rushed down to the national capital to appear on *Crossfire* with Tom Braden and Pat Buchanan. Buchanan, who had been President Nixon's speechwriter, held the conservative line, while Braden took the liberal point of view—strange, because he wasn't really liberal, and he used to work for the CIA. I found Pat extremely intelligent, and couldn't understand how he could possibly believe the hawkish and pro-nuclear views he espoused. But I was assured by his wife, whom I met in the green room after one of the shows, that indeed he did.

I usually won in these debates, but they were far from cosy. The travel they involved was exhausting. I would fly down to Washington, take a long taxi ride, do the show, and fly back—not exactly my idea of a relaxing day. Furthermore, I'm not sure what sort of education is provided by a noisy TV debate, apart from good theatre.

Too often after one of my trips, I would arrive in the Boston airport wiped out, never sure from which terminal I had departed and rarely remembering where I had parked. Laden with suitcases, I would stumble around knee-deep in snowdrifts on the roof of the parking garage, searching for my lost and buried car. And then the battery would be dead!

CHAPTER 19

I was standing with the PSR contingent in a New York street on a crisp, sparkling June day when it suddenly dawned on me that I would never make it to the podium on time. It was 12 June 1982, the day that one million people crowded the streets of New York to protest the continuing dangers of the nuclear arms race during the United Nations' second special session on disarmament. I was scheduled to speak at 12.45 and it was already 12.15. I fled through streets packed with every imaginable contingent, from Black Lesbians for Peace to the Church of Christ, the Mormons, Southern Baptists and Grandmothers for Peace. Never had the city witnessed such a huge crowd—all had come to bear witness to the monumental wickedness of the nuclear arms race.

I arrived backstage in Central Park distressed and short of breath with five minutes to spare. As I stood and watched Orson Welles being winched onto the stage in his wheelchair because of his massive size, I tried to imagine just what I would say in three minutes to this ocean of faces to focus their attention upon the dire probabilities if we continued to countenance the actions of the nuclear nations.

Orson gave a passionate speech about the gravity of the situation, and then it was my turn. 'Let me tell you what would happen if a nuclear bomb were dropped on Central Park,' I began. My voice was surprisingly confident, and I took courage: after all, I had said similar things before, all over the country. 'The bomb will come in on a missile travelling at about twenty times the speed of sound, moving on a ballistic trajectory. If it explodes at ground level on a clear day like today, it will release heat equivalent to that of the sun—several million degrees Celsius—in a fraction of a second. It will dig a hole three-quarters of a mile [1 kilometre] wide and eight hundred feet [250 metres] deep, converting all the people, buildings and earth and rocks below to radioactive fallout particles that will be shot up into the atmosphere in a mushroom cloud.

'Because the human body is composed mostly of water, it turns into gas when it is exposed to thousands of degrees Celsius. When the atomic bomb dropped on Hiroshima on 6 August 1945, a little boy was reaching up to catch a red dragonfly. There was a blinding flash, and he disappeared, leaving only the shadow of his body on the pavement behind him.

'Anyone who watches the flash without being vaporised will have his or her eyes melted by the intense heat . . . other people will be turned into charcoal. In a book called *Unforgettable Fire,* Hiroshima survivors drew pictures of scenes they remembered. One depicted a mother holding her baby, standing on one foot, running; she and the infant had been turned into a charcoal statue.'

I ended by quoting Richard Nixon, who said, 'Don't listen to what we say, watch what we do,' reminding the audience how horribly dangerous this was when applied to the Reagan administration. This became the quote of the week in the *New York Times.* When I finished, there was an eerie silence. Then wave after wave of applause broke over me. It felt wonderful to move so many people, knowing that the anti-nuclear movement had grown so fast. That was one of the most exciting moments of my life. I walked off the stage, feeling that the power of the people was immutable and would save the earth.

As I left the park, a young woman came racing up to me and said, 'Are you Helen Caldicott?'

'I am.'

'I was in the shower the other day and heard a voice on television say that every town and city with a population of 25 000 people or more in the United States is targeted with at least one bomb. I didn't know that, that's why I'm here'.

I'm sure that many thousands were there that day because of the enormous power wielded by the media to educate and influence people's thinking. Pat Kingsley, who had so facilitated my presence in the media, had helped to pack Central Park.

The *New York Times* devoted a lot of space to reporting the march as a local city event, saying that amazingly there was no rubbish left to clean up in the wake of one million people; it had been entirely peaceful. But at no point did the paper ever examine the issues that had created the largest political gathering in the history of the country, allotting only one small editorial to a discussion of the nuclear freeze movement. And it was dismissive to the point of arrogance, saying that judging by the march and rally, the freeze was supported by a vast spectrum of American citizens, from grandmothers to church groups to children, and that such support was unique in the history of the United States . . . but that the desired change was not feasible.

I couldn't believe this. Not feasible? When a million people were demanding a bilateral end to the nuclear arms race? When we were asking the USA and USSR to stop testing, developing, producing and deploying all nuclear weapons and delivery systems? Of course it was feasible, as well as simple and fair. The trouble was that we were up against the architects of the nuclear arms race, who greatly influenced the thinking of the press, men such as Henry Kissinger, Eugene Rostow, Fred Ikle, James Schlesinger, and the two Richards—Perle and Burt—among others, members of the old boys' club, and they were almost offended by an idea that had emanated from the very foundation of American society.

Nevertheless, the events of 12 June 1982 showed that the anti-nuclear movement was now a force to be reckoned with. And some members of the old boy's club did actually support us, including William Colby, the former chief of the CIA, and Paul Warnke, ambassador to the SALT II negotiations. Soon after the march, not to be outdone, the military–industrial complex, clearly intimidated by the show of popular pressure against them, retaliated and called for a major new engineering initiative in space, known as Star Wars, which would move the concept of nuclear war into space.

Reagan responded to the match in a derogatory fashion: you could get as many people at a rock concert. But he then began hijacking the language we used. 'Nuclear war must never be fought and can never be won,' he said. We were winning, yet not winning. The momentum of the movement was not to be stopped, though. In February 1982 Senators Ted Kennedy and Mark Hatfield had introduced a freeze resolution in the Senate, supported by 17 other senators; the House version of the resolution had 122 co-sponsors. In the same month Leonid Brezhnev urged a resumption of talks on limiting strategic arms, suggesting an interim freeze on the deployment of long-range cruise missiles, and a *Los Angeles Times*/CNN poll showed that Americans would support a freeze by a margin of 3–2 if the question was put on local ballots.

On 18 May, in reply to a Reagan proposal for informal talks aimed at reducing US–USSR arsenals of nuclear warheads by one-third, Brezhnev proposed that the freeze should go into effect as soon as the talks began. On 29 June, seventeen days after the march and nine days before the talks began in

Geneva, a US national mayors' conference adopted a resolution calling on President Reagan to begin talks with the Soviets on a mutual, verifiable freeze. But a month later Reagan aborted talks with Great Britain and the USSR on a comprehensive ban on nuclear testing, which had been in abeyance since 1980, saying he doubted that such a ban could be verified and that new weapons needed to be tested. He followed this up with a letter to House speaker Tip O'Neill urging Congress to kill any freeze resolution. Nevertheless, on 28 July Congress approved a measure proposed by Congressman Les Aspin to bar funds for developing, testing, procuring or operating any nuclear weapon that would undercut the SALT I or II treaty, except in cases of 'supreme national interest'.

The freeze resolution, sponsored by Congressman Ed Markey from Massachusetts, was to come up in Congress on 5 August—the day before the anniversary of Hiroshima. It was a conscience vote and not legally binding (called a sense of the Congress), but the fact that the freeze was being debated in the Congress was an enormous step forward for us. I had met Ed Markey, a passionate anti-nuclear campaigner, a year after the Three Mile Island disaster, at the PBS TV debate in Harrisburg. He was a lovely young man of Irish descent with blue eyes and dark hair and a playful but intelligent manner. His father had been a milkman and his first introduction to the nuclear issue occurred when he did a primary school project on milk contaminated with strontium 90 during the era of American and Soviet atmospheric testing in the 1950s and 1960s.

Needing further support for the resolution, I approached Tip O'Neill. On the day I dropped in to see him unannounced, he was chairing a session of Congress. His secretary informed him that I was there, and he came off the House floor to see me. I liked him at once, this big blustery man with a shock of white hair, a large red nose and a heart of gold.

'What can I do for you, doctor?' he asked in his Boston Irish brogue.

I explained why I had come, and asked him whether he would arrange to have *The Last Epidemic* played on the closed-circuit TV system in Congress, beaming it into the office of every member. He agreed. When the vote for the freeze resolution came up, he called it 'the single most important issue in my thirty-five years in Congress'.

On the evening of 5 August Ed and I kept in close touch as the vote proceeded. He finally called me late at night almost in tears. By a margin of only two votes—204 to 202—the House had rejected the call for an immediate freeze, approving Reagan's phoney option, a resolution to reduce arms. But the groundswell support for a freeze kept mounting, to the point where in November Reagan asserted that 'foreign agents' were helping to instigate the movement, and that majority backers were sincere but misguided. The National Conference of State Legislatures did not agree with him, voting on 10 December to support the freeze resolution by 29 votes to 8.

By 1983 newspaper polls showed that 80 per cent of the American public believed that nuclear war would not remain limited, be won, or be survived, and 77 per cent believed that nuclear weapons policy was too important to be left in the hands of the experts alone. This was clearly a revolution in the public's thinking on the issue.

The anti-nuclear education program was gaining ground. By the end of 1982 PSR membership was up to 30 000, with 153 chapters in 48 states. Our symposia had covered more than forty cities, with total attendances of more than forty thousand. As well, PSR had also developed a model curriculum on the medical consequences of nuclear war for medical schools; and 124 schools had included it in their courses.

The PSR symposia series inspired ABC to support the production of a chillingly dramatic film called *The Day After,* which depicted the medical and sociological consequences of a nuclear bomb dropping on Kansas City. It was broadcast in prime time on 30 November 1984. People worried that children should not watch this horrific event. Many Americans attended post-*Day After* events organised by freeze groups, churches, psychologists and educators. The debate at these events was intense. Interestingly, some poeple derided the film, arguing that a nuclear war would be much worse than the events depicted in the film. It was replayed in January 1989 and has become a classic.

I was enthusiastic to help any politician, state or federal, who supported the freeze. I attended fund-raisers in Oregon to help Congressmen Les Au Coin and Jim Weaver, in California to support Jim Bates and Jerry Brown, in Massachusetts for Ted Kennedy. I endorsed Michael Dukakis's gubernatorial campaign and I supported Ed Markey, Nick Mavroulis, Senator John Kerry, and Dick Celeste, Governor of Ohio. I gave detailed talks about nuclear technology for their fund-raisers, and they reciprocated by lobbying their congressional colleagues.

One of the staunchest supporters of the freeze was Tom Harkin from Iowa, who was running for the Senate for the first time in 1984. He is of medium build with dark hair and exudes a calm and knowledgeable demeanour that inspires confidence. For several days I flew around the state in a small private plane with him, his lawyer wife, Ruth, and their two small daughters, travelling from fund-raiser to fund-raiser, persuading the electorate to vote for Tom and to support the freeze. At several large functions as I was giving my speech about the medical consequences of nuclear war—first strike, counterforce or launch-on-warning—I was very moved by Tom. The baby sat on his knee during my speech, while he spooned baby food into her mouth. In fact, Tom seemed to care for the baby most of the time, even though he was in the middle of a senatorial campaign. A loving father, there was nothing artificial about him. He won his election.

Touring and lobbying for the freeze was hard, discouraging

work. I'll never forget standing outside the door of the Senate chamber one afternoon, after a particularly gruelling day of lobbying, watching the military–industrial lobbyists buttonhole the senators as they poured out the door. These lawmakers were often whisked away by the lobbyists to expensive lunches, hunting lodges and ball games at the weekends, all at taxpayers' expense because the cost of corporate lobbying is tax deductible. I felt like weeping with frustration. How could we compete against such power and money?

Fortunately, the freeze movement had several key supporters, including Ted Kennedy, who had sponsored the resolution in the Senate. He was always extremely hospitable and rather formal: like Tip O'Neill, he addressed me as 'Doctor'. I found his large office poignant, the walls covered with Kennedy photos and memorabilia. I consider him to be one of America's most humane politicians; for years he has pushed for a nationalised health care system, for decent wages and for justice in many areas. 'You've done more for this country than both your brothers combined,' I once told him.

Some freeze campaigners outside politics were extremely determined. At a fund-raising dinner in Beverly Hills I gave my usual hard-hitting and emotional speech. At the end a retired Superior Court judge and ex-mayor of Beverly Hills named Jack Tenner got up and fixed the audience with a beady eye. Dark, short, stocky and intense, he said, 'I can see thirty thousand dollars in this room, and nobody is leaving until we have collected.' He then accosted each person individually and, by God, he got the money. I've never seen anything so provocative in my life, and the crowd loved it.

But there were also some waverers. Late in October I was presented with the key to the city of San Francisco by its mayor, Diane Feinstein. It was a great honour. Some months later, however, when Bill and I, feeling particularly relaxed, were watching the news, the reporter announced that Feinstein had endorsed the decision of the Navy to home-port cruise missiles in San Francisco Bay. I was staggered. San Francisco, I thought, one of the biggest freeze supporters? What was Diane Feinstein thinking of? And what could I do about it?

Bill was smart. 'Why don't you give the key back?' he suggested. An excellent idea, I thought. But I couldn't find the damn thing. We had moved house from Newton to Annisquam by this stage, and I couldn't be sure we had packed it with everything else. Finally I ran it to ground in a corner of the garage and rang Feinstein.

'I'm going to give the key back,' I said.

There was a shocked pause. 'Nobody's ever done that before,' she said.

'Yes,' I said. 'But nobody's ever invited cruise missiles into a city that overwhelmingly supports a nuclear weapons freeze either.'

Soon after, I caught the plane to San Francisco and handed the key back to an alderman; Diane Feinstein was unavailable. She did, however, appear on a morning talk show with me to debate the issue. She discussed the new roads that would be built by the navy and potholes that would be filled; I talked about the children of the city burning in a nuclear holocaust. The show created a blaze of publicity for the cause, and I felt really good about it.

I travelled almost every night of the week throughout 1982, proselytising for the freeze, PSR and WAND. Half my life was spent in the air, and my dislike for aeroplanes abated as I boarded one after another. In those Reaganite days airports pulsed with military men; some places had special 'hospitality' lounges where they could relax, play pinball machines, and so on. Atlanta was the worst. It looked as if it were preparing for impending war, and I hated it.

Time after time in airports and on planes I overheard conversations between people who worked directly or indirectly for the military–industrial complex, which was a fiscal bonanza in those days (still is). One day in the Washington,

DC, airport I sat chatting with three men as we waited for our delayed flights: two made components for the cruise missile, the third was involved with the MX. They all seemed to love their work. Difficult though silence was, I held my tongue.

Most of the flights I took were uneventful, but some were terrifying. One hot, muggy afternoon I was flying back to Boston after visiting Washington, DC. I was feeling rather flat; my speech to the American Association of University Women had been received in a rather desultory fashion, probably because the husbands of some of the members worked for the nuclear industry. I overheard one flight attendant tell another, 'We're about to enter a thunderstorm and it's going to be bad.' I am terrified of storms when in the air, and I rushed to the lavatory for something to do. When the storm hit, the flight attendant banged on the door, ordering me to come out and sit in my seat. I was so afraid that I ran down the aisle with my pants down around my ankles, followed by the flight attendant, who ordered me to pull them up. I was too far gone to care: if we crashed, what does it matter where your pants are? When I got back to my seat, I quickly downed two cans of beer to soothe my shattered nerves and remained stony sober until we hit the tarmac. At that point the achohol crossed the blood–brain barrier, and I wove my way out of the plane with a sense of great relief.

Then there were the occasions when passengers got sick and I was the only doctor on board. Drugs and medical equipment are not carried on US domestic flights, the theory being that no plane is more than fifteen minutes away from the airport and help in an emergency. This doesn't always follow, of course. More than once I've had to try to treat a passenger who has had a heart attack, but all I could do was monitor the pulse and hope to God that the patient survived.

On one occasion a small boy had a severe allergic reaction and I was afraid he was about to go into anaphylactic shock. He had difficulty breathing and looked as if he was about to asphyxiate. The way to handle this is to make a small hole in the trachea or windpipe below the larynx and insert a hollow tube to make breathing possible. One of the flight crew had a penknife and I decided that if I pierced the trachea and cut a ballpoint pen in half, I could put the cylindrical barrel of the pen in the hole. Fortunately, none of this was necessary.

But the funniest time was on a flight from Australia to the States. I'd just settled down for the night, having eaten a lovely dinner with wine and taken my two sleeping tablets, when there was a call: 'Is there a doctor on board?' I made my way up the aisle to find a man slumped in his seat, grey and sweaty with shock, and a young, rather frantic medico attending to him. At that point an older, more distinguished man arrived, who happened to be the director of gastroenterology at the Royal Adelaide Hospital.

I looked at him and said, 'I've just taken two Normicon.'

'So have I,' he said. We had fifteen minutes to stabilise the man before the drug kicked in, which we did, but it was more by luck than by design.

✦

For the first time in my life during the early 1980s, I began to receive death threats. Initially these seemed to come not from people who resented being told of the dangers of nuclear war by a female Australian doctor, but from people who were mentally ill. In the 1980s there were a lot of them around, because Reagan was saving money by closing psychiatric hospitals and putting patients on the streets. And, of course, the US was—and still is—full of strange people carrying guns.

When I was about to campaign for Tom Harkin in Iowa, I received a letter from a man who said I should cut my throat before I arrived or he would have to do it for me. We alerted the police and the FBI kept this man locked in his house for two weeks during my visit. I grew accustomed to assessing my audiences and watching for signs of strange behaviour. Several times I bolted from the stage when a man in the audience stood and walked aggressively towards me, sometimes with a strange lump in his pocket. I often examined the podium before I spoke, wondering whether bullets penetrated wood or whether their trajectory would be aborted. In all, I had eight direct death threats, and probably many more that I never heard about. But in those days as I stood on a platform, I would say to myself, 'If I'm killed now, at least I'm doing the right thing,' and I felt good about that.

CHAPTER 20

The Playboy Mansion and Ronald Reagan

I stood before a gathering of film stars in the summer of 1983 at the Playboy mansion in Hollywood, a pile of a place built from the proceeds of that 'gynaecological' magazine, to tell them about nuclear war. It was a meeting to promote a forthcoming edition that featured excerpts from Robert Sheer's book *With Enough Shovels,* which described the administration's ludicrous defence plans for the American public in the event of a nuclear war. Hugh Hefner, dark haired and rather short, and not very interested in what was going on, was accompanied by the Playgirl of the Year, who was voluptuous in the extreme. Among the stars were Goldie Hawn, Sally Field, Jack Lemmon and Kris Kristofferson, who cried after my speech. For the first time I met Paul Newman, who smiled from those brilliant blue eyes, bowed and kissed my hand.

Paul spoke first, and though he was articulate and well prepared, I was surprised to find him so restrained. It was as if he was aware that he was a film star, but when he spoke against nuclear war, he had to be an ordinary person, very serious with no hint of acting. I knew he felt passionately about the subject, but as I was to observe on later occasions, he always pulled back when he discussed it, perhaps thinking that too much emotion would lessen his credibility.

My speech, on the other hand, was a real cry from the heart. Pat had told me in the car on the way to the mansion 'These people are film stars, be emotional with them'. I ended it by saying, 'We may be the only life in the whole universe, and when you leave tonight, I want you to look up at the stars and realise what this means to you and what you intend to do about it.' This got to them.

Shortly after I finished, a dark-haired intense young woman came up and introduced herself as Patti Davis. 'I'm Ronald Reagan's daughter,' she said, 'and I think you are the only person in the world who can change my father's mind about nuclear war. Will you see him?' This was a wonderful opportunity, one that I could only have dreamed of. 'Yes,' I said cautiously, 'I would love to. But he must be alone. I won't see him with Meese, Baker or Deaver.' I knew that they would speak for him, and if possible, I wanted to discover the man behind the image, and what he really thought.

'Okay,' said Patti. 'I'll get back to you in several days.'

Soon afterwards she rang me at home. 'We've got an hour with him at the end of his working day,' she said.

'What time is that?'

'Four o'clock,' she replied. Patti later told me that Reagan had agreed to meet me because he thought she was a communist, and to be fair to her, he thought he should talk to one of her friends with similar ideas.

On 6 December 1982 I flew to Washington, where I met Patti for lunch at a French restaurant near the White House. She was surrounded by Secret Service men conversing on their walkie-talkies, but they stayed outside the restaurant. She and I struck up an immediate rapport. There was no strain in our conversation, and neither of us was nervous. Patti started talking about her childhood easily, as if we had known each other for years. She said that when she was a teenager, she had hoped her father would help her become an actress in Hollywood, as Henry Fonda had helped his daughter Jane. 'But he went into politics instead,' she said, much to her disappointment. She added that the night he was elected, she was so upset she developed acute asthma and was admitted to hospital. 'I hate him being president,' she said.

Ronald and Nancy Reagan were a unit unto themselves with virtually no friends. 'I'm not close to her at all,' she said, 'but nobody is. They don't know what to think of Ronnie'—Patti's brother, a ballet dancer—'but they're certainly not close to him. He's a lovely, sensitive guy.'

The Reagan household wasn't particularly literary. 'While I was growing up, Dad rarely had a book in the house,' said Patti. 'But he always subscribed to the *Reader's Digest.*'

After lunch we returned to the hotel room where I was staying overnight. Patti had a short sleep while I prayed for a miracle—that I could influence Reagan and that he would do an about-face and support the freeze or some sort of nuclear disarmament. If I could change Reagan's mind, the course of world events could possibly be altered.

Then off we set in a big black limo, closely followed by the Secret Service. We swept down Pennsylvania Avenue and around the curved drive of the White House to the southern portico, where we were welcomed by a soldier wearing white gloves and taken into the downstairs library.

The word 'library', especially in the White House, may suggest musty, leather-bound tomes on floor-to-ceiling bookshelves lining oak-panelled walls, but this room wasn't like that. The walls were painted white and there were few books to be seen. The room had three tables, two small ones in the front and a large one in the back.

A few minutes later President Reagan entered, wearing a dark suit and tie and a white shirt. He looked softer than he did on television, his flushed pink face creased by deep wrinkles, his hair a medium brown. He seemed flustered and didn't take my hand, so I took his. 'It's nice to meet you, Mr President,' I said, adding that I was rather nervous about meeting him.

'No, no, you mustn't feel that,' he said in the familiar soft voice. He seemed ill at ease. I motioned to the head of the long table, where he cautiously sat, with me next to him and Patti on the other wide. During the whole of the following conversation he was very nervous, and I frequently found myself holding his hand to reassure him. This situation was rather disconcerting.

I started by saying he probably didn't know who I was; he interrupted and said he knew I was an Australian and that I had read Nevil Shute's *On the Beach* and was scared of nuclear war. I told him I had learned more about the subject when I began studying medicine in 1956, and although I had feared bringing my first baby into the world in 1963, I had had three babies because I loved children. 'I'm also a deeply religious person,' I said, 'and I consider what I'm doing to be a spiritual mission.' I was hoping, of course, to touch his heart by deliberately invoking his favourite deities: God and the family.

If he was receptive to this, he gave no sign. 'I don't want nuclear war either, he said, 'but our ways of preventing it differ. I believe in building more bombs.' Then he started talking about tactics and strategy, telling me that the Soviet Union was stronger than America, that it wanted the world to be taken over by communism. 'They already have a base ninety miles [145 milometres] off the American coast,' he said, referring to Cuba.

'But America sees capitalism as the only answer for the world,' I said. 'In that sense, the superpowers are mirrors of each other.'

He didn't take my point, saying only that the Soviets were

evil, godless communists. 'All of them?' I asked, but he declined to answer.

I asked whether he had ever met a Russian. 'No,' he said, 'but we hear from their émigrés.'

'America has the Soviet Union ringed by bases in Italy, Greece, Turkey, Britain, France and other countries,' I said, 'and many of them are equipped with nuclear weapons and missiles.'

'No, that's not right,' he said. But he gave no reason why he disagreed. He also declined to accept my assertion that the nuclear balance between NATO and the Warsaw Pact countries was approximately equal because of the forward-based systems in Britain and Germany, as well as the missiles in American submarines allocated to NATO.

'The Soviets have submarines, too,' he said.

I replied, 'The Pershing II missile can reach Moscow from its launching point in West Germany in six to ten minutes, which could induce the USSR to adopt a computer-directed launch-on-warning policy.'

'Ah,' said President Reagan, 'but the Soviet SS-20s can also reach Europe in six minutes.' He seemed not to realise the strategic significance that the Pershing IIs threatened the Soviet Command, Control and Communications system in Moscow, which could induce them to launch on warning, or initiate computerised nuclear war. He looked pleased, as if that clinched the argument.

At one point Patti interrupted the conversation with: 'Dad, I know that what Dr Caldicott is saying is correct because I have a 1982 Pentagon document to prove it.'

Unhesitatingly, he replied, 'It's a forgery.'

I tried again. 'The Soviet Union is flanked by communist countries that are hostile to it,' I said. 'And of the five nuclear armed nations in the world, each of three—Britain, France and China—could destroy the Soviet Union as an entity. The Soviets know that. Why would they provoke a nuclear war?'

'China doesn't have an adequate missile delivery system,'

he said. He then assured me that the Russian civil defence system was a very good one. I had been to Russia and seen the bad roads, plus the lack of up-to-date vehicular transport—among other things—and I quoted a 1979 CIA report that was highly sceptical about Soviet civil defence. I asked President Reagan where he got his data from. He didn't seem to know.

'Was it T. K. Jones?' I asked, naming one of the authors of the ludicrous civil defence system advocated for America. But to my astonishment, he didn't seem to know who Jones was.

We spoke about the money spent on defence. The President said the USSR had outspent the USA over the past years. I told him about the two CIA-prepared reports on Soviet defence spending—the Team A report and the Team B report—and said he was quoting from the latter, which had been proven inaccurate. He didn't seem to know the difference between the reports until I mentioned that the Team B report had been prepared under the guidance of George Bush when he was director of the CIA.

'George's report is the right one,' he said.

He wouldn't even entertain the thought of a nuclear freeze. 'That will lock the Soviets into a position of superiority,' he said.

'But America has more nuclear weapons,' I pointed out.

'The Soviets are ahead in megatonnage and missiles,' he replied.

'But missiles are only the delivery vehicles,' I said. 'The important thing to assess is the number of bombs.'

I told him America was ahead in the number of killer submarines; he stated that the Soviet Union was ahead. (In fact, the Warsaw Pact had 126 and NATO 110 nuclear-powered attack subs, but the NATO subs were substantially superior.) We got down to cases: President Reagan told me that the USSR had defied detente by building up a huge arms inventory with nuclear weapons, many tanks and troops. I showed him the data in the manual published by the Center for

Defense Information (CDI); although the Warsaw Pact had 63 000 tanks, NATO deployed more than 50 types of anti-tank weapons and had a total of almost half a million in Europe. NATO, stated the CDI manual, led the Warsaw Pact countries in the total number of ground forces in Europe.

'That's not right,' said President Reagan, adding that the former high-ranking Pentagon officials who ran the CDI were not credible. I showed him a CDI graph indicating that America led the Soviet Union in numbers of strategic weapons, both then and during the 1970s.

'I don't believe that graph,' he said.

And so it went. I made statements, and he contradicted me; he would assert something, and I would correct his facts. It was all done entirely without acrimony—in fact, the tone of the whole conversation was uniformly pleasant—but sometimes President Reagan seemed not to hear me, and I began to despair.

Then he pulled out some handwritten notes from his inside coat pocket, and quoted some material saying that the freeze campaign was orchestrated by Russia and that we were KGB dupes.

I looked at him. 'That's from *Reader's Digest*,' I said.

'No it's not, it's from my intelligence files.' These quotes were in fact taken directly from a recently published article by John Barron in the October 1982 issue of *Reader's Digest*.

He said that the huge rally on 12 June had been organised by communist and leftwing groups: 'You're being manipulated,' he said.

'You must think we're very unintelligent to allow this to happen,' I said, adding that I was one of the leaders of the anti-nuclear movement and that I had never met a communist in it.

'You might not know you're being manipulated,' he said. It was hopeless.

I told him I spoke as a citizen of the world and the whole world was frightened of nuclear war. I then read to him a statement made by an eight-year-old girl, Rachel Conn: 'I know the big countries of the world think they have to have nuclear weapons to be strong, and that they think they have to have more nuclear weapons than the other countries or else they wouldn't be strong. I think it would be better to be less strong than to blow up the world.'

He did not respond to this statement, but instead pulled from his pocket two sheets of paper: one a map of Oregon showing the concentric rings of destruction from a nuclear explosion, the other a map of the USA showing the location of nuclear weapons facilities. 'These are handed out to grade-school students in Oregon,' he told me, 'and I don't think children should be frightened like this.'

'Maybe not like that,' I said, 'but this is the reality of the world in which they live, and people pick up information from television anyway, as Rachel did.'

We left it there. I stood up, took President Reagan's hand and thanked him for his time.

It had been the most disconcerting hour and a quarter of my life. Reagan reminded me of the Peter Sellers role of Chauncey Gardner in the movie *Being There*, the character whose entire life experience came from watching TV and films. Certainly President Reagan had been unfailingly pleasant and courteous to me, but the last thing the world needed was a nice but totally uninformed old guy who might just decide to commit it to radioactive dust.

I left the White House hardly able to walk from shock and staggered back to the unreal world of my hotel: low lights, music, sophisticated people drinking at the bar. I felt like rushing up to them and saying, 'Do you know what I've just heard?' The media, who had gotten wind of the interview, were hungry for details and my impression of the president; nobody ever got close enough to question him at length. (I later discovered that my interview with Reagan was longer than any other person's during his eight years in office, including members of his staff; even his close friend and confidant Don Regan had never had an extended period alone with him.)

Because I had promised the president I would not talk to the press, I said nothing, until one reporter got under my guard and asked for an informal, off-the-record background briefing. I gave him one, which he promptly published. I was furious, but could do nothing about this. When I wrote to Reagan apologising for this breach of etiquette, I received a handwritten reply, saying he understood and that once upon a time the press had been gentlemen, but now they could no longer be trusted.

At ten the following morning I rang Patti to speak to her. I asked if the president was up yet, and she said, 'No, I've just been down to the family quarters and there's no sign of movement.' I couldn't believe it. Not up by ten in the morning, with the working day over at four in the afternoon? The President of the United States?

Later I met an employee of the State Department who had been asked to write a brief on the countries of Central America for Reagan to study before he went there. The man told me he showed the paper to his nine-year-old son, who said he understood it. Then he sent the paper off to the White House. It was returned with a note: 'Too complex, please simplify.'

In spite of my depressing conversation with President Reagan, in spite of the opposition to the freeze movement that he expressed on behalf of conservative forces, our work came to fruition on 4 May 1983. The freeze resolution went back to Congress for the second time, and Congress voted 278–149 to pass a non-binding resolution calling on Reagan to negotiate a mutual and verifiable freeze and to reduce the number of nuclear weapons.

CHAPTER 21

Humanity was almost converted to radioactive dust in 1983, the year I saw President Reagan and the year that Congress endorsed the freeze. During a belligerent NATO exercise when US fighter planes were buzzing Soviet nuclear facilities in Eastern Europe, the Russians decided that the exercise was for real and the Americans were about to strike, so they decided to go first. A double KGB-CIA agent in London who heard of the impending attack contacted Prime Minister Thatcher, who then called Reagan and woke him in the middle of the night with the news. Luckily he had the sense to abort the exercise, and nuclear war was averted.

My intuition about the probabilty of nuclear war had therefore been accurate. Some people called me a fanatic, but fanaticism is appropriate when life on earth is in the balance.

We knew PSR was really hitting the big time when Edward Teller attacked us. This world-famous physicist, the father of the hydrogen bomb, was the man who persuaded President Reagan to initiate the Star Wars program. In the *American Medical News* of 30 July 1982 he was quoted from a lengthy interview.

> Who are these physicians who call themselves Physicians for Social Responsibility? Does that mean that all other physicians not belonging to this small group are not responsibile? . . . The so-called Physicians for Social Responsibility are, in fact, highly irresponsible. The only way to prevent nuclear war is for America to regain its nuclear strength so that the Soviets will not be tempted to strike. The actions of the dove, of the people of peace, will cause war, not prevent war.
>
> We are now in a period of danger and during the next ten to twenty years that danger will become exceedingly great. We must arm a strong America to extend the period in which the Soviet leadership must hesitate . . . The medical profession can make an enormous contribution if only it can help cure this nation of its tragic neurosis—the neurosis that 'a nuclear war is unthinkable'. If we accept the myth that a nuclear war is unthinkable, then we will not think about it and we will not do anything about it. The danger to our way of life will grow greater every month.

What a feather in our cap! It was akin to being on Nixon's Black List.

Amazingly, by the end of 1983 every single medical organisation and society in the country had passed resolutions against nuclear war. And by the end of 1982 PSR had gleaned $1.5 million from direct mailing, my fund-raising at parties and meetings, and charitable foundations.

We appointed a great new executive director, Tom Halsted, formerly of the Arms Control and Disarmament Agency, who then persuaded us to employ Jane Wales, a Carter administration deputy assistant secretary of state and White House coordinator of public liaison, to run a Washington PSR office and to lobby congressional staff and members. Jane was in her mid-thirties, willowy and tall, with a dark complexion and smoldering brown eyes, and political savvy. It was so exciting to have a Washington office with ready access to Congress; Jane would be able to 'work' the Congress with alacrity.

Meanwhile PSR continued its meteoric ascent in the political, medical and scientific worlds. *Time* magazine described it as possibly the most effective group in the anti-nuclear movement. But trouble was brewing.

The second meeting of International Physicians for the Prevention of Nuclear War (IPPNW) was held in Cambridge, England, in April 1982 and was attended by 160 physicians from 31 countries. Several 'stars' were present, including Nobel laureates such as Willi Brandt, and the meeting looked extremely impressive. I was not asked to speak, except to chair a workshop on national organisations. I had grave misgivings about going at all, but I needed to know what was happening to the fledgling medical groups around the world.

I thought the conference very dull. Bernard Lown presided in a dictatorial fashion, and little attempt was made to gather together the various national groups in a democratic fashion to discuss their mutual political problems and share their goals and successes. The official PSR report on the meeting stated: 'There was a sense that PSR's identity was not clear to most European participants. No significant communication between Soviet physicians and other participants was observed.'

On the last night of the conference I was sitting on some stairs relaxing when several young Swedish doctors approached me and began discussing the Nobel Peace Prize. I asked warily, 'Has Lown been talking to you about Nobel Prizes?'

'Yes,' they said. 'Don't you think IPPNW deserves it?'

I was startled. Were they serious? How could we be eligible for a Nobel Prize when we hadn't caused the eradication of a single nuclear weapon and our educational work had just begun? As doctors, we were doing this work for humanity, not for Nobel Prizes. And Lown had done nothing in terms of education or activism except to hold two 'international' meetings. Most of the national groups had been started either directly because of Claire Ryle and me, or because they were emulating the successful PSR model.

On the other hand, the public profile of PSR continued to grow. In five short years we had become the eleventh largest medical organisation in the United States. I was now ready to use our influence as leaders of a 'revolution in thinking' to nail the military–industrial complex, to focus our efforts on the horror of Reagan's Star Wars agenda, and to mobilise grassroots support for the freeze and for bilateral nuclear disarmament. We had to go for it; our mission was becoming more urgent by the day. Now that we had definite political clout, we were ready to significantly influence the nuclear and militaristic thinking within the United States, NATO and indeed the USSR.

My speeches changed. It was no longer enough to move people to tears by describing the symptoms, the medical consequences of nuclear war. It was now time to examine the reasons why the world was in such a predicament. As doctors we were obliged to examine the causes of this nuclear disease. I therefore encouraged audiences to look at the relevant institutions that had created the nuclear monster. The military–industrial complex still reigned supreme, as did Reagan; *nothing* would change unless we focussed our attention upon these issues.

This approach threatened some people. While it was thoroughly acceptable to discuss the awful medical consequences of nuclear war, it was going a bit far to examine the reasons behind the nuclear build-up. Americans are a patriotic people who are generally loath to stand up and criticise their government. Ronald Reagan was probably the most popular president in US history. But I had met him, I'd read his fascinating and scary psychological history, and I considered it imperative that for their own safety, the American people understand the person they had put into the White House: a nice old man who didn't have a grip on things, someone whose Hollywood-inspired ideas of the world could lead the planet to destruction. I also began talking at length about the corporations that made nuclear weapons, as well as the dynamics of what was called the Iron Triangle—the corporations, the Pentagon and the Congress—and the revolving door through which people moved readily from one to the other.

I knew I was overstepping the bounds for some people, including a few of the doctors on the PSR executive. They didn't want to rock the boat. They worried that if we started to tell the truth about Reagan and the Pentagon, we would lose the support of our conservative colleagues; our newly acquired power would disappear, our funding would diminish and membership recruitment would cease. I ignored their fears: were they not aware that our membership drive was more successful than at any point in our history? I was the one who was recruiting the doctors and raising the funds and I refused to truckle to such fear-engendered conservatism.

The 1982 board meeting was held in Chicago in September, arranged by Richard Gardiner and his chapter. A new board was elected, mainly consisting of previous board members. Some of the old guard attended, including Bernard Lown. The atmosphere was unusually tense. However, the meeting reached unanimity on several important issues. We were vehemently opposed to the Reagan administration's policy of recruiting hospitals to support the Civilian Military Contingency Hospital System, mandating that hospitals be ready to treat the military casualties of nuclear war. For physicians to endorse these fantasy plans, we said, meant that we were endorsing plans for a global holocaust. Directors of some hospitals later accused of us abrogating our responsibilities as physicians and surgeons; one medical editorial that took this line was headed: 'Hell no, we won't sew.'

Jack Geiger, the Arthur C. Logan professor of community medicine at the City Hospital, New York, had been involved in our symposia for some time. He is a short man with an agitated manner, dark, balding hair and thick myopic glasses; he chain smokes and is very articulate. He always did the 'bombing run', describing the medical effects of a nuclear bomb dropping on whatever city in which he happened to be speaking. Jack wanted to be on the PSR board, but as we had just elected a new board, there was no room for him.

On the other hand, I knew the board could use his expertise, and I greatly respected his abilities as a speaker. After discussing the situation with him, I decided to step aside and give him my place on the board. This simply opened up one more seat on the board; I would still be PSR president, and an *ex officio* board member. I was pleased with this decision, but I thought it was strange that Jack never thanked me, assuming his seat on the board as if it belonged to him by right.

I continued to travel, but began to feel that things at PSR were not as they had been. Snippets of gossip and information filtered through indicating that the feeling of mutual respect and egalitarianism I had tried so hard to promote within the organisation and the board itself was being undermined. It seemed to me that Jack Geiger was constantly criticising the fund-raising work for which I was totally responsible, without offering to help, and I felt frustrated. He was a stickler for correct procedure and used 'Robert's Rules of Order' with élan; over time our meetings became a nightmare of rules and proposals, voting and agenda items, with little substance. A small army of subcommittees appeared. These events stifled open debate; spontaneity fast disappeared.

I was determined that nothing would impede the task at hand, and I continued to speak the truth. On one occasion Jack and I appeared together in California. The meeting took place in the cavernous foyer of a government building that housed the area's municipal offices. Hundreds of workers came out to hear us, hanging over the balconies and standing all the way down the stairs. I was very moved by this occasion and delighted to be working with Jack, whose articulateness I so greatly admired.

Trying for a light note, I introduced him by quoting some lines from the carol 'Good King Wenceslas': 'In his master's steps he trod. Where the snow lay dinted,' by which I meant that Jack was a kind of a mentor because he was so articulate and was one of the founders of the original PSR in the 1960s. As we drove away from the meeting, Pat Kingsley was upset. '*Never* say things like that about Jack. You're the person setting the pace, not Jack. Don't hand your power over to him and give him an opening.' I really had no idea what she was talking about. It had not consciously occurred to me that Jack would use his new position on the board to undermine me.

It was shortly after this episode that Brian Lord of *Nightline* scheduled me to appear on the show. The timing was bad: the announcement had just been made that cruise and Pershing II missiles had been deployed in Europe and, without having a chance to do the necessary homework in terms of numbers, I was pitted against Richard Burt of the State Department. From the start I was at a disadvantage. I had no idea exactly how many missiles were to be deployed; I understood only the strategic technologies of these weapons and their medical and ecological consequences.

This wasn't good enough for the anchor, Ted Koppel, who speedily showed the audience that Richard Burt had the figures and I did not. Burt was suave and self-assured; without this data I floundered about, discussing the psychological and medical effects of the arms race on our children. Koppel interrupted: 'Stop the emotion, let's talk about facts.'

If my wits had been about me, I would have replied, 'That's the kind of thinking that will kill us all,' but I didn't. I was feeling rather intimidated, so my mind was less agile than it could have been. After the show, as I lay on the back seat of a huge black limo en route to Philadelphia, where I was to speak at a Jewish temple the next day, I reviewed the interview with a sinking heart. How would my enemies at PSR react? I had a strong sense that they would use my performance on *Nightline* as ammunition against me.

I had heard tell that Jack implied that I was too emotional, that I was not a good lobbyist, and I was too political. These weren't new criticisms: I had heard them from others as well. There was no answer to them, really, except that the prospect of a nuclear war and the end of the world is a somewhat emotive issue. I was a darn good lobbyist, and it was now necessary to be political.

Jack also asserted that I made mistakes, that my data were not accurate. Yet I had frequently observed that he and his scientific colleagues also made mistakes when speaking, but I never held those against them: they were sometimes tired and they were human, just as I was. I often found that those who accused me of factual errors had not read the particular information I was quoting. To do this work, I kept up to date and read widely—two newspapers a day plus every significant book published on the subject—so I could effectively debate generals, defence officials, prime ministers and presidents. Credibility was imperative.

But constant travelling from city to city giving speeches every day produced exhaustion. Sometimes I was simply so tired that I would shortcut a certain train of logic and go from A to Z, falsely assuming that the audience would understand. Thus I produced confusion, and people sometimes thought that my facts were wrong. They were not. I was just tired. The only time I really did not know my stuff was during the *Nightline* debate with Richard Burt.

Things came to a head at an executive committee meeting on 3 November 1982 in Boston. I had arranged to leave in the middle to receive a peace award from the Massachusetts Audubon Society. Jack arrived late from New York on a cold night, irritable and testy. Almost immediately, he tabled a proposal to move the office of president downwards and laterally to the equivalent of the executive director—in other words, to substantially diminish the office.

I was shocked, as were the rest of the board. This was a really hostile act, directed solely at me. Everybody in the room understood and the meeting went very quiet. At a totally inauspicious time I had to vacate the chair to Richard Gardiner and leave to receive my award. I returned to the board meeting as soon as I decently could. The debate was acrimonious; fights broke out and the atmosphere became increasingly poisonous. Jack's proposal was argued back and forth. Most people on the committee didn't know how to react, and a few sided with Jack. His hostility was completely foreign to us.

It was devastating. PSR had always been such a happy group. To all of us who cared about it, it was much more than an organisation: it was a kind of surrogate family, whose members loved and trusted each other, working together with tremendous energy and creativity. And though Jack's plan was not accepted, and there was no formal vote, our trust in each other had been shattered, and we never recovered. The meeting ended at two a.m. Judy Lipton and Richard Gardiner stayed with me that night. Judy hugged me the next morning and wept. The organisation we had created was being destroyed.

Next day I had lunch with Tom Winship of the *Boston Globe.* I was clearly shaken, and after one look at me, he asked 'Have the men been getting to you?' It was almost as if he had been expecting this to happen.

Over the next few days I had a number of speaking engagements, ending with an address to a large Catholic conference in Minneapolis set up by the Archdiocese of Minnesota. After this speech, for the first time, I had time to analyse what had happened. Why was Jack Geiger so hostile? I rang Pat and poured out the whole story. She listened in silence. The first thing she said was: 'I think I'm responsible. I gave you all the publicity, and Jack is jealous.' I couldn't see how she was to blame and told her so, denying the possibility for myself as well. But in retrospect I can see she had a point.

When I put the phone down, I sat alone in that large Minneapolis hotel room and thought. Would Jack succeed next time? Would the executive committee really consider downgrading the position of president? I didn't know what the ramifications of Jack's attack on me would be, but I needed to do some lobbying.

I spent hundreds of dollars calling each executive member in turn: Jonathan Fine, Jennifer Leaning, Tom Winters, Henry Abraham and others. It was a demeaning experience. My colleagues were clearly confused; Jack's persuasive powers had obviously influenced them, and they didn't know whom to believe. I rang Bob Scrivener, my confidant at the Rockefeller Family Fund, and told him that PSR was experiencing problems. He was calm and reassuring. 'All organisations go through this,' he said. 'It's a reaction to rapid growth. You have been incredibly successful in a very short time. What you need is a diagnostic management team to come in and assess the problem.' When Bob told me it would cost $27 000, money that PSR didn't have, I balked. He said, 'We'll pay for it.' He advised us to use the Planning and Management Assistance Project, a Washington-based firm run by Susan Gross and her partner Karl Mathiason.

In January 1983 PSR held its annual general meeting and board meeting in San Francisco. It soon became clear that Jack had done a great deal of intensive lobbying: a majority of Geiger supporters were elected to the board. I looked around and knew I was in trouble. Though I had never taken Jack on publicly, I decided it was now or never. Rules of behaviour needed to be established. After the results had been announced, I said from the chair: 'There is to be no further backbiting and gossip, and that means you, Jack. There is to be only honest communication from now on.' He seemed to accept that proposition. People were shocked that I should castigate him in public, but they were also pleased.

There had been some difficulties between the executive committee and Tom Halsted, the executive director, and at that meeting he submitted his resignation. I felt bad for him, but thought his departure was inevitable. Jennifer Leaning, a tall, lithe, determined woman with a rather beautiful, sculptured face, who was a very competent emergency room physician at the Cambridge City Hospital, became acting executive director and took time off from her medical career to restore order to a chaotic office situation. The staff needed reassurance, financial matters were crying out for attention, and there was an increasing backlog of policy issues. Raine Lee, blonde-haired and sweet-tempered, was already on the PSR staff, and together with treasurer Sid Alexander, took over the finances.

Because I was so grateful for the work that Jennifer had done, I invited her to accompany me when I visited George F. Kennan at his Princeton University office on 4 January. Kennan, then a distinguished elder statesman in his eighties, and formerly ambassador to the Soviet Union, was a man of medium height, balding, who carried an air of gentle authority. During the 1940s, after the end of the war, he wrote a paper for the State Department under the pseudonym of 'X', which initiated the philosophy of containment of the Soviet Union. But in recent years he had become deeply concerned about the galloping nuclear arms race. He had just co-authored an article in *Foreign Affairs* magazine arguing that the security needs of NATO would be better served with a policy of 'no first use' of nuclear weapons, directly contradicting the belligerent US policy. I wanted his support for a five-year plan I had devised for bilateral nuclear disarmament with the Soviet Union in response to Reagan's new five-year plan for 'rearming' America.

The meeting went very well: Kennan agreed to consider supporting the proposal, and Jennifer was enthusiastic and impressed. However, on the way home in the car she attempted to persuade me that a fellow by the name of Irwin Redlenner should be the new PSR chairman. Warning bells went off: Redlenner, a paediatrician, was a relative newcomer to the executive committee and was closely aligned to Geiger. It suddenly became clear to me where Jennifer now stood. Oh Gawd!

A month later the executive committee considered my proposal to initiate a diagnostic review of PSR by Scrivener's Planning and Management Assistance Project. People felt that the last few committee meetings had constituted a kind of bloodletting, that the acute organisational chaos was over and emotional rifts were now healing; we had weathered the trauma and were now recovering, and there was no point in unearthing more problems. Jack Geiger strongly opposed the idea. However, I felt it was important to investigate the dynamics still operating within the executive committee and at board level. In the end I prevailed.

This meeting also discussed allotting Irwin Redlenner, newly elected, the sum of $15 000 to chair the meetings, which seemed entirely inappropriate—none of us ever received money for our work, it was a labour of love. Jack and his supporters were strongly in favour; clearly they had cooked up the plan with Irwin before the meeting. The vote passed.

Jane Wales in the Washington office was firing on all cylinders: PSR was becoming an effective lobbying group on legislation related to nuclear weapons and the arms budget. Individual congressional representatives vote according to their consciences or in response to pressure from their constituents or lobbyists in the American system, not along party lines as in Australia, which provides far more latitude to achieve a particular policy.

As our power and influence grew, I presented the executive committee with enthusiastic reports about my appearances and meetings. For example, a debate with Richard Perle at the American Newspaper Editors Association, an upcoming meeting with Congressman Ed Markey, a meeting with Admiral Noel Gaylor and Sargent Shriver in the Watergate complex to further discuss our five-year plan for bilateral disarmament, a debate with Edward Teller and an address to the National Press Club in Washington. But this produced discomfort. Jack and his followers decided that my National Press Club speech and all other speeches should be vetted and written by the PSR executive. They said that as president of PSR I spoke for the membership, and so everything I said should be checked. The organisation should be seen to use its power wisely, they said. I flatly refused to consider such a thing. 'You clip my wings and I'll flee.' At a time when our power and prestige were at their peak, why would they think to inhibit the very thing that had provided such success? My speeches had always been extempore; written words never have the power of a spontaneous call to action.

My mouth was watering in anticipation of the Perle debate. Assistant secretary of defense and one of the architects of Reagan's aggressive nuclear strategy, Perle had been named the 'prince of darkness' by his colleagues in the Pentagon. I later discovered that while Bill and I were away on speaking tour of Australia in April, Jack had expressed doubts about the Perle debate to the executive. He reiterated that the executive committee needed to review what I said, and Jane Wales pointed out that the issue was whether anyone in PSR should become embroiled in a detailed debate on the technical aspects of strategic nuclear weapons. In other words, they thought I should confine my remarks to the medical effects of nuclear war.

The debate format was cooked up by Tom Winship and me. He initially suggested Teller, but I preferred Perle, who would be much more of a challenge. He wouldn't have a leg to stand on when overwhelmed by the medical data relating to a nuclear attack. In the event Perle cancelled, and his replacement was his deputy, who was a pushover. If Perle was scared to debate me, what was PSR so nervous about? Clearly it wasn't nervousness; the internal debate was about power and control.

Jennifer Leaning was about to return to her medical job after a noble effort, so we now needed a permanent executive director. After an intensive search, we decided that Jane Wales would be perfect. Her political and lobbying skills were impeccable, she was efficient, and she was very smart. There was hesitation among some of the members, but I pushed hard for her and won.

Problems of philosophy continued to plague us. The March executive committee meeting turned into a disturbing discussion about our fundamental approach towards nuclear weapons. We needed to formalise our support for the notion of complete bilateral elimination—the correct attitude, I felt, for a group of doctors whose job it was to save lives. Jack Geiger and several supporters disagreed—the political climate was too conservative for such a radical proposal. Jack used his persuasive powers to steer the debate, and in the end the executive committee voted to abstain from supporting abolition. I was distressed, and insisted that we were jettisoning our principles.

Meanwhile, other PSR members were also entering the public arena. Jack Geiger had been to Nuremberg, West Germany; Irwin Redlenner had been working with Peter Watkins, the English writer and director of the influential anti-nuclear movie *The War Game* to develop another documentary on the same theme; Jennifer Leaning was addressing various bodies on anti-nuclear issues.

One of the many highlights for me in the first half of 1983 was my debate with Edward Teller at Clemson University in South Carolina. When I was initially approached by the college, I agreed to debate him only if I had the last word. But Teller had apparently not been told he was to confront me in a public format, and his fury knew no bounds when he learned this on arrival at the airport. He informed his hosts that he would not participate unless he could be the last speaker. An hour before the televised debate, the four participants—Admiral Gene LaRoque and I, Edward Teller and actor Charlton Heston—met with the college officials in the boardroom at Teller's instigation.

Teller was belligerent, saying that he would go to the press and destroy the university publicly if he was not given the final word. I insisted on my initial contract, remembering clearly Teller's brutal treatment and destruction of his former colleague Robert Oppenheimer. Clearly he always got his way through such tactics, and he wasn't going to treat me like that; furthermore, I'm a woman. Teller grew more and more nasty, I held firm, and the poor college officials were almost sliding under the table. After thirty minutes of intense intimidation from Teller, I thought, 'Damn, it's only a debate,' and capitulated as gracefully as possible. The college president was so relieved that he almost hugged me.

The televised debate began before an audience of college students and faculty members, and proceeded along well-travelled lines. Teller enumerated what he saw as the strategic disadvantages of the United States versus the Soviet Union in nuclear terms; I marshalled facts and figures to prove that his argument was nonsense in medical terms. Gene LaRoque backed me up strongly. Charlton Heston turned out to be a hard-line hawk who, I think, would have blown up the Soviet Union given half a chance. I found it difficult to get past the sonorous, Moses-like voice he assumed, presumably to maximise his credibility. Judging by audience reaction, Gene and I prevailed. This gave me great satisfaction, particularly as we were facing an intrinsically conservative Southern audience.

Several days later, at the instigation of a local Methodist minister, I flew to Omaha to visit the Strategic Air Command base. The first thing that amazed me was their motto, 'Peace is Our Profession', arching over the entrance gate, a wonderful example of Orwellian doublespeak. I was very much looking forward to seeing the control centre and the B52s, but wasn't allowed anywhere near that stuff, although public tours are marched through there every day. I think they considered me too dangerous. Instead, I was whisked away and given two briefings. One compared the American and Soviet arsenals, pointing out the deficiencies of the United States in practically all weapons and equipment; the other involved the Air Force's interpretation of the nuclear freeze, which was similar to the demeaning analysis of President Reagan. It was humiliating to have to sit through such a mass of lies and half truths. But as I asked penetrating and difficult questions, more and more officers wearing medal-covered uniforms quietly slipped through the doorway and sat on chairs lining the walls. I felt as if I was being surrounded, and asked my minister friend why this had happened. He replied, 'There is safety in numbers.'

Then I was taken up to see the commander-in-chief, General Bennie L. Davis. His office was straight out of *Dr Strangelove*, with tall models of missiles adorning every table. I assumed a pleasant demeanour, but gave him as good as I got, answering his veiled hostile statements with a great deal of data. At the end I asked him if he had grandchildren. He stopped and said, 'Yes.' 'How old?' I asked, and he said softly, 'Two and six months.' That cracked his aggressive pose; we shook hands and I left.

Later I read that General Davis had testified before Congress, reassuring people that the American strategy was not one of mutual assured destruction (MAD), but was now counterforce and first-strike nuclear war—in other words, winnable nuclear war. I knew that he was difficult, but had I known his posture on these issues. I would have moved in even more strongly.

CHAPTER 22

In April 1983 we arrived in New Zealand after a never-ending flight that brought on severe jet lag and were met at the Auckland airport by some kindly people who drove us to their house in the hills, where they plied us with homemade bread, home-grown tomatoes, lettuce and eggs. Then they beetled off and left us with their house for the night. The time was two p.m. Bill and I looked at each other and said, 'Let's just lie down for a couple of minutes.'

That was it; we woke sixteen hours later on top of the blankets in the same positions in which we had gone to sleep. I asked, 'What do you want for breakfast?' and he said, 'The lot.' So I cooked up a feast of bacon, sausages, eggs, tomatoes, toast and marmalade—rarely had we been so hungry. Then we were ready to take New Zealand by storm.

We started on the southern tip of the south island, Bill working one side and I the other, speaking in every little town and city all the way up. Then we repeated the exercise in the north island, culminating in two huge public meetings, one in Wellington, which sits on a beautiful harbour, and one in the YWCA hall in Auckland—a light, airy, hilly city with charming old wooden houses and an old-fashioned feel to the place.

One of the most recent chapters of IPPNW had been formed in New Zealand, and this group together with the New Zealand Peace Foundation ably organised the tour. The New Zealand doctors were more effective than the Australian group and were well led by the president, Derek North, professor of medicine at Auckland Medical School and by Dr Ian Prior, a ball of energy from Wellington. Derek pumped me for information about the arms race, so I gave him lists of books to read. He is a good-looking, quiet, forceful man with tremendous authority and he endowed the New Zealand IPPNW with great credibility.

These two groups worked us to the bone. I don't think I've ever been so tired, a combination of jet lag, burnout, hard work and sleep deficit. Apparently, before we arrived, the Peace Foundation had trouble convincing the media that we were newsworthy, but the advantageous publicity surrounding *If You Love This Planet*, which had just been nominated for an Academy Award, certainly helped. The trip lasted ten days and was a great success. In Wellington I briefed a parliamentary committee on the strategic risks of nuclear war, and all over the country we spoke at media conferences, at receptions for local MPs, for trade unionists and church workers, as well as for the New Zealand IPPNW doctors. As we moved north, the media coverage reached saturation point, and several of our TV interviews were saved and rebroadcast weeks later.

The ANZUS Treaty (formed from the initial letters of its three signatories: Australia, New Zealand and the United States, and uniting the three countries in foreign policy and military strategies) forced Australia and New Zealand to accept American nuclear-armed and nuclear-powered ships into their ports. Following the 1975 defeat of New Zealand's anti-nuclear Labour government, the conservative National Party government allowed port access of US nuclear-powered ships every fifteen months. Public disapproval had been swift and effective: New Zealand, being a small nation, can readily mobilise demonstrations. American nuclear submarines had been attacked by peace boats; one young man, armed with a bucket of yellow paint, even had the temerity to mount a submarine and convert it into a 'yellow submarine'. By May 1982 the USS *Truxton* had been attacked by several dozen Peace Squadron boats in Auckland Harbour, supported by 1000 marchers; in August 1983, some months after our visit, 120 Peace Squadron boats launched a direct confrontation against another nuclear ship, and 6000 Aucklanders took to the streets in their lunch hour.

Our visit proved to be very important for the New Zealand anti-nuclear movement; after we left, concerned people mobilised in renewed and hugely effective protests. For instance, in solidarity with the International Women's Peace Day of Action for Nuclear Disarmament, spearheaded by the Greenham Common women's peace camp in England on 24 May, 25 000 women, the largest gathering of women in the history of New Zealand, marched up Queen Street, Auckland. On that same day women in Wellington circled the Department of Defence, and similar scenes were repeated throughout the country. The women of New Zealand were magnificent; they showed themselves to be strong, uncompromising and fiercely principled.

Finally, in June 1984 Marilyn Waring, a member of the ruling National Party, crossed the House floor to vote with the opposition on an anti-nuclear motion, bringing down the government and precipitating a federal election, which was won on 14 July by the anti-nuclear Labour Party. One of this party's first actions was to ban all nuclear ships from New Zealand ports. This meant a confrontation with the United States, who promptly removed New Zealand from the ANZUS

Treaty, theoretically excluding that country from US protection in the event of war.

In response, the new prime minister, David Lange, said, 'New Zealand cannot live easily in a region that has become the cockpit of superpower confrontation, and Labour does not want nuclear powers playing war games in Pacific waters ... exclusion of nuclear weapons is not an unfriendly gesture towards any nuclear power; rather 'exclusion' is an unfriendly gesture towards nuclear weapons.' He also said, 'We refuse to sit in the dress circle of the nuclear theatre.' Courageous words—what a pity an Australian leader has never had the courage to speak them.

From New Zealand Bill and I went on to Australia to be reunited with our two elder children. Philip and Penny had left the States for Australia after graduating from high school, and before long Philip wrote to us; 'I've fallen in love with this country, and I'm never coming back.' He bummed around for a while; Penny found herself selling clothes in Sportsgirl. She hated having to look busy arranging and rearranging clothes on the racks as the hours dragged by. 'I've left everything and come to nothing,' she wrote to us, and added she had consoled herself by eating chocolate and drinking Coke, gaining seven kilos. She's a skinny girl and I couldn't imagine what she looked like then.

At the beginning of 1983, however, Penny and Phil had both been accepted at the University of Sydney, Phil to do arts-law and Penny to study for an arts degree in maths, government, biology and psychology. One of the masters at Wesley College, attached to the university, arranged for them to live in residency, and during our Sydney visit Bill and I stayed there as well. I was delighted to see that both Penny and Philip seemed to be enjoying college life.

Bill and I gave speeches at a formal Wesley College dinner,

the students dressed in typical English-style black undergraduate gowns, seated side by side at long refectory tables. The speeches were okay, but we were very tired. When some smart-ass students spent the whole night outside our room making sounds like descending rockets and exploding bombs, we were too weary to get out of bed and blast them—the little buggers.

The Australian tour was less spectacular than New Zealand's, though we spoke at anti-nuclear seminars and meetings all over the country. Initially this trip was financially supported by the Australian Council of Trade Unions under the banner of the Amalgamated Metal Workers' Union, whose boss, Laurie Carmichael, had been a staunch anti-nuclear supporter from the beginning. However, just before we left the States, Laurie pulled the funding. From that time on I had grave doubts about his fundamental commitment to our cause, and we decided to fund this part of the trip ourselves.

It was at a press conference in the Sydney Town Hall that an ABC radio reporter led me into a small, dark room and said, 'How would you feel if you won an Academy Award?' I had no idea what he was talking about. This is how, in typical low-key Aussie fashion, I learned that *If You Love This Planet* had won an Oscar. The award attracted surprisingly little publicity in Australia; only Canada celebrated the event (which was not surprising, as the film had been made by the National Film Board of Canada).

Our return to the United States signalled more turmoil at PSR. Apart from receiving honorary degress from the Medical College of Pennsylvania and the Universities of Massachusetts and Notre Dame, there was precious little joy in the next few months.

In June 1983 Susan Gross and Karl Mathiason, the directors of the Planning and Management Assistance Project, invited me to Washington to talk about their report on PSR. I was quite excited about the prospect. They took me to a Japanese restaurant for lunch. We started off with small talk. Then, with tears running down her cheeks, Susan suddenly said, 'You are too important a leader in the peace movement to have to endure attacks from Jack Geiger. You should leave PSR.' I was stunned. Never did I expect that this would be the conclusion they would reach. Rather, I thought they would give an objective analysis of the players in the power struggle and help us to understand it so we could move ahead with increased harmony. Furthermore, if Jack was the attacker why shouldn't he be the one to leave?

But I was so bamboozled by this stage that I wasn't thinking clearly. In retrospect, I realise that I need not have accepted the report, with which I disagreed. But my ability to analyse, let alone act on my best instincts, was by that time severely depleted. I moved like an automaton, hardly in control, certainly not acting as a mature adult.

Here was my Waterloo. Ironically, without my insistence that the executive committee cooperate with the investigation, we would not have reached this crisis. Better that I had let sleeping dogs lie. I later heard that Jack had told Susan, 'I have the numbers,' meaning that he had the majority of the board on his side. Knowing that, the thrust of her report was to accept the status quo.

The report was detailed, but flawed in its logic. It said that our organisation was like an adolescent that needed to stretch its wings and escape from its mother—me, presumably. Up to this point, it said, I had done all the fund-raising and recruitment of new members, but now other directors of the board needed to step in and take some responsibility. That point was absolutely true. I had been encouragingin g this approach for some time.

There were many more suggestions, but fundamentally Susan's message was clear. PSR now needed a new president. The report talked about me: 'Her vision, her creativity, her commitment, her ability to inspire and activate, her brilliant intuitive sense of strategy and her drive to achieve what at first seems impossible have been a key factor in the organisation's success and a major reason why the organisation has come so far so quickly.' But, it added: 'In any organisation's life a point is reached where a charismatic leader can become overpowering rather than empowering.' I did not agree with this conclusion. The board had been working brilliantly together; PSR had been in the midst of its biggest growth period just as Jack arrived on the scene. Clearly the report did not reflect the true state of affairs.

Susan acknowledged that I had operated as PSR's chief executive, really pulling the executive committee, the board and the staff along behind me. 'It is essential for the president to see his or her job as not only leading the way in speaking out, but inspiring, encouraging and enabling other doctors to exercise leadership and become spokespersons for PSR on this issue too,' said the report.

> Indeed, we see as part of the president's role not only serving as PSR's ambassador to the medical profession, the media, policy and opinion makers and the public at large, but serving as a statesman to PSR's own chapters and members. Regular presidential contact with the chapters may in fact be one of the keys to their feeling a greater sense of connectedness and recognition within the institution, and it would probably also be a great boost to their membership recruitment and retention.

This, in fact, had been precisely my own philosophy from the beginning. I made regular visits to the chapters. But I was only one human being, and I couldn't be everywhere all the time, so that inevitably some of the chapters may have felt out of touch. I can see now that my enormous energy and staying power was in a way a handicap, because although I encouraged the others to accept responsibility, they were content for the most part to let me do the work.

The Gross report added that frequently, charismatic

leaders' contributions to the growth and development of an organisation are not acknowledged, and the members resist them and rebel against them as part of the separation process. Yet I continued to feel that if Jack Geiger had not sown seeds of doubt, most members of the board would have supported me. I carried a huge load, not just for PSR but for the freeze, WAND, the international anti-nuclear movement, and my family. Some sympathy or even empathy would have been therapeutic for us all. But love, mutual support and honesty had long gone from PSR. The dynamics of power and control now held sway.

The tension that had built up over the last few months become almost unbearable. I could have coped with the exhaustion associated with constant travelling and speech giving, but when I was under attack from my own people, my surrogate family, I started to fall apart. I became ill and developed difficulty swallowing solid food, a condition called dysphagia; I lost weight.

On the day of the annual board meeting, I sat in the corner of the ferry terminal on Boston Harbour, knowing that I was about to participate in my own execution. The ferry transported me to Thompson Island, a retreat in the middle of the harbour, where I chaired the meeting like an automaton, waiting only for discussion on the Gross report. Finally the moment came. After Susan presented it, the board seemed acutely uncomfortable. They accepted the report passively, reluctant to enter into any deeper discussions. Aware that a lot was going on below the surface, I broke the silence. Looking in turn at each of the eighteen board members, I said, 'Truth and honesty are the most important aspects of communication. None of you has ever said what you think about me and how we have come to this end.' And I invited them to say what they thought, in turn, round the table.

They were dreadfully embarrassed. Most of them stumbled through poorly rehearsed and ill-thought-out reasons why I should leave PSR. I had heard them before—I was too emotional, sometimes my data were inaccurate, I was not a good lobbyist, arguments that echoed Jack's stated objections; others had clearly been swept along on the tide of recrimination and didn't really know what they thought. Only one board member actively supported me. Judy Lipton said, 'Helen has laboured under the burden of organisational responsibility, and now it is important to see whether we can move with her at her pace. If we did, PSR would be immeasurably strengthened.' I was grateful for Judy's words, but it was clear to me that the mandate of the board had disappeared. Under these circumstances I had only one option. I resigned as president.

I disagreed strongly with the report. Judy was right. It was not time for me to move on; I'd just been re-elected president unanimously by the board. Furthermore, PSR was at the height of its political power, and we were about to fly. The dynamics had nothing to do with a disorganised group, but with the jealousy of one man, and a general timidity about the political power we could now wield. I remember at one previous board meeting Peter Joseph said tentatively, 'Now we are so powerful, we must be very careful,' to which I replied, 'Now we are so powerful, we can really go for it.'

I was shattered. The organisation I had created with such fervour and excitement had been taken from me, and I was left without purpose. I could cope with, and indeed expected, attacks from the CIA, but not from those with whom I worked. We were supposed to be on the cutting edge of the peace movement, but had ourselves been torn apart by strife and internecine intrigue. What an irony.

What disheartened me most was that many of the people once dear to me had sided with Jack and his cohorts. The 'old guard' also supported Jack, and those who disagreed kept quiet. None of our 30 000 rank-and-file members knew what was happening. If I had had my wits and fighting spirit about me, I could have written to each of them and said, 'It's

Geiger or me,' and there would have been no competition. But I was in too much despair. The only board members who showed signs of outrage at what had happened were Richard Gardiner and Judy Lipton, both of whom left PSR shortly afterwards. They were my only allies.

On 19 September I stood in my pink and lime green kitchen chairing another PSR board meeting, which would replace me as president. My heart sank as the operator connected the eighteen board members from around the country. They elected Sid Alexander, a nice, malleable guy who made no waves. The execution was complete.

At one point during the lengthy discussion I said, 'It's not clear how choosing a more conservative president for PSR will affect membership growth, and it's not clear that a more conservative membership will allow PSR to assume the critical role for which it is cast in the crucial year ahead. It is a marked advantage to have a president who could appeal to the press and the public; at this point Sid Alexander is not known.' My pleas fell on deaf ears. But 1984 was a presidential election year: if Reagan was re-elected, the United States and the world were in serious trouble. PSR was in an extraordinarily influential position to start educating the population about the Iron Triangle and the dynamics of Reagan's nuclear policies. We were entering a very dangerous period. Another four years of Reagan would be a disaster.

Two weeks after the PSR board meeting, the annual IPPNW general meeting was held in Holland, but I was too disconsolate, too grief-stricken, to attend.

I had intended to take part in the next PSR board meeting in September but decided I couldn't face it, so I rang from a distant airport to offer my apologies.

Jane Wales held a farewell dinner for me in a slap-up hotel in Washington, DC towards the end of the year. Congresspeople, admirals and other public figures gave me extremely complimentary plaudits. None of the board members made a speech; Jack sat at the back of the room looking as if he would like to fade into the wallpaper. It was the strangest affair: it was an excellent fund-raiser for PSR, but at the same time I felt as if I were being bought off with nice speeches by people who had no idea why I was resigning as president. I wore a beautiful long dress in burgundy silk with an embroidered jacket. There was dancing at the end of the dinner and I took off the jacket and danced with an abandon that said: 'I don't give a damn what any of you think.' I felt as if I were dancing on my own grave. My dear Pat, loyal as ever, came from Los Angeles; when I went to her room to see her after the show was over, she looked how I felt.

At the beginning of 1984 I resigned from the board of directors. My letter of resignation said, in part:

> [F]or the past two years the board has become relatively nonproductive—mired in bureaucracy, bickering and ill will. Above all, honesty was lost, with resultant destruction of the original structures. This dynamic was due in large part to a negative influence displayed by some of its most powerful members.
>
> Unfortunately, this negativity has also impeded the function of the executive committee for a similar length of time. These dynamics, which six months ago forced me to resign as president, now prevent me from playing a constructive role on the board.
>
> ... I worry about the lack of inspirational guidance and leadership from the top. Without dynamic leadership addressing the real problems, the crucial issues will pass us by and we will become extinct by failure to evolve. I would suggest that you all consider clearly where you want PSR to go and the best way to achieve these goals.
>
> I think our work is only one-third complete. Indeed we taught the American media that nuclear war will be 'bad for their health' but these same elements have no comprehension of the new generation of missiles, C3I [command control, communication and intelligence, a complex system whereby the Pentagon had the world wired up for nuclear war], the Iron

Triangle and the dynamics of the Reagan administration.

In no way do I wish to sever my relationship with PSR. I am proud to be President Emeritus. I will always be available for consultation, grand rounds, etc., and should the internal dynamics of the board change, I would welcome re-election to the board of directors.

I write you this letter because we have an enormous lesson to learn from this experience—as goes PSR, so goes the world . . . if we cannot work together in an honest environment peacefully and creatively to save the world, who will? Our social responsibility is to be the example.

I salute you with deep respect and love and I wish you strength, goodwill and inspiration for the future. You have a huge responsibility.

I received no reply to this letter. The only feedback came from Jane Wales, who reported the board's reaction; 'That letter didn't do you any good.'

I didn't write it to do myself 'good', merely to state the truth. My frustration was intense. I believe to this day that if I had stayed to push for a more radical approach and circumstances had been different, we would by now be well on the way to bilateral nuclear disarmament. As it is, despite the end of the Cold War, very few bombs have been decommissioned. The missiles are in the process of being dismantled, certainly, but at the instigation of the United States, most American bombs are merely being placed in storage for possible future use. Meanwhile, the Pentagon is in Russia decommissioning Russian bombs—what an opportunity to eradicate nuclear weapons!

PSR had been infiltrated by the FBI some time before my resignation; under the Freedom of Information legislation we obtained a copy of the informer's report. But it did us little good: almost all the relevant words had been blacked out. To this day I don't know the identity of the infiltrator.

Shortly after I left, a revised history of PSR was sent to its members, its author anonymous, stating that the movement began in 1961, founded by Lown, Geiger, Seidel and Alexander, and had been in continuous operation ever since. I was not a part of the revisited history, and neither were most of the other people who had done the pioneering work of the new PSR. It's important to note that the creative work of this new organisation was done by a handful of people. This is true of most great achievements. I was away when this document was delivered to our house, but Bill was so infuriated he wrote several letters to the board in protest.

In retrospect I see that betrayal was the name of the game. It crept up slowly and surely over several years, and I seemed powerless to stop it. I was attacked from the rear, and I was defenceless. The paradox was that if I'd learned to be devious (something I tried to do), I'd have lost my openness, naïveté and optimism and belief that everyone is basically good—the qualities that made me a good leader. Instead I lost the organisation I led, precisely because I couldn't learn to be devious.

Even so, I eventually dropped out of the work because I was devastated that dishonest dynamics could operate within one of the leading peace organisations of the country, and the effective tool I had helped create to move the world towards disarmament had been kidnapped from under my wing. It took me many years to recover from this insult, but I was helped somewhat when reading Carl Jung's *Man and his Symbols* to discover that archetypal leaders are always betrayed or destroyed.

I knew that Bernard Lown was promoting IPPNW for the Nobel Peace Prize; in 1984 Linus Pauling told me that he had nominated me. I had already expressed my view that seeking acclaim like this was an abrogation of our goals, since we had not caused the decommissioning of a single nuclear weapon. I naturally assumed that the Nobel committee would do its work thoroughly, investigate the dynamics of the international physicians' movement and come to the same conclusion.

Bernard Lown claimed over one million members for IPPNW because the Russians said that every doctor in the Soviet Union was automatically a member. This was specious; PSR claimed the largest national membership, about 30 000 members, some 7000 of whom were associates (not medicos). The Canadian medical group, which patterned itself after PSR, claimed thousands of members, while other countries contributed much smaller numbers to the IPPNW whole. However, the Soviet doctors did have some influence. They invited three American doctors—Jim Muller, Bernard Lown and John Pastore—to speak uncensored on prime-time Soviet television for an hour, complete with interpreters, to discuss the medical implicatons of nuclear war. This program was replayed several times. A vast audience watched, including Mikhail Gorbachev, then minister of agriculture. When he assumed the presidency of the Soviet Union in 1985, he moved to end the Cold War because of his real fear of nuclear war. His attitude was undoubtedly influenced by what the American doctors had said, and I salute Jim Muller and Bernard Lown for making this possible.

The 1985 IPPNW conference was to be held in Budapest. I was attending as a visitor, with Philip and Bill; Penny was now a medical student (after one year in arts at the University of Sydney, she had been accepted to study medicine at the University of Newcastle) and a delegate to the conference. I attended one uncomfortable plenary session where Victor Sidel gave the now revised history of PSR.

I had been asked by organiser Dr Susan Hollan to give a speech. It was to be in a hall at some distance from the conference hotel, along winding lanes and roads. Nevertheless, the word got around, and the place was packed. I was introduced by Dr Henry Abraham, who, though he acknowledged my skill as an orator, studiously avoided any mention of the history of the physicians movement. Something was fishy!

I launched into a powerful speech about the arms race, Star Wars, C3I and the newly emerging nuclear technology, which was greeted by a prolonged standing ovation. Several members of the German delegation rushed up asking if I could open the Cologne conference the following year. I cautiously agreed, warning that Lown was unlikely to sanction the idea.

I revisited Germany several months later, but instead of showing its initial enthusiasm, the IPPNW delegation had cooled off. Lown had clearly advised against me as the keynote speaker in Cologne, and they were now too embarrassed to look me in the eye. What surprised me was that deep in their hearts these men knew the truth, and that their initial impulse had been correct.

After Budapest, Bill and I were invited to tour Ireland by Dr Mary Dunphy, president of the Irish Medical Association Against Nuclear War. Mary was a petite attractive woman who wore very high-heeled shoes and who often was accompanied by her husband, Sean, and two young babies. On the morning we were to embark on the tour, Bill and I were waiting to be interviewed in a Dublin TV studio when the interviewer remarked vaguely, 'The Nobel Peace Prize has just been announced'. I pricked up my ears and asked, 'Who won it?' 'Some international group of doctors' was the reply. Lown had done it.

The Nobel ceremony was held later in 1985. I received a form letter from Lown, thanking me for my work and inviting me to attend. I didn't. I felt as if I had been kicked in the guts. Chasov and Lown as co-presidents accepted the medals, and Lown gave a speech calling for a test-ban treaty. I mourned the lost opportunity. I would have called for the bilateral elimination of weapons within the next five years and exposed the nefarious activities of the Reagan administration, which was spending more money on weapons than all past presidents combined. In other words, I would have emulated

Bishop Desmond Tutu, who, when he received his Nobel Peace Prize in 1984, blew the wickedness of the South African apartheid system apart in front of the whole world.

Looking back through the retrospectoscope, I can see that I learned many lessons from these traumatic events. True, I was to become depressed for several years because I had lost the tool I had created to prevent nuclear war, and the bifrontal attack, both within PSR and from IPPNW, was difficult to countenance at the time. But the whole saga was a prelude to an even more traumatic personal crisis from which I eventually recovered, learning much about life and myself. So these events were not the end, but the beginning of a new existence.

I learned that, to a degree, I had become arrogant, that I needed to encompass humility within the equation of my life—a difficult lesson to learn at any time, particularly for a physician. I learned that living life as a damaged victim is self destructive, and above all, I learned to recognise, understand and analyse human behaviour and motivation both in myself and in others. So in a strange way the actions of Lown and Geiger were gifts.

CHAPTER 23

One freezing Boston morning early in 1984, after my resignation from PSR, Bill and I were lying in bed together in the blue and green spare room, where we slept in the winter to save heating expenses, when he suddenly said that he was very depressed and had been so for several years. Sometimes, he said, he wanted to run away and yet was trapped because we had so many expenses and responsibilities. I had no idea that he felt this way.

Why shouldn't he feel depressed when his wife and the mother of his children was rarely at home? I can see now that I had been insensitive to his needs and to those of our relationship. It was true that I was impelled to do the work to which I felt I had been called, but it was also true that I enjoyed the notoriety and prestige that accompanied it. I ignored the price that Bill paid as I followed my calling, however noble it was. The urgency of the work should not,

I now realise, have offset my responsibilities to our family.

For eight years he had been conducting research on hypertension in a grim, yellow, isolated basement lab at Harvard while I rushed around the world, full of excitement and enthusiasm. The comparison between our two lifestyles could not have been more stark. Depression doesn't predispose to creative research, and Bill's real love had been teaching and running a vital radiology department. Night after night he stayed at home holding the fort with nobody to talk to, minding the children. I called him every day when I was away and we spoke at length, but that was poor compensation.

He finally decided to leave Children's Hospital and proffered his resignation. His colleagues were deeply shocked by his decision, not understanding how he could give up such a prestigious position on the faculty at Harvard. But Bill felt as free as a breeze. His department gave an elegant farewell dinner at a new Boston hotel, during which he made a very touching speech about the need to move on in life and the sense of freedom associated with finding one's true passion and separating from stale activities that cease to serve the soul. He also announced his intention to work full time in the peace movement because 1984 promised to be a strategic year in the history of the world.

I was deeply moved by Bill's decision. He was courageous to give up a prestigious job, although it was one that offered no satisfaction. Now he had time to work at something which inspired him. He threw his lot in with the national freeze campaign and with Women's Action for Nuclear Disarmament and we began to speak side by side at functions.

Although we had initially called WAND Women's Party for Survival (WPS), people kept assuring me that there was no room for a third party in the American political system. We also received calls from 'survivalists' who wanted to know how to survive a nuclear war by hiding in caves equipped with caches of food and guns. This was the antithesis of our goal, which was to create a huge grass-roots movement of dedicated women to pressure the government to initiate bilateral nuclear disarmament. So we changed the name.

At first we operated from the Cambridge home of Mary Beth Williams, mother of small children, an early enthusiast who became president. Then we sublet a small office in Watertown from PSR: as they got bigger and moved out, we moved in. We operated on a shoestring, even supplying our own toilet paper, soap and office supplies. Luckily an anonymous donor gave us a generous contribution that year to cover the rent.

Our first major event was a Women's Day march in Washington during the autumn of 1980. Diane Aronson, a dynamic volunteer, arranged transportation by bus and train, and 8000–10 000 people met at the Capitol and marched to Lafayette Square in front of the White House, where I gave a speech. The day was spectacularly successful and proved that the 'women's' concept had enormous potential. Since that day we have celebrated every Mother's Day, which was originally founded by Julia Ward Howe to commemorate the notion of peace, with a slap-up ball or elegant lunches in Boston to honour women who devoted themselves to the cause.

We experienced some difficult teething problems in the early days involving money and other things, but we were fortunate in the quality of the women who joined us. One was Sayre Sheldon, professor in English literature at Boston University, a tall and elegant woman with a patrician face and bearing. In a magazine article, she described her initial experience with WAND: 'We were a national organisation founded by one woman who went around the country sowing her message like a nuclear Johnny Appleseed, while here in Cambridge a handful of women were responsible for setting up a program to make effective activists out of all these converts.' She went on to say that the group was strong in energy, creativity and commitment but weak in experience, recognition and funds. She mentioned that it had a refreshing lack of

hierarchy and protocol, and that opinions and feelings were freely expressed.

I worked simultaneously with PSR and WAND through the early 1980s, promoting the latter at general public meetings, where I recruited men as well as women. The speeches I gave before medical audiences were entirely different from those for a general audience. Doctors appreciate hard data and no emotion, whereas one needs to use appropriate emotion before a general audience to keep them engaged and stimulated.

WAND grew rapidly, contributions and membership rolling in. By the mid-1980s the group had 125 chapters and 25 000 members—almost the same as PSR. The two grew in parallel. It was exciting to watch these two fledgling organisations develop such momentum and political dynamism. I found that women tended to be less confident than men when I suggested they become involved politically. When after they were fired up by a speech I suggested they run for Congress, they often backed away saying, 'Who, me?' And if their husbands or partners questioned their grip on the subject, they tended to drop the idea for the sake of domestic harmony.

We equipped ourselves with computers, published newslet ters, hired a field director and turned ourselves into a lobby group. We trained women to speak publicly, to develop their confidence and express their passion about nuclear war. They desperately needed information concerning the arcane statistics and data relevant to the arms race, so we prepared a series of fact sheets. Two of our members wrote a manual on lobbying, and we also made a lobbying video featuring Republican Congresswoman Claudine Schneider and Democratic Congressman Nick Mavroulis. We established a direct mail campaign, which like PSR's was extremely effective. Within several years we were collecting $1.5 million per year, about the same as PSR—not bad for a non-profit organisation. Contributions large and small arrived from thousands of people, as well as from foundations. WAND hired staff, as did PSR, but I never asked for nor received a salary from either. Along with thousands of other women, my contribution was only to do the work, though I was lucky enough to be compensated with honoraria for some of my speeches. This money helped defray the considerable expenses incurred in doing this work.

Although women numbered 53 per cent of the American population, they comprised only 2 per cent of the congressional delegation. This had to change, so we decided to encourage more women to enter politics. We developed the motto '200 women in Congress by the year 2000' and supported all good female candidates in state and federal elections by sending both money and speakers to their fund-raising functions.

After my resignation from PSR in 1983, I was much more comfortable working with WAND, where I was able to spread my wings and fly, than with doctors who attempted to confine me to ground level. WAND stepped into the breach with alacrity, organising my life down to the minute, and I was ready to work. It was 1984, the watershed year I thought would determine the fate of the earth.

Speaking requests reached almost unmanageable levels. We moved into high gear, drawing up a list of eight Senate and twenty-two congressional campaigns that needed our support. The WAND staff prioritised these invitations, sending me to these particular congressional districts to address public meetings and raise money for the candidates.

Half a million women in fifteen states were not registered to vote, so WAND geared up to help them to register. Unlike Australia, voting is not compulsory in the United States, and it is often difficult for poor women in particular to register, let alone vote. WAND women throughout the country also worked like mad to educate the public and the media about the arms race, and we actively encouraged people to make personal donations of $1000 to the candidate of their choice. It really did feel like a race for survival.

The WAND Political Action Committee officially endorsed

candidates who strongly opposed Reagan's military build-up and who would therefore vote against all new nuclear systems. Sometimes we assisted these candidates financially; at other times we provided a bank of volunteers to help them with their campaigns. We also joined with the National Nuclear Weapons Freeze Campaign, working closely with the two Randys—Randy Forsberg, the freeze maker, and Randy Keiler, the deeply religious man who directed the freeze movement. We distributed freeze information in our national newsletter and sent a mailing to the chapters once a month. We also established a Washington lobbying office run by the efficient, charming; curly-haired Nancy Donaldson, who wooed and cajoled the congresspeople. We became the most important group in Washington to effect legislation on nuclear weapons and delivery systems.

Nationwide the freeze campaign and other peace groups now numbered about 5700—a force to be reckoned with. To utilise this enormous political power, the American peace movement decided to concentrate its activities on the 1984 presidential elections. By the fall of 1984 polls showed that 96 per cent of the American people believed that there could be no winner in an all-out nuclear war. We had a mandate.

Women in large numbers gave up their personal lives to join the struggle to save the earth. The story of Terry Schraeder is typical. Tall and willowy, dark haired and blue eyed, she was one of thirty-five people who attended my speech at the University of Utah in 1981. She was to later say, 'As I listened to her describe the faces of burned children, I knew the horror of nuclear war had been etched into my soul.' After hearing me speak again in the same location in 1984, to 250 people, she booked me to appear on the evening TV news magazine show where she worked as a medical reporter.

In the make-up room that night, I asked if she was attached to her job. She answered, 'No, I would consider quitting,' which she did. Two months later she drove 4000 kilometres across the country alone to work in a funky little office in

Arlington as the WAND media director. At the tender age of twenty-four she booked me on *Nightline*, called press conferences with Marlo Thomas, Sally Field and Lily Tomlin, juggled requests from reporters from the *New York Times*, *Good Morning, America* and National Public Radio. Terry was but one of the many thousands of fine, dedicated women who helped to educate the American people about nuclear war.

The Democratic nominee for president was Walter Mondale. He had never spoken out forcefully about the dangers of nuclear war, but we in the peace movement felt that we could mould and influence his opinions after he learned what a huge gift we could supply in terms of votes. Almost immediately after announcing his candidacy, he made the exciting choice of Geraldine Ferraro as his running mate. Women around the country, including me, were ecstatic that this lively, intelligent congresswoman had been chosen. I was disturbed a little later, however, when, during a debate with George Bush, she was asked whether she would press the nuclear button. Geraldine looked straight at the camera and said, 'Yes.' Her answer reflected the political realities in this macho society, but I was appalled.

I met Mondale briefly at the International Machinists and Aerospace Workers national convention in the Midwest, where I was a keynote speaker. I gave my usual rap, hoping that the nominee would be there to hear, but he arrived late. I was anxiously hoping to have a talk with him to guide him in the right direction because I was keenly aware of the somewhat hawkish policies of his advisers. Democrats were always more conservative than Republicans when it came to the issue of nuclear weapons and US foreign policy (Reagan was an exception). But I was able only to shake hands with him as I stood in a long queue back stage. At that very moment, unbeknownst to me, the assembly I had just addressed was voting to appoint me an honorary member. The only other such appointees had been Jack Kennedy and Walter Mondale himself.

The year 1984 was pretty exciting in many ways. I was invited to attend the Democratic National Convention in Moscone Center, San Francisco on 16 July by Dick and Dagmar Celeste, the governor and first lady of Ohio and my dear friends. The aim was to get me onto the platform before the microphone, so I could address the convention and focus attention upon the single most important issue of that election year, but no such luck. I did get to within a metre or so of the microphone, but there were too many minders guarding it. So near and yet so far: I knew that what I had to say could have jerked the convention around, but it was not to be.

The highlight of the event was Jesse Jackson's speech. Looking tiny in that vast hall, surrounded by tens of thousands of people, some wearing Uncle Sam outfits and many carrying signs, balloons and badges, he was further dwarfed by a huge screen behind the podium that magnified his every expression and movement. He started off slowly in his typical style, but brought us to our feet when after a thrilling crescendo he shouted, 'I'd rather have Roosevelt in a wheelchair than Reagan on a horse!'

'Oh, Jesse!' we yelled. We were all so high when he finished that the whole audience held hands, swaying together and singing 'We Shall Overcome' with tears pouring down our faces.

In June of 1984 Morrow published my book *Missile Envy.* I coined the phrase during one of my speeches, and it seemed to fit the situation perfectly. It described the extraordinary one-upmanship characterising the superpower obsession with superiority, the 'mine's bigger than yours' syndrome.

The book began with a personal account of my beliefs. Its first words were: 'I write this book with a tremendous sense of urgency—as a mother, as a paediatrician, and as a woman—aware that we live on a planet that is terminally ill.' It was a litany of facts, figures, data, technology and the psychological dynamics behind the nuclear arms race. I wrote much of it in Annisquam when I stayed there alone during the summer of 1983. I hoped desperately that the book would play a significant role in preventing Reagan from securing a second term. I did an exhausting three-week book tour in June 1984, and by the end I had repeated myself so often that my tongue turned to cardboard and could hardly articulate the arcane language of the arms race.

On 4 August, just before my birthday, WAND gave me a party at Annisquam. It was a hot, muggy day, and about thirty women of all ages and sizes wandered around in bathing suits on our spacious back lawn leading down to the serene waters of Lobster Cove. Early in proceedings a clown suddenly appeared and read out a crazy birthday telegram addressed to me from no one in particular. Then the action started. Those wonderful women had written and rehearsed a fantastic song and dance routine about WAND and me, and I laughed until I cried. They were so loving and funny. It was an extraordinary feeling to be united with them in this work for a great common goal.

CHAPTER 24

Sunday, 9 September 1984 was a beautiful, clear autumn day. I felt very much at peace with the world and in love with Bill. But instead of staying in Annisquam and enjoying life, I fulfilled an agreement to fly down to New York that afternoon to speak at one of the YMCAs in a rather sad part of town. Everything told me not to go, but as I almost never broke engagements, I obediently drove to Logan Airport and boarded the plane. This was my pattern during those years. On the one hand, I was so desperate about the nuclear situation that I would accept in a totally indiscriminate fashion almost every invitation that came my way. On the other, I was profoundly tired and needed some time out to recuperate and refresh myself.

Nobody met me at La Guardia, so I took a taxi to the Y, where I was shown to a small, dingy bedroom in which I sat during that sunny afternoon, wishing to hell I was somewhere else. About six people turned up to hear me speak. As the evening dragged on, I was bereft. Why had I left Bill and our summer paradise for this sterile experience? I'm not sure how Bill felt, but he was probably inured by now to my leaving him in the midst of a weekend's intimacy. I'm sure that he would have preferred me to stay.

I forgot my despair a couple of days later in Washington, when I participated in a Women's Conference on Preventing Nuclear War organised by the Center for Defense Information and the actress Joanne Woodward. It was held in an imposing room in the Capitol; Pat Kingsley brought Sally Field and Lily Tomlin, and the program featured prominent women speakers. Having recently completed *Missile Envy,* I was brimming with facts and figures about Congress's irresponsible appropriation of money for nuclear weapons—in 1984 it totalled more than $300 billion a year—when two-thirds of the world's children were either malnourished or actually starving. Out came all this information in a torrent; at one point pointing towards the Congressional Halls, I said, 'This place is full of corporate prostitutes!' Next morning's write-up in the *Washington Post* used much of my speech, including that quote.

Following my speech a tall, earnest, bespectacled woman approached me and, with some reverence in her voice, said, 'Joan Kroc would like to see you.' I had no idea who this Joan Kroc was, but obediently followed her. She ushered me into a small room where I was greeted by a handsome and beautifully dressed blonde woman in her early fifties who turned out to be the heiress of the McDonald's hamburger chain fortune.

She told me she had been very impressed with my speech, and without much ado announced she was prepared to spend $11 million to put me on television to defeat Reagan. She took my breath away; I hardly dared believe that such good fortune could suddenly appear. With some difficulty I kept my cool, and said, 'All right.'

For several days I walked on air. Then Joan discovered I

was not a US citizen. She didn't think it was appropriate for a non-American to enter into the fray of American politics, and confront the president, so she backed away.

Soon afterwards I flew up to Maine to support the campaign of Libby Mitchell, Maine's House majority leader, who was challenging the superhawk Republican senator William Cohen. A group of children met me at the airport, gave me flowers and sang to me. They were very sweet, but I wanted to get going quickly: I was impatient to share the information from *Missile Envy* with the people of Maine. Shortly after my arrival, Libby held a press conference. I didn't pull any punches in my criticism of Cohen, who endorsed and voted for almost every nuclear weapon that came down the pike. Many in the audience liked Cohen; they seemed to have little idea of his participation in the nuclear arms race or how avidly he supported the military–industrial complex.

The next day I spoke at a junior high school. This is never easy; it's difficult to speak to relatively young children about nuclear war at the best of times, for the issues are so complex and frightening. The ideal format in primary schools is a free-wheeling discussion because, surprisingly enough, children often know more about these subjects and think more deeply about them than their parents do, and they really need an adult whom they trust to confirm their knowledge and validate their fears. So without the children's responses I can be at a loss when speaking to them—it's rather like walking through a crowd of people blindfolded. But I worked very hard with this group, giving some of the unadorned medical details, many of which they seemed to know already. I told them that their parents needed to vote the right way in this election to make sure they had a safe future.

At the end a girl of about ten was crying. She raised her hand and asked me: 'Does this mean I won't live?'

I said, 'I don't know, darling, but that's why I'm here, to make sure that you do.'

The headmaster and other teachers were enthusiastic and

grateful as they walked Libby and me to the car. We felt sure that we had done a good job. Unfortunately, the television cameras concentrated on the little girl who cried, and that night the TV news reported that Dr Caldicott had told the children that they would die in a nuclear war. Television can so distort a message and play havoc with the truth—on this occasion it seemed to me the distortion was deliberate.

That broadcast had a detrimental effect upon Libby's Senate campaign. I felt very bad about this; I still regret that of the twenty-nine WAND-supported candidates she was one whose chances of election I did not improve.

On 2 October I met a woman with the extraordinary name of Minerva (her father used to read the Greek myths and legends) Neiditz at a Connecticut fund-raiser. Closely involved with the Democrats, she decided that my speaking skills should be harnessed to the Mondale presidential campaign. This was wonderful news: it meant that the message could be spread far and wide. Minerva obtained permission for me to be a Mondale surrogate, authorised to speak for him along the campaign trail.

From that point onwards the Democratic Party took me over. We made television ads in which I said: 'If you're a parent who loves a child in America, then this is the most important election of your life. A recent poll shows that most American children believe they will die in a nuclear holocaust. I believe America's children are right. Tensions between America and Russia are high and the nuclear arms race is out of control. As a paediatrician and a mother I urge you to vote for Walter Mondale and Geraldine Ferraro. For your children's sake.'

I was living in a state of high excitement. What could stop us? I had only to consider the groundwork that WAND, PSR, the freeze and all other peace groups had done. We had moved the American public from almost zero support for ending the arms race in 1978 to 80 per cent support for a freeze by 1983—a revolution in thinking. If Mondale talked about the threat of nuclear war with passion, he couldn't fail to win. It seemed to me that all he needed to do was to appear on television with a doctor who clinically outlined the dangers of a nuclear attack. Then he would reassure the people in a statesmanlike way that if elected, he would stop the arms race and move rapidly to bilateral nuclear disarmament. If I had been Mondale, that's what I would have done, but I wasn't. This was not naive thinking: I understood the pulse of the American people at that time and this strategy would not have failed.

I moved through October at a frantic pace. The Democrats scheduled me to speak in three cities a day; towards the end of the month I became a walking zombie. Often I woke in the morning not knowing which city I was in. This must be what it feels like to campaign for president. I became so tired that even after a hot bath, meditation and a restful book, I still slept fitfully, constantly dreaming of ways to prevent nuclear war. The only respite I found was in reading *Pilgrim at Tinker Creek* by Annie Dillard.

Two pre-election debates were arranged between Reagan and Mondale, the first in mid-October. The subject was domestic policy. Mondale did very well, speaking crisply and lucidly, all his information at his fingertips. In contrast, Reagan was dithery and doddery. He couldn't remember his facts, and he did so badly that the next day the *Wall Street Journal* speculated that he was developing Alzheimer's disease, which has now been confirmed.

I was delighted with the outcome of the debate. This was our chance: if Mondale performed as well during the foreign policy debate, we had the election in the bag. All he had to do was use the expertise and knowledge we had given him, to appear to be a statesman. I knew that Mondale was basically a good Democrat, but I wasn't sure that he had a great deal of passionate commitment to our issue, or indeed any others.

I was in California on the evening of the definitive debate.

On this occasion Reagan was much more self assured, even folksy. He pushed the Strategic Defense Initiative line—Star Wars—assuring the American people that it would protect them from a nuclear attack. On the other hand, Mondale fumbled, failing to take the initiative and, to my deep consternation, sounding like a greater hawk than Reagan. Not once did he mention the freeze, not once did he use the data we had provided him about nuclear war, and not once did he mention the mandate he had from the huge peace movement. Reagan won the debate hands down.

The election was decided that night, and I knew it. I was appalled and depressed. God help us, after all the amazing work we had done, with an electorate primed and ready to go, ready to heed our message, we were being represented by this man, so inadequate in the face of immense danger.

In the months following Mondale's devastating defeat I found it difficult to keep going with the same enthusiasm. We had all worked so hard for Democratic candidates in the House, the Senate and the presidency, and Mondale had let us down. He had seemed not to understand the gravity of the nuclear situation, he clearly had not bothered to study the literature nor to listen to millions of his constituents. In essence, he betrayed us. Now we were in for another four years of chaos and damage. If we survived.

Why had the peace movement failed? Why had we fared so badly?

There were a couple of obvious answers. People didn't like our criticism of President Reagan, who appeared to be so strong and authoritative. I believe that at a fundamental level people enjoy being cared for by supposedly strong leaders. This gives them the freedom to avoid the true responsibilities and autonomy of adulthood, with all its attendant details. They can then behave as adolescents needing a father or a mother figure. And Reagan fitted this pattern. It was a pity that the father the American people had chosen was not a creative, vital figure, but such a destructive one—I called him the Pied Piper of Armageddon.

I decided to make a full investigation into the reasons for our failure, and went to see John Martilla, a Boston political consultant who had masterminded campaigns for Congressman Ed Markey and Senator John Kerry. John is a warm, responsive man and was interested in the problem. He suggested that he do several studies, working with Diane Aronson, the executive director of WAND, on the project. Joan Kroc agreed to fund this enterprise. John and his staff interviewed 1000 citizens, 100 key press people, reviewed two years of nightly network news, spoke to 35 members of Congress and their staffers and analysed more than 100 grassroots organisations. All this took about a year; the results appeared in a once-only magazine called *Turnabout*, published by WAND in 1986.

Some of the findings were disturbing. Although 70 to 80 per cent of the general public had supported the freeze consistently for three years, from 1982 to 1984, the media saw the movement mainly as an interesting grassroots social phenomenon. They never took the freeze seriously as a credible arms control initiative. In my view this was mainly because the Washington media coterie was almost exclusively male. It was a closed shop relying on a small battery of arms control 'experts' trained in public relations by corporations or by the Pentagon to supply reporters with relevant information or to give them critical commentary on any new initiatives. The experts also included past architects of the arms race such as Henry Kissinger, James Schlesinger and Harold Brown. These people and their views did much to shape the national media's political evaluation of the freeze. As one reporter commented, 'The experts came up with sixteen technical reasons never to be in favour of the freeze'.

But the people who criticised us were never publicly pitted

against the leaders of the freeze movement in a freewheeling debate. So, quietly, with no stated reason, the media simply wrote off a grassroots movement supported by 80 per cent of American citizens. They were quite happy to write about marches, freeze conventions, and so on—colour pieces—but when the freeze came to Washington as a piece of legislation for adoption, they never took it seriously. The presence in Central Park of one million people from every corner of the nation did not seem to have political significance. In essence, the media reported the freeze movement as a trivial diversion. And given that the media managers were male, it is not outside the realm of possibility to suggest they might have reacted this way because the instigators of the freeze— Randy Forsberg and I—happened to be two capable and intelligent women.

On the other hand, the freeze earned a great deal of respect from legislators in Congress and their staff. Our lobbyists were well informed and worked closely with Congresspeople. But the legislators did tell *Turnabout* that we must be prepared to compromise our views on certain votes, such as the MX missile—the 'Peacekeeper'—and Star Wars. This we found difficult, if not impossible.

The public poll was very interesting, too. While most respondents liked Reagan, they disliked his insistence on manufacturing nuclear weapons. They wanted less money spent on these and favoured negotiation with the Soviet Union. Reagan and his advisers noted these trends in public opinion, so they moved into damage control mode. The president changed his rhetoric from talk of evil empires and fighting and winning nuclear wars to 'meaningful arms control'. He told the American people that the freeze wasn't good enough; he wanted a 'zero option' ending all deployment of nuclear missiles while allowing both countries to build more nuclear weapons. This, he said, would provide true equality between the superpowers, while the freeze would leave the Soviets at a comparative advantage because of their 'massive nuclear build-up' during the 1970s—all lies.

The introduction of this zero option undercut the peace movement. It made people think that the president and the proponents of the freeze differed only on strategy, not in principle, and the suggestion that those behind the freeze were naive about the Soviet Union created doubts about some movement leaders who, like me, were critical of the United States' policy position. This 'new' Reagan, then, was more palatable to the public, and seemed reassuring and avuncular, and this alone weakened the peace movement.

John Martilla and his advisers recommended that the movement develop more effective communication with the media, arms control experts and policymakers. We should devote greater resources to obtaining free media coverage, to fostering frank communications between the movement and members and staff of the House and Senate.

The 'movement' was really an ad hoc, heterogeneous collection of millions of people across the country arranged in disparate and individual units—churches, psychologists, lawyers, real estate brokers, artists, the Sane and Freeze groups, and many more. The leaders occasionally got together to discuss strategy, particularly those based in Washington. But I rarely participated in these conferences because I was continually on the road, recruiting more people and groups. However, we all agreed on a common goal: to freeze the production, development, deployment and testing of nuclear weapons with eventual elimination of same.

The recommendation I found most exciting was that we should establish a National Strategic Planning and Communications Center staffed by former admirals, generals and experts in the freeze and arms control movement. Every time Reagan lied, we would demand and obtain equal time to tell the truth and in the process educate the public more deeply about the issues. We also needed to create substantial news stories of our own, using both top-level policy issues and interesting grassroots stories.

I wanted to start on this right away. Unfortunately, Joan

Kroc, our guardian angel, declined to provide further funding. The way to create this media centre, I knew, was to initiate and run a major fund-raising drive, to use my credibility in the movement to galvanise support, to promote enthusiasm, to get it really moving. But I was tired and depressed. By the time the *Turnabout* report came out in 1986, I lacked the stamina and enthusiasm to really get it going. The study had been my initiative, it was obviously up to me to follow through; nobody else in the peace movement took up the challenge. And now, for the first time, I couldn't do it either.

CHAPTER 25

In 1986 Bill and I took a few days' rest in Crete. I loved it: I read a book on kundalini, meditated, swam topless and lay in the sun for hours. We ate creamy yoghurt, fresh, crunchy bread, fried octopus and olives and drank thick black coffee. I felt warm, brown and relaxed when we left the island, and very close to Bill. In fact, I had fallen in love with him all over again. We always became close when we had time to relax and talk together. I must have been Greek in a previous life because I always feel so at home wandering among the dry, brown hills, smelling the orange blossom mingled with the pungent whiffs of roast lamb and garlic, or sitting beside the turquoise Mediterranean totally at peace.

We'd just completed a strenuous but fascinating tour of Asia—including China, Thailand, Vietnam and Japan—for the anniversary of Hiroshima and Nagasaki. China was beyond compare. I'd never seen such a mass of human beings. This was before the advent of capitalism and the people were still fascinated by white-skinned foreigners and our strange way of life. Millions of silent bicycles filled the streets, and the general impression was one of gentleness and ancient tradition, despite the recent traumas of the Cultural Revolution.

Hanoi and Ho Chi Minh City were something else. My brother Richard was the Australian ambassador in Hanoi, so we stayed with him in his small, white, mossy French colonial villa, typical of the buildings in Hanoi. Run-down and somewhat dilapidated, the town and its shy people nevertheless had an air of dignity, despite the deprivations imposed upon this small nation by the war and its aftermath. In comparison, Ho Chi Minh City (Saigon) felt as if it had been sullied by the never-ending succession of colonial regimes—Japanese, English, French and American. The people seemed sullen and withdrawn, deprived by the American withdrawal of their materialistic, if exploited, lifestyle. The country was still wracked by the ecological insults of the war: once-lush tropical forests had been replaced by blackened, sterile countryside, never to recover from the insult of millions of litres of defoliating dioxin.

Throughout this trip the knowledge of what happened to me and our movement was never far below the surface. I seemed to be in a state of limbo, but my sense of defeat was always there: the PSR/IPPNW betrayal, Mondale's defeat in the 1984 election, Reagan's triumph. The more I thought about this, the more depressed I became. We had worked so hard for so long, thought we had made so many gains for peace. And we were right back where we had started. Not a single bomb had been decommissioned; we had made not one whit of difference to the might of the military–industrial complex.

Defeated, tired, angry and to some extent bitter, I lost the ability to deliver my message with simplicity and purity. My audiences sensed this change of mood; in my despair I castigated them, and my frustration and anger polluted the message. But still they arrived in droves to hear me speak. I'm not sure what kept them coming at that point.

How much more could I do? I wondered. Could I summon the energy to go on fighting?

Our next stop was Frankfurt, and once again I had to switch into peace activist mode. I still felt passionately about the cause, but I was flagging. In Berlin we had to face a meeting of fifty anti-nuclear doctors; sentiment against nuclear America ran high, and the event was an excellent one. Interestingly, several reporters took us aside and told us off the record that they opposed the deployment of cruise and Pershing missiles. I felt lifted by this, but I dropped the ball when we had lunch with Professor Horst Richter, a psychiatrist who wanted to hear all about the power struggle within the doctors' movement. I thought I was objective enough by then, but as I spoke, I grew upset and realised that I was still feeling vulnerable.

The ongoing enormity of our task was epitomised in Holland. On attending a small meeting in Amsterdam sponsored by the Interchurch Peace Council, the group that had worked so hard to oppose the deployment of cruise missiles in Holland, my friend Laurens Hogebrink told us that the US Embassy in Holland had totally manipulated the Dutch media and the politicians to accept missile deployment in the face of majority opposition.

As the tour progressed, the more doubtful I became. Could I go on? Compared to the might of the Pentagon and military–industrial complex, the peace movement had no power. I had thought we could win, that with Mondale in the White House and the people of the United States behind us, we would overcome the pro-nuclear forces and right would triumph. I hadn't understood how much American history and tradition—faith in technology, belief in peace through strength, fear of communism, trust in political and business institutions, willingness to trust and love a leader who looked strong—was against us.

I was only forty-seven years old. I felt as if I had been rushing from one end of the globe to the other for years. The speeches, the seminars, the tours, the writing . . . I had loved all of it, felt high on the adrenalin of believing I was making a difference, that my efforts would help to change the world. They hadn't. And I was depressed, discouraged. Was this all my life amounted to? Maybe it was time to go.

But before I made a final decision, something happened that showed me the world *must* sit up and take notice of the nuclear horror: Chernobyl.

The nuclear reactor at Chernobyl in the USSR suffered a meltdown on 26 April 1986. More than 25 people died, at least 300 were injured, 90 000 were evacuated. The fallout spread over much of Europe. Radioactive elements that remain poisonous for hundreds or thousands of years rained down on some of the world's best agricultural land in the Ukraine and Europe.

By 1990 it was predicted that 800 000 children in the Soviet Union could be at risk for developing leukemia in the wake of the Chernobyl accident. It was also reported that many babies in the fallout area had been born without arms or legs and with other gross deformities. Doctors now estimate that about 160 000 children below the age of seven living in the Ukraine in radioactively contaminated areas are at risk of developing thyroid cancer from radioactive iodine 131. Another 12 000 are also at risk because they drank contaminated milk and inhaled radioactive iodine before being evacuated from the 30 kilometre zone around the reactor.

In Belorus alone 2697 villages, with a combined population of two million, have been seriously contaminated. People in the Soviet Union and Europe are still eating radioactive food; food grown in contaminated areas will be radioactive for thousands of years. Some Soviet doctors and environmentalists have estimated that a total of 3.5 million people are at risk of cancer or leukemia.

'Now,' I thought, 'now they'll have to see.' I summoned

facts and figures about this latest horror and set to work. I spoke to groups all over the United States about the medical consequences of Chernobyl, wrote, gave TV interviews. I impressed on every audience that Chernobyl was but a small example of a greater horror to follow. I summoned up every last skerrick of energy I possessed to tell people, once again, what I had been telling them for years.

But they weren't listening. Most American commentators took the line that Soviet reactors were obviously more dangerous than US reactors, and that the Russians don't care about their people. They used the catastrophe to attack the Russians. In 1986 the Cold War was as hot as ever, despite the fact that Mikhail Gorbachev was now president of the Soviet Union. I was accused of being alarmist, a scaremonger . . . and now, emotionally depleted by the PSR debacle and the Mondale defeat, I lacked the strength to fight back effectively.

CHAPTER 26

I'd reached the end of my tether. No more to give; nothing more to do. It's called burnout. So—home, James, and don't spare the horses. Although Bill wasn't so keen about returning to Australia, that's all I could think of—to join the children and be a family again.

So in the autumn of 1986 Bill and I stood on the back lawn of the house in Annisquam, our arms around each other, drinking in the peace of Lobster Cove for the last time. We'd sold the house and were about to move to Bermagui.

On the trip home we ventured into India for the first time. I'd always been reluctant to go there and face the poverty, but we'd been invited by a group of Indian physicians and scientists who strongly opposed their country's nuclear power and weapons program. The last gasp of the wilting activist. I must say it was not easy to see so much preventable disease. In parts of India I felt as if I were walking around in a pathology museum with diseases on display which had long since gone in the West. Why would the world condone tuberculosis, leprosy, polio, malnutrition, all the other horrors India presents, while spending so much on weapons of mass destruction?

Westerners are not necessarily welcome on the Indian subcontinent. While our academic hosts were thrilled that we had come, resentments of the British Raj linger, and it was obvious that we were related to the English and came from one of the world's richer countries. On the other hand, I was astounded to learn that there is enormous wealth in India, enough to care for all if it were redistributed. We spent a glorious couple of days on an old English houseboat floating on Lake Dahl in Kashmir, where, searching for answers to my own dilemma, I devoured Gandhi's autobiography.

From Kashmir we flew north to Katmandu in Nepal, past the glorious Himalayas, taking a bus to the small town of Pokhara at the foot of the mountains. We stopped at a roadside village for lunch—I was still shaking with fear after my first experience of Indian public transport—and I noticed a group of curious people standing around. I walked over and found a Western man was lying on the ground experiencing an epileptic fit. We later discovered that he was a Swiss tourist who had complained of a headache that morning. His face was blue, his eyes were rolled up, and his breathing was stertorous.

My medical training came to the fore. I laid him on his side and propped his mouth open with a spoon to provide a patent airway; it was all I could do. The nearest decent hospital was hundreds of kilometres away, and I was unable to organise a taxi. I felt powerless and impotent. Later I discovered that the man made it to hospital and lived. Apparently there was a virulent epidemic of encephalitis in the area, almost certainly the cause of his seizure.

The trip was a difficult one. I was still quite depressed, and Bill seemed to have retreated into a world of his own. On a train trip winding up the mountains to Poona, I read *Women*

Who Love Too Much. Every sentence was like a knife piercing my heart. I saw for the first time that I was codependent with Bill, trying to please him at every turn but unsure of my own identity emotionally. No wonder he needed to maintain a distance. Mind you, I'm sure my exhaustion and depression aggravated the situation.

It was then that I understood I was in serious trouble. Bill did not discuss his feelings with me, we seemed only to talk about travel arrangements and ordinary practicalities. It felt as if he resented me; his feelings must have been a result of all the time I had spent away from home for the last sixteen years. Was this emotional standoff to be the culmination of our years in the States, the end of everything we had worked for?

My spirits lifted, however, when we hit the tarmac at Sydney airport. Home at last. To smell the hot-pepper scent of the bush at midday, to hear the magpies and kookaburras singing in the morning, to eat a hot meat pie with tomato sauce, to devour a honeycomb-and-cholocate Violet Crumble bar and bite into a big, fat cream bun! Now I knew I was home!

I discovered that during our time in the States, I had lost touch with my Australian sense of humour. I hadn't realised how heavily this depends on irony, much more than does the more literal American sense of humour, and I found I was taking people's comments at face value. It took me a while to get used to the rather sardonic, leg-pulling way of relating to people that is so Australian.

We bought a box trailer in Sydney, attached it to the back of our car, loaded it with our gear, and set off for our house in Bermagui, buying a kitchen full of food on the way. I even bought an apron in the supermarket, symbolic of my wish to be a full-time wife and homemaker.

I threw myself wholeheartedly into my new life. After the years of travel and snatched meals in the USA, it was bliss to be able to invite people home, to plan meals, to nurture and care for them. I indulged my domestic nature, and loved it.

During the heat of the day I walked through the silent bush to pick bulging, warm, soft blackberries to bake pies which we slathered in cream. Bill dug a vegetable garden, fenced a flower garden for me, and built a roomy deck at the side of the house. He, too, apparently revelled in our new domesticity. But the undercurrents were still there; our communication was minimal.

The kids came to visit. Philip, who had spent several years as a ski bum in Austria, now decided to bicycle around Australia. He bought a tiny one-man tent and cooking utensils, and off he set. He rode several thousand kilometres from southern New South Wales into Queensland, where he met and fell in love with a beautiful English girl. He cut his trip short and caught the bus to Darwin to join her.

I came across them later in Alice Springs when I visited on a speaking trip. They seemed very sweet and peaceful together. I still felt I had to do what I could for the anti-nuclear cause, so I took part in a lively demonstration at Pine Gap, a huge CIA spy base. Protesters breached the outer barbed wire fence and were captured by police. Two men climbed a pole surmounted by an observation camera and stuck themselves to the pole with superglue. The police took hours using solvents to unglue them.

I accidentally impaled myself on barbed wire and gouged my legs deeply. Blood poured into my sandals, while the police stood and watched. I was furious: 'Aren't you employed to care for us instead of protecting US facilities?' I asked. Eventually they (reluctantly) assisted me. Unfortunately, as usual, the demonstration achieved nothing but a flurry of publicity.

After the initial novelty of homecoming, I found great difficulty letting go of my life in the States. Here I was, attempting to be a contented, happy person, but I couldn't control my thoughts or my feelings. I was lonely, bereft, emotionally sterile; I was so anxious that sleeping was difficult. When I did sleep, I dreamed about Bernard Lown and Jack Geiger and awoke with my heart thudding. It would have helped, I think, to talk this over with Bill, but that wasn't possible. Clearly I missed the States and my friends and even the work, although it had exhausted me.

Bill and I decided we both wanted to spend some individual time with our children, getting to know them as adults and—in my case, at least—making up for the times I hadn't been there for them when they were younger. Penny had always felt closer to Bill than to me, partly, I think, because I had been away so often during her adolescence. She always loved talking; when she was little, she used to lie on the foot of our bed at night and chat for hours. While I was away during the 1980s, she talked to Bill; I knew she resented my absences.

At the end of 1987 when Penny had finished third year of medical school, she decided to take the following year off to travel. She and I arranged to spend several months together; I thought perhaps we could bond again, as we had been so close in the past from time to time.

We met in Geneva and went to the Greek island of Santorini for several weeks. I had been away from the States and the political work for more than a year, but I still couldn't let go. I was obsessed by news events, devouring the *Herald Tribune* every day, almost like a drug. I also felt irrational and experienced inappropriate outbursts of anger. When an Englishman we met dared to praise Margaret Thatcher, to Pen's acute embarrassment, I lost my head and told him at great length what an evil, war-mongering person she was. I also began to obsess about getting older. I was intensely jealous of the beautiful young bodies on the beach but was not able to take my eyes off them. The strength of these feelings was puzzling and alarming: I didn't understand what was happening to me.

Nevertheless, Pen and I had some precious time together. I explained to her the dynamics of my anti-nuclear work, the story of PSR, the extraordinary machinations surrounding the award of the Nobel Peace Prize. It was a great relief to talk to Pen about these things, to explain how I felt about what I had done. Until then she really had not understood the significance of all these events.

We became closer and closer, and did some mad things together. We hired two little puttering mopeds and sped around Santorini with the wind streaming through our hair, stopping at quaint old churches and eating at little roadside cafés. On our last night on the island we drank dreadfully expensive strawberry daiquiris as we watched a radiant red Mediterranean sunset, then ate fried calamari and creamy yoghurt. We felt very happy and united.

It got better. I had been invited to participate in an international women's conference in Moscow and decided to take Pen with me, though she was doubtful about this because she felt it would be another official event that would take me away from her. But we had a wonderful time together, talking through the long white Moscow nights in our hotel with close friends: Diane Cirincione, who came from the same town in Italy as Sophia Loren and looked like her; Vivienne Verdon Roe, a dark-haired English beauty who had just won an Oscar for her documentary *Women, America, and the World*; and her assistant Molly Rush, who was large, wise, and warmly friendly.

There were no hours of darkness during the warm nights; we were near the Arctic circle, where the sun never sets—hence the term 'white nights'. Sprawled on the twin beds in our room, the five of us exchanged confidences as only women can. I was in purgatory with my undefined and unresolved emotional distress; Penny had just met an attractive young Frenchman, Eric d'Indy, in Calcutta, but was torn because she had a boyfriend back in Australia; Vivienne and Molly were each dealing with their own unresolved childhood difficulties. We became very close despite a wide discrepancy in ages, and I think we helped each other. For three or four nights we talked for hours into the early morning, alternately laughing and crying as we achieved an intimacy whose depth belied its transitory nature. It was a special time.

The conference was wonderfully colourful. It seemed that all the world's women were represented: attendees from Africa in outrageously colourful costumes with huge hats like butterflies, Peruvian women in black top hats, and Indian women in shimmering saris. I gave a talk about nuclear power, and during questions a robust Russian woman got up and talked about the rosy apples ripening on the trees at Chernobyl, laced with radioactive toxins. The openness of discussion was unique, a result of Gorbachev's recent rise to power.

At the close of the conference three thousand delegates attended a meeting in the Kremlin. There was only one man in the hall: Mikhail Gorbachev, who sat on a long platform flanked by women, including his wife, Raisa. His speech began in a pedantic and predictable fashion as he praised the conditions of Soviet women. He said they enjoyed equal work, equal pay, and a good education—the usual propaganda. Then suddenly he added that they had to stand in long queues to buy food and cook meals while their men drank vodka and read the paper. I sat up. Here was something very different.

Gorbachev got to the heart of his speech: the overwhelming threat of nuclear war. I listened almost incredulously as he said that for him this was the single most important issue in the world. He spoke with such passion about the horrifying medical consequences of this potential catastrophe. It was obvious the subject was burned into his soul. It became clear that he did not want the Cold War to end simply because of the economic consequences of the arms race, but because he knew that Russian flesh burns at the same temperature as American flesh. 'Maybe,' I thought, 'this is the man who will bring the Cold War to an end.'

As he finished his speech, hundreds of children danced down the aisles, dressed in white shirts and red shorts or skirts and handing red carnations to the women, while rousing

Russian folk tunes stirred the audience. Two children, one Russian and one American, handed Gorbachev a crystal globe of the world. I watched his body language very carefully. He turned his back to the audience after he received the gift, pulled out his handkerchief, and wiped his eyes. It was a private moment, and I couldn't begin to imagine Ronald Reagan behaving like this. Although he was emotional, Reagan could never have given this sort of credence to the notion that the earth must be saved for both Russian and American children—that extended beyond the realm of his reality.

As the music began again, Gorbachev looked to the woman on his left, picked up her hand, and held it aloft, then did the same to the woman on his right. Suddenly we were all holding hands and swaying to the music as tears of hope and love for the children rolled down our cheeks. But as Raisa Gorbachev left the podium when the crowd was dispersing, she was accosted by Petra Kelly, who insisted that Gorbachev do something about the political prisoners in the Soviet Union. Petra never stopped: there was always something that needed fixing, and she always went to the top. She was absolutely uncompromising in her morality. As well as leading the peace movement in West Germany, she led demonstrations on the Alexanderplatz in East Berlin against Russian nuclear missiles. The Germans described her as 'a candle burning at both ends, and always for others'.

That night we were given a magnificent banquet in the Kremlin, complete with caviar, champagne, and blintzes. Russian dance music played, and I became quite inebriated with the glory of the whole thing. I was dancing down one of the aisles between the laden tables when I came face to face with Eduard Shevardnadze, Gorbachev's minister for foreign affairs. I took his hand in mine and thanked him for his statesmanship and work on ending the arms race with the US secretary of state George Shultz.

Pen and I then went to Tiblisi, the capital of Georgia,

where we were feted with the tastiest Mideastern food, fresh cherries, peaches and apricots washed down by the most delicious smooth red wine I have ever tasted. The climate was Mediterranean, one of dry heat. The back gardens of the houses looked just like those in Adelaide, full of trees laden with fruit. It breaks my heart to think of the dreadful rifts in Georgia later, and the stress that Shevardnadze endured when he subsequently became president of Georgia.

After Georgia Pen and I flew to Dublin to attend another international women's conference, this time of social workers and psychologists at Trinity College. It was fascinating; each day there were workshop sessions and seminars covering every issue relevant to women, from rape in marriage to political leadership and economics. Pen and I found it exciting sharing our experience from different workshops, and our enjoyment strengthened the tie between us. The closeness we had shared in Greece and Moscow was enhanced, and we became bonded at a very deep level by an understanding and vision of women that we had never experienced before. It was almost an emotional awakening, a love affair between mother and daughter.

Ireland felt very familiar—the sense of humour, the ubiquitous pubs, the twinkly eyed people. But there was the repressive presence of the Catholic Church. My eye was taken by huge young families and black-clad priests in the streets. Divorce, contraception and abortion were still illegal. Pen and I participated in a 'take back the night' march, the first ever to be held in Dublin. Hundreds of us blocked the streets, trams and cars were delayed, and there was a feeling of fear amongst the women—how would the authorities and the church react? Women had a long way to go in Ireland.

One of the workshops I attended jolted me considerably. It was a discussion of the feelings of a rape victim: the loss of self esteem, self blame, concession of power to the rapist, and social ostracism because nobody could really identify with her. With a shock I realised that I had been psychologically raped by some of my colleages in PSR and IPPNW: I recognised all of those feelings within myself.

Shaken by this realisation, I decided in my final keynote address to describe the dreadful events that had taken place within these organisations. Ever the good girl, I finished without mentioning the names of the men about whom I felt most disturbed. Then a woman in the front row shouted: 'Name them!' I hesitated, then did. And only then did I see how extraordinarily inhibited women can be, even after years of consciousness-raising and education. It was an immense relief to be truly honest; my revelations were met with enormous sympathy and understanding.

Pen left me at our Dublin hotel to visit Eric in France. This decision had been blessed by our 'white night' companions in Moscow, and Pen and I parted feeling closer than we had ever been. Later she wrote me this letter.

Ma:

I just wanted to say what a precious time we spent together. I will never forget it. I feel like a new level of understanding and friendship was reached, and that it can only grow with more time together. I really feel that it was the best thing we have ever done together, and it was wonderful to feel our relationship and communication and to see you transform from being depressed to feeling once again confidence in yourself and what you believe, and motivated by this to become active again in the nuclear and women's issues (so intimately related).

I have always been proud of you and respected what you have done, but I never really understood the incredible impact you have had and will have in the future, nor have I realised your incredible charisma and vision. You say your mother was the most wonderful woman you knew; well, I feel the same about you.

It was really joyous to learn together and especially to learn from you. Thank you for the opportunity to share all we did together—I feel new and strong.

It will be lovely to see you again. I love you very much.

Love,

Pen

I flew home from Dublin feeling a renewed sense of self esteem, if only from acknowledging that the turmoil of emotion I had experienced was indeed valid and that I wasn't going mad. And I knew that my daughter loved me and supported me in my personal struggle. The relief was tremendous.

Pen and I experienced something that my mother and I never had. Granted, Mum and I were very close during the time in Adelaide when I stayed with her and we cared for the babies together. There was a new degree of love and respect between us. The children were the vehicle of our newfound closeness, but the honesty and depths of our feelings about and for each other that Pen and I had achieved on this trip eluded us. If only Mum were alive now, with my present state of knowledge and wisdom I would insist that we communicate honestly no matter how much she procrastinated and tried to manipulate the situation. I have now a new philosophy—never put off today what you must do for the sake of honesty and intimacy, because there is no guarantee that there will be a tomorrow.

CHAPTER 27

Soon after our return to Australia we bought an apartment at Rushcutters Bay that overlooked a glorious view of the Cruising Yacht Club of Australia on Sydney Harbour. This was our townhouse. In December 1987 we came up from Bermagui to celebrate our twenty-fifth wedding anniversary. For several days before the anniversary date, the 8th, I noticed Penny and the boys creeping around the apartment, bristling with secrets.

When the day arrived, the kids instructed us to don some nice clothes, then they ushered us into the car and took us for a long drive. We arrived at a jetty, where a launch awaited us. Our dear, sweet children had hired his boat, asked our best friends to join us, and cooked a most glorious meal to celebrate the occasion. We cruised around the harbour at sunset drinking champagne and eating fresh salmon. It was wonderful, and I should have been the happiest person in the world. Bill did give me a wonderful long, intense kiss while everybody sang 'Happy Anniversary', but at some level I experienced a sense of great foreboding.

One morning some weeks earlier Bill had joined me on my early morning walk along the beach and told me he needed time alone to find himself. I was a little shocked but also pleased that he had made a definitive decision for himself, and I endorsed the notion that at our age, forty-nine, it is sometimes necessary to take stock of one's life. He said he wanted to drive around Australia and put some distance, both metaphorically and literally, between us so he could develop a new perspective on life. But he was not to act upon this impulse for about a year.

My old nemesis of depression reappeared. It was partly to do with the aging process, partly because I had no real goal in life now and partly because Bill and I continued to be distant from one another. And menopause had come to me early, at the age of forty-six. The hot flushes were very unpleasant, often triggered by mild anxiety that normally would never bother me. Some years earlier in Annisquam I used to throw off the blankets and lie naked in bed as the snow fluttered down outside. My gynaecologist had advised hormone replacement therapy.

Along with these symptoms came a degree of amnesia—difficulty in remembering names and places—which was unnerving, to say the least. Perhaps these are signs of impending Alzheimer's disease, I thought, not knowing that depression plus menopause can predispose to transient memory loss. Until recently the gynaecological profession had never really examined the physical and psychological consequences of menopause, and I was shocked to find that it was left to women themselves to do the seminal work on these topics.

It was difficult to reconcile myself to the fact that this was the end of my years of fertility; I did not really desire another baby, but there is a degree of grief associated with this realisation. The physical reality of aging is unpleasant and requires a degree of adjustment. Deepening wrinkles, loss of skin elasticity and occasional aches and pains in the old joints were things I had to face. It is a rite of passage in life's journey, a profound adjustment similar to that required in adolescence.

I also sensed that society, Australia in particular, doesn't take older women seriously. Society is geared towards youth, in both the advertising and consumer world, and the wealth of wisdom and experience of older people is almost ignored, to the detriment of all. It's interesting to note that elephants are the only other species to suffer the inconvenience of menopause.

Early in 1988 Bill travelled to Brisbane to address several union meetings. Simultaneously, I left on a gruelling six-week speaking tour of the United States and Canada, which turned out to be one of the most arduous lecture tours I have ever undertaken. The Canadian government had decided to construct a whole raft of nuclear submarines that were expensive and militarily unnecessary. Consequently, audiences in Canada were very receptive to my anti-nuclear message. I covered the length and breadth of the country, from Yellowknife on the Arctic Circle to Winnipeg and Calgary in the west, to Montreal, Halifax, Windsor, and St Johns in Newfoundland on the far east coast.

Most of the time I was escorted by a woman from one of the activist organisations, who was experiencing a turbulent emotional time. We had long and intense conversations, and I began to see that I had repressed many of my own feelings in order to live compatibly with Bill. Now that there was the perspective of distance between us, I realised that I was very unhappy with him. Speaking frankly for the first time was a great relief; I am sure she did more for my basic mental health in those six weeks than any counsellor.

The tour raised a lot of money for the peace movement,

and to our delight, eventually the government reversed its decision about the submarines. One night while waiting in a dark, freezing airport, I suddenly knew I could no longer live with Bill unless we obtained some counselling. But my insight stopped there. I couldn't visualise the emotional consequences of living alone after twenty-five years. I just pictured myself living in a small flat on Sydney Harbour surrounded by tall gum trees full of currawongs and screaming parrots, my bedroom beautifully decorated with lace and flowery prints.

On my return from this trip I told Bill that I couldn't go on unless we agreed to obtain some professional help. He consented, and the counselling was useful as far as it went, but when we returned to Bermagui after each weekly session, we continued to live our lives side by side, at an emotional distance.

It was during this period that a photographer named Gordon McQuilten came to visit with his family. A shy and passionate man and an avid member of the Australian Labor Party, he was worried about the party, which was moving from egalitarian socialist principles towards market rationalism. Paul Keating, then treasurer, had deregulated Australia's banks, floated the dollar and encouraged foreigners to buy up Australian-owned industry and land, as well as reducing our protective tariffs. Gore Vidal has said that 'America has one political party with two right wings', which has unfortunately become true for Australia as well.

Over the weekend of his visit Gordon and I decided to form Green Labor, a wing of the Labor Party with emphasis on environmental issues. When we announced its formation to the press, disillusioned Labor voters flocked to us in great relief. But with my marriage about to fall apart, I was in no fit state to be heavily involved in the running of the organisation, which continued to exist for some time.

Then I was off again, this time to Denmark for a tour arranged by Danish unions to speak about the nuclear arms race. But I felt as if I was on automatic pilot; although everybody looked after me with great care, I was lonely beyond belief, feeling like a satellite that had left the earth's orbit and was careering off into space without direction or reason.

After Denmark I went to France to stay with the d'Indy family, whose son Eric, much to everybody's delight, had just become engaged to Penny. They lived in a chateau named Les Faux (the oak trees), built by Eric's great-grandfather, the French composer Vincent d'Indy, and situated on a mountainside overlooking the beautiful countryside of Ardèche. Eric's parents and I liked each other on sight. His brothers and sisters were delightful, and all spoke enough English for us to become friends.

I felt secure at Les Faux, and it was there I had a very clear dream, which turned out to be a portent. In it I was walking down a road past the Adelaide Children's Hospital and stopped to talk to Bill, who was working in the park opposite. Then a glamorous university friend of mine walked past wearing a beautiful suit of ivory silk.

I said to Bill, 'You've been having an affair with her recently.'

'Not recently,' he said. 'For years.'

Then I was suddenly at a party with all the children. Penny, I knew, would give me all the support I needed; Will, the youngest, was the most vulnerable and would be most badly damaged. I woke with a sense of foreboding.

On the way home I flew to Perth for yet another speech, then headed for Sydney. I landed at the airport at 5.55 p.m. on 6 August, the eve of my fiftieth birthday. Bill met me at the airport with the news that he had decided to leave me. Although I had known the writing was on the wall, I took years to recover.

CHAPTER 28

We told the children two days later as we sat in our dining room overlooking Sydney Harbour. They had no idea what we were going to say.

I turned to Bill. 'Tell them.'

'I've decided to leave Mum.'

They were shocked. Pen then developed a severe migraine that confined her to bed for the next two days; the boys went onto automatic pilot. Phil went back to his restaurant job and denied that anything disastrous had occurred; Will, who was about to turn twenty-one, fled to Perth shortly after. His birthday should have been a time of joyous celebration, but it was largely devoid of joy.

After spending about a week in Sydney trying to come to terms with Bill's decision, I returned on my own to Bermagui, where reality hit. I would fall asleep at night after hours of nightmarish tossing and turning, and the moment I lost consciousness, I would awaken automatically with the dreadful knowledge that my world had collapsed. Eating became impossible, and I started to fade away. Bill and I talked occasionally by phone; we swapped residences intermittently. Sometimes he came down to Bermagui and I went to Sydney. We passed each other on the road, but we seldom met.

Friends advised me to return to medicine and lose myself in my work, but I knew that was not right. I walked around my flower garden under a leaden winter sky listening to the huge rollers crash on the beach while black, funereal cockatoos circled and screeched eerily overhead. And I obsessed: *What did I do wrong in the last twenty-six years? What could I have done differently?* My sense of guilt was ever present.

I would wake at five in the morning, reliving every detail of our marriage, then, at one stage I would frantically paint the brown doors white as if to expunge the sickening reality of my life. One night alone in the double bed, I listened with dread to a strange crescendo of noises on the verandah. Was I about to be attacked? Finally, after gathering the courage to investigate, I found only a large possum clambering up the wooden post outside the bedroom.

It's not easy to be alone at fifty after twenty-six years of marriage, menopausal, with no apparent prospect of love ever again. Furthermore, never in my life did I expect to be divorced. It was a taboo in my family after my father's traumatic childhood experience. I was in it for life. After a time I became involved in a few superficial relationships, but they offered nothing like the intimacy of a long and loving marriage. This, of course, only exacerbated my sense of loneliness.

I drove for aimless hours in the car, often travelling very fast, as if perpetual movement could somehow eliminate the pain—to no avail. About three months after Bill left, I woke suddenly at three in the morning, sat up in bed and thought, 'I have no money. What about my old age?' Until that moment I had been so engrossed in emotional despair that money hadn't entered the equation. It was up to me now. I decided to make use of my reputation as a lecturer to earn money in the United States and in Canada. I would also write more books, and if necessary I could always return to medicine. In fact, I was considerably better off than most women of my age in a similar position.

But life continued to pursue me with extraordinary experiences. I was asked to attend a conference in Iceland to commemorate a century of women's rights; Iceland had been the first country in the world to give women the vote. It was a fascinating place, and it was here that President Reagan and Chairman Gorbachev met in Reykjavik in 1987 to discuss the nuclear arms race.

I was taken to the tiny house where the two leaders had met. There I was told the full story by the caretaker and an Icelandic government official—a story which for understandable reasons did not make its way into the mainstream press accounts. Gorbachev and Reagan met in a small downstairs sitting room; next door sat George Shultz and Edouard Shevardnadze. Reagan and the American delegation had come unprepared for a very sophisticated Soviet initiative. As Gorbachev presented Reagan with more and more facts and figures, Reagan would become confused and run upstairs to ask questions of Richard Perle, who was in the bathroom, the only extra space available. Perle frantically wrote numbers for Reagan on strips of lavatory paper. To compound the farce, members of the KGB, stationed in the cellar beneath the sitting room, imbibed copious vodka as was their custom, and by accident one of them set fire to a wastepaper basket; it was quite by chance that the fire was discovered. Despite the most extraordinary external security, the world leaders were placed in great jeopardy by their own keepers.

Nevertheless, during that weekend Reagan and Gorbachev almost agreed to eliminate the nuclear arsenals of the superpowers. It stands as one of the most significant conference of the twentieth century, perhaps in the history of the human race. But Reagan would not compromise on Star Wars. The whole argument unravelled because Gorbachev insisted that this program must be eliminated. The exercise, however, made George Shultz a statesman, and from that point on he worked brilliantly with Shevardnadze to fashion some substantial disarmament treaties.

Penny married Eric on 17 December, four months after Bill's departure. It was fun to plan the wedding—the gowns, bridal veils, flowers, wedding breakfast and guest list, something I had looked forward to ever since she was born. But the circumstances were not easy.

The ceremony was held at a beautiful Mediterranean-style villa in the valley adjacent to our house at Bermagui. Pen was radiant in an ivory silk princess-line dress trimmed with ice-pink piping. Eric, dazed, seemed to float through the day. My nieces Mary Alice and Anna played Bach's Double Violin Concerto as Pen made her entrance into the courtyard. The wedding table groaned with decorated fish, glazed ham, beautiful breads and cheeses and a French profiterole wedding cake, all to be washed down with red wine. Philip, the master of ceremonies, gave the occasion a light touch; Will's speech, as always, was straight and to the point. He said he loved his sister very much, and it was a gorgeous wedding. And indeed, it was a wonderful day, although difficult for me because it was the first time I'd seen Bill since we split.

Soon after, Phil and I flew to Paris to attend Pen and Eric's second marriage ceremony, this one in a small Catholic church called Notre Dame. It was here I was reminded that Penny was marrying an aristocrat—Eric was the Count d'Indy—and a more unlikely countess you couldn't hope to meet. Her clothes were anything but haute couture, her manners sometimes left much to be desired, and she refused to take Eric's name, remaining plain Penny Caldicott. She was a daughter of whom I was very proud. She and Eric returned to Australia exhausted after days of celebration and meeting with the many near and distant French relatives, and she entered her final year of medicine.

Meanwhile, Philip and I spent the next two weeks wandering the streets of Paris in the middle of winter; the best time to see that city, sans tourists. What a magnificent creation of humankind's ingenuity and passion. We walked for mile upon mile drinking in the sights, sounds and people, taking in the Jewish section, the Arab sector, the Louvre with the I. M. Pei glass pyramids, the Pompidou museum and the Musée de Gare. We ate delicious homemade food in little basement restaurants. But a sense of desolation never left me despite the beauty and grandeur of Paris. Phil and I ended up at St Anton in the Austrian alps, where I tentatively learned to ski while Phil swept downhill in long, curving arabesques.

CHAPTER 29

Once back in Australia, on one occasion I was speeding with absolute disregard for my own safety or that of others, when a policeman pulled me over. I had no excuse except, as I said in near despair, 'My husband's left me.' He looked at me with complete sympathy and said, 'My wife's just had a baby with my best friend.' We almost fell into each other's arms, and he told me how to write to the judge to extricate myself from the fine.

Bill rang me several months after Pen's wedding to tell me the news that I had been dreading. He said he had been 'seeing' another woman. I hadn't adjusted to the fact that my marriage was at an end, let alone that I had been replaced. That was one of the most difficult moments of my life. Abandonment and betrayal together.

Meanwhile, I set off on a journey to find some answers to this excruciating dilemma. I was more open to new ideas than

I had ever been in my life; it would have been exciting if I hadn't felt so terrible. I met some Sunyasins who lived with my neighbour Shunny at Bermagui and listened to their philosophies; they were interesting as far as they went, but not right for me. I smoked some dope, which was quite brave, but it was of no help—it seemed to exacerbate my despair. I attended a sweat lodge and sat naked with about ten other dripping, sweaty people in a tiny tent full of heat and steam, and rolled naked in the frosty grass under the vibrant, starry sky. Next morning the soles of my feet were puffy and painful. Clearly *this* experience was not the answer either.

It was time to become involved in local environmental issues. The old-growth forests of south-east New South Wales were about to be converted to woodchips by the voracious Japanese giant Harris Daishowa, and there was an active conservation movement in the Bermagui area. The obvious question was—why had the federal government invited the Japanese to destroy some of our last remaining stands of ancient forest?

Twice I was arrested for obstructing the loggers. The first time, I took my friend Lee Gold, newly arrived from Toronto, straight to the demonstration, and she was also arrested, saying, 'They're my forests too!' We both went to court. As I gave evidence, I felt I was in a holy place, defending the life of the trees. I said to the judge, 'As you practise the ethics of law, so I was practising the ethics of medicine.' Lee and I were freed.

Emboldened by this experience, at about three one morning I arose from my bed and drove several hundred kilometres to a stand of old-growth trees that were about to be decimated. I arrived as the sun rose; several people had already blocked the entrance to the logging area with a car. I lay under this vehicle, chaining myself to the left rear wheel with several other people. After about an hour three policemen arrived, saw what we had done, and drove away. Some minutes later a band of burly loggers came into view. They lifted the car under which we were lying and slammed it down at the side of the track, almost flattening my head.

The police returned some time later, and I accosted them, demanding: 'Why did you allow this to happen?' It was evident to me that they had given their tacit approval for the loggers to do their dirty work. One of them grabbed me roughly and threw me into the back of a paddy wagon along with some other people, several of whom were bleeding. We were driven at top speed along winding dirt roads, thrown from side to side in the van, until we reached the Bodalla police station. Here, for the first time, I confronted 'the law'. They removed everything I had, my purse and means of identification—even my shoelaces so I couldn't hang myself. I refused to be fingerprinted on the grounds that I was not a criminal. The whole affair was such an invasion of privacy. They then led me to a gaol cell and slammed the door behind me.

The cell was cold and lonely. In one corner lay a dirty ticking-covered mattress with an old grey army blanket, in the other a stainless-steel lavatory pan without a seat. I paced this cell for several hours like a caged lion, having no idea when they would return. Finally, a policeman came and got me, insisting that I sign an admission that I had been trespassing. I refused and told them that the forest belonged to me, as it did to the rest of the Australian people. Furthermore, no signs had been posted warning people off. One cop grabbed me by the arm and threatened to throw me back into the cell. I didn't want to go back in, so I signed under sufferance and was permitted to leave.

Months later I was summoned to appear in court and prosecuted by the New South Wales Forestry Department. Several hundred other protesters with similar offences had been acquitted, but not me. My solicitor referred me to a Sydney barrister, who agreed to defend me gratis. Pen happened to be in town on the day of the hearing, and she went to court with me. I looked quiet, elegant and non-threatening in a pink silk blouse, skirt and pearls. Pen sat beside me holding my hand. The atmosphere was intimidating. Policemen were lined up giving evidence in black leather jackets, with guns on their hips—a relatively new phenomenon. I was very anxious: would I end up with a criminal record? Would I go to gaol?

The proceedings began. The policeman who appeared for the prosecution read out the wrong name from my conviction document. The magistrate interrupted to ask why.

'We put the wrong name on by mistake,' admitted the policeman.

There were several more hours of testimony, then the magistrate called a recess. After what seemed a very long time, he recalled the court. The policeman appearing for the prosecution continued to give evidence, when the magistrate suddenly interrupted and read out a statement acquitting me on the grounds that the original documents had been mislabelled. That's what he'd been up to during the intermission. He seemed very irritated with the police.

We could hardly believe our ears. He finished reading, and I was free. Pen and I behaved exactly like people in a TV courtroom drama: we stood up and embraced with joy and relief.

At about this time I was asked to speak at a public meeting in a North Sydney church. The church was packed; my message of global environmental disaster was well received, and as a result I was asked to run for the Labor Party in the 1990 federal election, contesting the seat of North Sydney against a well-heeled conservative incumbent named John Spender. Despite my disillusionment with Labor, I accepted: perhaps I could help reform from within.

However, Labor's right wing section in New South Wales, which controlled the party machine, was unhappy about my selection. These people had very definite ideas about what I should and shouldn't say, which I refused to accept. I disagreed with many of their policies—uranium mining, economic rationalism, the watering-down of the great Australian union movement—and was not loath to say so. They transcribed my speeches and showed me their corrections, clearly not wanting me to win. They haggled about small barbeque events instead of endorsing large public meetings through which I believed I could easily have mobilised the entire electorate. They preferred a member of the opposition in Parliament to an irritant within their own party.

After several weeks I told them to get lost and left the Labor Party. I have no doubt that the right-wing machine was relieved to see me go. I gave my side of the story to the press, but it had little interest. That ended my concern with politics for the time being.

Still searching for answers to my personal problems, I booked into a rebirthing centre in the Melbourne suburb of Richmond. It was very strange. Run by a doctor, it consisted of a huge room covered from floor to ceiling in red sail cloth, with padded walls and floor lit by dull red lights, apparently to resemble a womb. I was encouraged to thrash around the floor, screaming if necessary, to re-enact my birth. With architects, lawyers and other professional people I went through ten days of floor thrashing as we screamed out opinions of lovers, husbands, parents, wives and friends. When this was over, I felt no better, with no further insight into my problems. The doctor's daughter mentioned that a better course known as the Hoffman Process was on offer in Byron Bay in northern New South Wales, so I enrolled for this five-day event, paid a large fee, and set off. The course was intended to lead to the understanding that unless I changed, I would be buried with my problems unresolved, as my parents had been. But after five days I felt more insecure and unsettled than ever. Clearly this was not the answer either. So I decided impulsively to fulfill a long-time ambition and see the Amazon before it was totally decimated by logging. I invited Will to acompany me; he agreed, and off we set.

We flew first to the Galapagos, just off the coast of Ecuador, protected islands of wild volcanic rocks and giant cacti, where red and blue lacquered crabs scurried between rock crevices and the surrounding turquoise seas were alive with porpoises, sea lions, giant turtles and fish. After two weeks of this paradise we flew to Venezuela to travel down the Orinoco River, a tributary of the Amazon, for ten days in a dugout canoe. The journey was breathtakingly beautiful. Sweet perfumed air slid past our faces as we floated into the pink dawn, swaying in our hammocks in the bow of the boat. The forest on either shore was densely matted with vines and a huge variety of flower-covered trees. At night blood-curdling screams penetrated the jungle as distant monkeys and other unknown creatures prowled their territory. But jungles are for insects and not for people. We were bitten on every available square millimetre of skin.

I had arranged for us to be dropped off at a specific town at the end of the journey, but our guides feared that the river rapids were too turbulent to negotiate at that point. After a heated argument, they let us off at a town they designated, introducing us to a kind family who arranged that a truck would pick us up the next day to drive us to the large town of São Gabriel. There we could catch a plane to Manaus and thence to Rio de Janeiro.

The trip through the jungle to São Gabriel was eventful. Neither Will nor I spoke the language; Will had learned Spanish at school, but it bears little resemblance to Portuguese, the language of Brazil. And the truck could go only a certain distance before the road disappeared; a track of deep red mud stretched several kilometres through the jungle before the road began again. We had to get out of the truck and walk. Huge mosquitoes dive-bombed us, sweat ran off our faces and down our necks, and we sank up to our thighs in the red mud. We arrived in São Gabriel in a disgusting condition.

Next day we flew to Manaus, a European town complete with opera house in the middle of the Amazon jungle. We had had enough of exploring after our São Gabriel trek, and spent our time in the airport waiting for our plane to Rio, where Will was staying behind for a while. I felt desolate, perhaps as a reaction to the trip. I was still mourning Bill and Will's parting words as I boarded the bus to leave him were: 'Mum, you can't let another person ruin your whole life.' He was right: his words became a mantra for me.

But I continued to feel alone, worthless, unloved. During one of my depressive interludes a writer for the now-defunct *Ita* magazine came to Bermagui to interview me about my past work and plans for the future. I was in no shape to give a dispassionate and thoughtful interview, and when I spoke of my problems, she suggested changing the topic to separation in midlife. I agreed, and the photographer who accompanied her took me down to the beach for several pictures. Before I knew it, I was on the cover with a line reading: 'The Devastation of Helen Caldicott: My Husband Left Me for Another Woman.' Penny rang me when the story appeared; I was in the United States on a speaking tour. Bill hated the story, she said, and had rung Ita Buttrose, the editor, to deny it. What was he talking about? What wasn't true? My feelings?

I was surprised to discover that the publication lifted my mood. I had needed to make a statement, to have my side of the story heard, to validate the experience.However, in hindsight, I can see that the expression of such raw emotion in public was a difficult experience for all concerned. While it helped me in the short run, its overall effect was not beneficial.

After eighteen months searching for answers, asking every other person what they thought, it suddenly dawned upon me one day as I was tending my garden at Bermagui that no one could help me. We are born alone and we die alone, and I gathered strength from this quite profound insight. In the meantime, my fifty-first birthday was around the corner, and I decided that unless I took the matter into my own hands, all my birthdays would be anniversaries of grief, like my fiftieth. So I organised a party to which I asked my dear friends from Bermagui. It was a cold night in August, and I built a big fire in the sitting-room fireplace. I cooked chocolate cakes and pavlovas, and it was a great party. Eventually everybody left except a fisherman, a dark and attractive man about my height who sat on the floor beside me as we talked in front of the fire. The next morning I woke to find him in my bed. I couldn't have been given a nicer birthday present.

Things were definitely improving, I thought: I was over the worst. And then Pen told me that Bill had decided to live in Bermagui with his new 'partner'. I was very disturbed. My house was my security blanket, my friends my support system. How could he invade my territory and spoil it for me? And how could he use our daughter as an emissary—didn't he have the courage to talk to me about this himself? I decided that enough is enough, so I rang him and demanded a meeting.

We met for lunch at a restaurant overlooking Sydney Harbour, both very nervous as we sat down together. We spoke of ordinary things to begin with, and to my surprise and relief, our conversation was very pleasant. But he then said that having driven around Australia, he had concluded that the very nicest place on the whole continent was Bermagui. He added that ever since he had left me, he had wanted to live there. He remained affable, and nothing I said—'Australia is a huge place, why choose Bermagui?'—could change his mind. No matter how much I begged him not to intrude upon my community and support system, he remained implacable.

Shortly after this meeting, I was driving back to Bermagui when the car suddenly died on the outskirts of Batemans Bay, the nearest sizeable town to the north. I hitched a ride into town, arranged to have the car towed, and waited for hours while the mechanic searched for the appropriate part of the engine. It happened to be a national holiday. Happy families marched by in joyous celebration while a band played and I sat huddled in the corner of the garage feeling absolutely isolated. I had nothing left.

I didn't want to go on living. 'I'll end it all,' I thought.

But I needed to be responsible and give it some thought. I had enough sleeping pills; I could prescribe more if necessary. Nobody would find me in my isolated Bermagui house until I was dead. Then I visualised my three kids standing around my grave, and I knew I couldn't do it. I couldn't traumatise their lives, but I resented them for even existing.

About a week later Bill came down for several days while he looked for a place to live. He was staying in a small house in the next valley and invited me for dinner. It was a strange occasion. Bill's first words to me were unexpected: 'I hope you haven't come to seduce me.' I stared at him; nothing then could have been further from my mind.

He cooked lamb chops and boiled potatoes, then proceeded to tell me enthusiastically and in great detail all about his round-Australia trip. Eventually I grew tired of this and said, 'Let's talk about real things.' We settled down into couches facing each other and talked frankly until two or three the next morning about our lives and our children. It was extraordinary, like the good times when we were married. We were very comfortable with each other; it seemed that this, at least, had not changed. I could quite easily have stayed the night, as if we were still married. But we were not.

The next morning was hot and dry, raked by a blistering north wind. I had asked Bill to come around and help me start our old Sears lawnmower, and was looking forward to continuing our newly amicable relationship, hoping against hope that he'd change his mind about the separation. But he was efficient and brisk, announcing that he wanted to settle our property arrangements as soon as possible, to have our marriage over. I was devastated yet again.

Some weeks later I filed for divorce.

CHAPTER 30

Shortly after I had decided to divorce Bill I visited Surfers Paradise in Queensland to speak to the Australian Intensive Care Society about the medical implications of the ecological crisis. On the way home I stopped off in Byron Bay to see the one friend I had made during the Hoffman Process some months before.

Cape Byron forms the southern border of a vast sweeping bay defined at the northern end by serrated rugged mountains that are volcanic in origin. The tallest of these is Mt Warning, an Aboriginal sacred peak that rises above the rest like a jagged tooth and is a local landmark. The bay is turquoise, with breakers that lazily roll onto white sandy beaches. At sunset the whole bay, water, breakers and sky, turns pink, like an ethereal painting.

At the time, Byron Bay was transforming itself from a sleepy beach town with three pubs, a few stores and a petrol station or two to the rather glitzy place it now is. Heavily influenced by the Aquarius festival, held in the town of Nimbin in the early 1970s soon after Woodstock, the Byron Bay area is widely recognised as a mecca for alternative lifestyles and progressive thinking.

The morning after I arrived, I woke at about five feeling distressed about my Bermagui situation and walked down a street lined by weeping bangalow palms to the beach. I entered the warm water and dived into the towering blue-green waves. At that moment I suddenly decided to live in Byron Bay.

At nine a.m. on the knocker I went to the nearest real estate agent and asked to see some houses. My Hoffman friend also took me to see one that had been constructed by a former shipwright. It stood on seven acres of land near the town, with a view of the distant mountains, including Mt Warning. The owner, my friend said, was motivated to make a quick sale.

It was an odd-looking place, with a steep, concave roof. It looked like a Balinese temple on stilts. The living room was spacious and oddly shaped; huge sliding glass windows faced onto a patch of tropical rainforest. Glorious birds sang in the trees outside the bedroom on the second floor, and down by the path was a lake filled with exotic native blue waterlilies. The large floor plan looked strange, so I went away and looked at other properties. But I was pulled back to the temple house. The minute I walked into it the second time, I fell in love with it, the way one does with a person. I secured the sale within an hour.

As I flew home, I knew I had made exactly the right decision. This was the first house I had ever owned alone, and it symbolised my new life facing into an optimistic future.

My neighbour Shunny and Will helped me pack the contents of Bermagui into a removalist's van; I knew exactly where everything would go in the new house. Bill happened to be camping nearby at the sandy mouth of the Murrah River with Doc—our old friend from Adelaide days—as I was moving, but, thank God, he left me alone. As we were about to drive away, I went into the empty, echoing house and thought: 'This has been a place of grief.' I was exultant. This phase of my life was over.

We drove into town and Shunny, Will and I sat on the lawn in front of the fish and chip shop at Bermagui, eating hot chips in farewell—hot chips seemed a metaphor for beginnings and endings at Bermagui.

The new house was even more beautiful than I remembered: all windows, no screens or curtains, nature was visible from every room. The roof was unlined silver galvanised iron, the rafters and walls were white. The floor was made of beautiful pink box gum. My poor plants, carefully uprooted from Bermagui and partially defoliated on the windy trip, snuggled into a warm patch of loam beneath a Bennets ash tree, decided they liked the new climate and promptly grew new leaves.

The next morning I woke to glorious birdsong and heavenly tropical scent. Outside my bedroom window stretched a green valley, a fig tree with a white, triangular trunk glowing in the distance with the volcanic peaks rising above. However, all was not totally blissful: a little later I discovered that one of the biggest piggeries in Australia lay just over the hill. Some mornings the pigs squealed as if their throats were being cut, and occasionally the wind brought their raw smell into my house. But this was the only defect.

After Will helped me unpack, he returned to the wilds of Sydney, leaving me alone in my new paradise. I wandered round the garden, picking warm, golden mangoes, deep red mulberries, and cherry guavas, stuffing them into my mouth and letting the juice run down my chin. I picked the heavenly blue waterlilies, filling the house with their perfume, and roamed through the patch of rainforest set about with ancient hoop pines, bangalow palms, box gums and umbrella trees.

But nature was not all benign. Within days there was news of a cyclone gathering force off the Queensland coast to the north. Could my new house withstand the onslaught? I removed all furniture from the verandahs, fastened the windows, battened down, and waited. I was afraid. Here I was, all alone, wondering whether my house would take off like Dorothy's in *The Wizard of Oz*.

The cyclone hit with gale force winds that blew everything flat. I was terrified that my huge windows would pop their sockets and soar into the air or through the house. Then came the eerie calm of the eye of the storm, when the air was heavy and dense and not a sound was heard. Even the birds were still. An hour later the wind hurled itself at the house from the opposite direction. I cowered inside, venturing out only when the storm was over. All seemed to be well, and the house was intact; I was pleased that I had weathered this storm. I was strong and able to cope with any contingency alone. The storm mirrored the emotional storm from which I had just emerged. A fitting end to the old life and the beginning of the new.

I was bored, knowing no one except my one busy friend, so I enrolled in a scuba diving course. The world under the sea is a completely different universe. Fish of every size and colour flicked past—vivid blue, yellow and purple, speckled with phosphorescence. Schools of fish brushed against our bodies as we all, humans and fish alike, drifted back and forth with the ebb and flow of the currents. Huge ancient turtles, harmless wobbegong sharks and poisonous eels grazed the sandy bottom. A rock cod the size of a Volkswagen fled at the first sight of black-clad divers passing the entrance of its cave.

I loved it. I may have been a woman of fifty-one, but life wasn't over. There was more fun to be had.

Shortly after I arrived in Byron Bay, I lunched with Nick Shand, editor of a small progressive local newspaper, the *Brunswick Echo.* Nick, who had followed my career, was very supportive of my work. It was early in 1990 and the federal election had just been announced; Nick suggested I run as an independent candidate for the seat of Richmond, saying that we need more women in Parliament.

'No,' I told him. 'I'm sick of campaigns.'

He thought for a monent, then asked, 'What do you think of Gorbachev and his moves to end the Cold War?'

I spoke enthusiastically in support. Nick then asked me, 'What has Australia done to support Gorbachev?'

'Oh my God', I thought, as the implications of his words sank in. My work would not be complete unless I supported Gorbachev and his initiatives. I needed to help those in power understand the implications of *glasnost* and *perestroika*, to ensure that Australia, my homeland, took its role in maintaining a safer world. This really had to do with the integrity of my life's work. I would run for Parliament.

I drove home feeling absolutely certain that I had made the right decision. Almost as soon as I announced my intentions, my new house was full of people, strangers who quickly became part of my life: journalists, writers, PR people, secretaries and grassroots campaign workers. Many of them knew about my career over the years, and they too were deeply concerned about the nuclear and environmental issues confronting the world. These volunteers worked with a dedication that resembled the women in WAND and the doctors of PSR. Within days we had two telephone lines, a fax machine, a photocopier, and a campaign.

Our sense of camaraderie was enhanced by our common goal—to evict Charles Blunt, the leader of the National Party from his seat. The National Party had held Richmond for almost a century and considered this seat to belong to them, but their policies were becoming less relevant in a country whose citizens were increasingly flocking to the cities.

Furthermore, graft and corruption sullied the National Party at that time, and it was further compromised by their most prominent member, the Premier of Queensland, Joh Bjelke-Petersen, whose conservative, somewhat nutty policies were making him the laughing-stock of the country. He had recently announced his intention of running for prime minister, supported by the Liberal Party.

The Australian Labor Party, which also ran a candidate in Richmond, had been in power since 1983: this was their fourth election campaign. Many Australians were beginning to feel, I think, that the Labor and Liberal parties were becoming indistinguishable: a common piece of graffiti said that ALP stood for Another Liberal Party. People were sick of the two-party system anyway, and were looking for independent alternatives.

Our bumper stickers were on the knocker—STOP THE ROT, VOTE CALDICOTT—and my supporters stuck them up all over the electorate. We had only three weeks before the election. Fund-raisers contributed $14 000 and I gave $12 000 which paid for several television advertisements. Wearing my stethoscope and appearing with a small child, I said, 'If you want this child to have a future, vote for me.' The message was simple, but it appealed particularly to women in the district.

A week before the election I arrived at a local radio station to debate the issues with Charles Blunt and the other candidates. Blunt arrived in his black Commonwealth car surrounded by minders and was seated in a studio apart from the other candidates. This demonstration of elitism and exclusivity cut right across the Australian egalitarian tradition. That day I knew in my bones that he was going to lose, although I had no idea who would replace him.

One hectic afternoon my lawyer rang to say that my divorce was official. My new friends and I drank several bottles of celebratory champagne, but we were terribly busy. Later when I had time to think and feel, I felt very sad, but nothing like the agony of grief I had experienced when Bill and I first separated.

After three weeks of frenzied activity we faced the people on 24 March. It was a day of nail-biting tension: how would the voters of Richmond respond to my pro-conservation message?

That night the house filled with people in party clothes until it was overflowing, and the phones rang off the hook. Caldicott, Caldicott, Caldicott: we were consistently winning most booths. Good God, we had a chance. The TV was blaring out the result from the national tally centre. One of the commentators suddenly announced: 'There's been an upset in Richmond, Charles Blunt is in trouble.' Cheers filled the room. Next we heard. 'It's Helen Caldicott' in shocked tones from the commentator.

Whether I won or lost, however, Charles Blunt's vote had been split to such an extent that he couldn't win. The election was a cliffhanger, and there was a real possibility that two independents might hold the balance of power in the new Parliament. This was almost too good to be true. But the vote in Richmond was clearly too close to be decided that night, so we contented ourselves with a party and drank to the possibilities.

The election in Richmond was big national news. I flew to Sydney for a press conference and TV interviews. It was wonderful being able to say my piece, and a picture of me smiling appeared on the front page of the *Sydney Morning Herald*, accompanying a broad-ranging interview about issues close to my heart. But as usual, I said something controversial. This time it was: 'Every family should have only one child.' I was thinking of the severe overpopulation problem facing the earth. Some people were offended—but I was right. The next day I was interviewed by *60 Minutes* with Ted Mack, the other independent who was elected to Parliament. The show was watched by hundreds of thousands of people because the election was so close and the results in Richmond were still not confirmed.

Because I was exuberant, excited and therefore unguarded, some people perceived my mood as aggressive. They were turned off by my enthusiasm, which they perceived as anger. Since my sojourn in America I'd lost my ability to be deferential and assume the false modesty required of women in Australia. As a forceful, intelligent female, I was found threatening.

Over the next week the votes in Richmond were all recounted by government scrutineers, whom we facetiously called the 'scrutes'. Everyone expected me to win most of the Australian Democrat preferences, but because of their position on the ticket, I only got half of them. Consequently the Labor Party candidate, Neville Newell, squeaked home instead. By splitting the National Party vote, I helped the Labor Party and Bob Hawke back into power. Had I known this would be the result, I would never have run in the first place.

Three days after the final count was announced, I threw a dinner party for my closest campaign workers. The sense of camaraderie reminded me strongly of PSR in its early days; we did not want to admit we had been defeated, to let go of each other and say goodbye.

I was dejected: so close and yet so far. My sense of depression lasted for weeks. I couldn't believe I had lost to the Labor Party. Had I won, I would have flown home from Parliament each weekend, held a large public meeting, updated my electorate on past and future legislation, then asked their advice about my voting agenda. Armed with true democratic input, I would then have returned to Australia's capital and voted according to the wisdom and wishes of my people. But it was not to be.

CHAPTER 31

Three days after the election result I departed for another US speaking tour. When I returned after three weeks on the lecture circuit, I felt lost.

As a child I had sought a spiritual life but had not found it. My parents were agnostics who did not contemplate or accept the spiritual. When I became a physician, my quest for God was sidetracked and I took on my parents' scepticism. But now, at fifty-one, I found myself needing something more, some understanding of why I had had to spend all those years in the wilderness. What meaning had my life had? What was its purpose to be in the future? And how was I to deal with the continuing pain following the ending of my marriage and my years of work in the States?

I sought the help of a local psychologist, who introduced me to a group of people who, although not religious in the conventional sense, had an extraordinary amount of wisdom both spiritual and psychological. I joined the community and worked with the group for several years, experiencing for the first time in my life the presence of a higher power.

I found I was better able to communicate with people and to see the beauty of their souls shining through their eyes. The sense of impotence and anger I had known abated, for I learned to accept and honour my own being. Every soul is unique: social conformity compromises the soul's integrity. Of course, I had learned some of this from reading *The Female Eunuch*, but the liberation I now felt was something quite different.

I now saw that I was part of a larger plan, that I was not alone as I had always felt. This is the essence of all religious experience, but it was only through my work with the group that I learned to accept it. My soul had a specific destiny, and if I used this newfound knowledge to understand myself and others, I would, of necessity, bring a new dimension to my work.

The healing techniques which were taught by the group caused me to question some aspects of Western medicine. I had always prided myself upon my scientific knowledge, and like most physicians, I had been rather arrogant. If any patient challenged me, I turned a deaf ear and felt irritated. However, because of this new knowledge, I understood I had not really been trained to heal, and it became obvious to me that traditional medicine only goes halfway. Doctors are adept at surgical procedures, scientific diagnoses and prescribing drugs. We handle bodies well: we ignore the soul.

I spent three years with Will in my Balinese temple-house. We mowed grass, planted eucalypts on land degraded by cattle grazing, and planned and planted a permaculture garden of tropical fruits: mangoes, papayas, guavas, bananas and coffee plants. We mulched, pruned and watered it, and in two years it grew into a small forest. We also regenerated patches of indigenous tropical rainforest, and Will became so enamoured with the variety of local species that he decided to enroll in university to study for a degree in coastal management. During those years, I wrote *If You Love This Planet*, which dealt with the global ecological crisis; I also updated *Nuclear Madness*. I wrote in my dining room, which looked out onto the rainforest basking in the tropical warmth.

Penny gave birth to Micky, my first grandchild. I had felt during her pregnancy that I definitely wasn't old enough to be a grandmother, but when he came, those apprehensions disappeared. It was a rite of passage—this skinny little human being, perfect in every way, was even more beautiful to me than my own three babies. Never did I expect to experience these feelings.

Micky is an absolute character, spontaneously crazy, affectionate and sweet. Like his mother before him, he has developed his own Micky form of language that we all now use.

Almost two years later Rachel arrived. She is the spitting image of Pen as a baby, a celluloid doll with chubby pink arms and legs and a soft round face. As an infant she looked exactly like a Buddha, and she still radiates a golden aura. She is calm and placid, the opposite of her brother.

In 1991 Philip was married to a young Englishwoman in my Balinese house.

After three years of living in the tropical paradise of Byron Bay, I moved with others in the group to cold, rainy Victoria. I had spent my childhood there in the bone-chilling cold, and I had vowed never to return.

In Victoria I found a log cabin on Brandy Creek, accompanied by nearly half a hectare of cottage garden dripping with roses, honeysuckle, columbines, wisteria and hydrangeas, not far from the small town of Warragul. The cabin was surrounded by lush green hills in some of the richest dairy country of eastern Australia. Deep in the back yard gurgled a spring-fed creek that was once the home of platypus and blackfish. Huge willows hung over the water, and I could swear Tolkien's hobbits lived under the trees on the creek. Two black sheep came with the house, but I gave them away because they enjoyed eating the baby eucalypts I planted on the spare block next door. I gutted the interior of the house, making it a light, airy, comfortable dwelling in a dell overlooked by the hills and dales of Gippsland.

If I wore enough underclothes and boots, the cold climate wasn't so bad, and the potbelly stove lent cosiness to the log cabin. But even in this comfortable retreat, politics surfaced. After giving a fund-raising speech for a Labor Party candidate in Melbourne, the candidate informed me that hidden away in the policy of the Liberal Party was a small clause condoning the use of nuclear power and uranium enrichment plants for Australia.

The people of Australia would have been furious if they knew this, but when I attempted to inform the national media, they were once again strangely uninterested. I bought two half-page ads in the Melbourne *Age* and the *Sydney Morning Herald* to warn of the covert Liberal Party policy. I designed the ad, using a beguiling photograph of Micky dressed in his striped pyjamas. The caption read, 'Does this child have a safe future?' The ads, plus a small TV commercial, set me back $30 000, but then how much is a safe future worth?

The story was not carried by the media. However, on 4 January 1994 the Liberal Party policy committee publicly and officially revoked its nuclear policy, saying it was clearly not acceptable to the Australian public. Obviously many of its followers had seen the ads and internal pressure had been exerted to change the nuclear agenda. Yet again it was proven that small, well-planned actions can profoundly affect the political agenda.

I know I had no choice but to leave the practice of medicine in 1980 and follow a different path. But it remains my vocation and all my political work since has been guided by its principles. The problem of impending nuclear war was to me an acute global clinical emergency. What needed to be done was to delineate the history of the nuclear arms race: to present a kind of clinical examination of the planet: the number of bombs and where they had metastasised; the pathology of a nuclear attack; the aetiology, or cause, of this crisis, which involved human psychology; and the cure—a universal commitment by the global community to abolish these weapons.

Never in all those years of political activity did I believe the arms race and the Cold War would end. In fact, I was desperate. But they did end—a miracle occurred. The work of the international peace movement helped to pave the way for a Russian, Mikhail Gorbachev, to perform the final act. He sanctioned the collapse of the Berlin Wall, and the ever-present tension between the nuclear superpowers dissolved with the disintegration of the Soviet Union. This, I believe, was the single most important event of the twentieth century.

When the Cold War ended, so did my desperation. And my spiritual work now provided its replacement: a joyful passion for life in all its aspects. For I believe a spiritual life should be full of joy and it is this which I seek for myself and wish to give to others.

As I look back, I can see that the desperate passion I felt was that of a mother and a paediatrician who cared for sick and dying children. I was filled with the ferocity of a lioness protecting her cubs. In no way was I going to allow the incidence of genetic and malignant disease to increase amongst the world's children because of nuclear technology.

However, the work of global preventive paediatrics is not over. The lives of my grandchildren are now threatened with ongoing ozone depletion, the perils of global warming, pollution of the air, water and soil with a multiplicity of chemicals and radioisotopes, deforestation, and species extinction combined with the rampant overpopulation of human beings.

I paid a personal price for the intense political work that I conducted over a twenty-five-year time span, through the pain I inflicted on myself and those dear to me. That said, I must continue.

I N D E X

Also available from Random House Australia

Judy Cassab Diaries

'Judy Cassab's life is a triumph of the spirit'
YVONNE PRESTON, *CANBERRA TIMES*

Since she was twelve years old, the age she started painting, Judy Cassab has kept a diary, recording details of her family, her work, and events of the day. *Diaries* is a selection from a lifetime of journal entries, which portray an exceptional woman, a successful and driven artist, mother, wife and friend.

Judy Cassab's life is part of the story of our times: the story of the trauma of war, of displacement and migration and the struggle to find a new life in a new land. It is also the story of one of Australia's finest painters, an artist with the astonishing gift of capturing people's souls as well as their likenesses, who was also able to portray the spirit of the land in a strikingly original way. Running through this extraordinary life, strengthening and enriching it at every turn, is a beautiful and moving love story.

Diaries tells the story of a life lived passionately and to the fullest. It is a rich, fascinating and inspirational self-portrait of a courageous and vital woman, whose determination to live shines through her writing.

'The golden threads which run through Judy Cassab's life are passion and love.' MORRIS WEST

'Cassab's diaries provide a deeply moving self portrait of a perpetually curious woman, often plagued by self-doubt, who has lived her life with passion, courage and generosity. Today Cassab still sparkles with life. "You are a magnificent woman," says her husband of fifty-six years. And she is.'
SUZY BALDWIN, *VOGUE*

'Judy Cassab's diaries span fifty years and record the enormous changes in society and in her own life during this time . . . An impressive achievement intertwining the personal and the public in many beautifully observed moments and with honesty and humour.'
JUDGES' REPORT, KIBBLE AWARDS FOR LITERATURE, 1996

Australian RRP $45 hardback $19.95 paperback

Jobs for the Girls
Caro Llewellyn and Skye Rogers

Motivated by a desire to share their own experiences and discover how other women succeed, Caro Llewellyn and Skye Rogers have compiled this fascinating collection of interviews with 24 women from around Australia who run their own businesses.

With engaging frankness, each of the women talk in detail about their experiences, from the moment they decided to take the plunge through to where they are today. Recurring themes include the challenge of balancing work and family life, securing financial support, working in a partnership, and coping with the everyday crises that inevitably occur.

From dog washing to whale watching, through opera singing, jewellery making, magazine publishing, fashion, building construction, real estate, childcare and a whole host of others, each of these women know well the challenges and joys of self-determination.

If you are one of the many Australian women considering a business of your own and you want information or inspiration, or if you just want to dream about the possibilities, then this book is for you!

A refreshing, practical and inspirational book for anyone considering a business of their own.